D0023204

The Fenians in Context

Series
Topics in Modern Irish History
General Editor: R. V. Comerford

Published
Priest, Politics and Society in Post-famine Ireland
A Study of County Tipperary, 1850-1891
James O'Shea

Towards a National University: William Delaney S.J.
(1835-1924) and an Era of Initiative in Irish Education
Thomas Morrissey S.J.

The Context of Fenianism: Irish Politics and Society, 1848-1882
R. V. Comerford

By the same author
Charles J. Kickham (1828-82): A Study in Irish Nationalism and Literature (Wolfhound Press, 1979)

Dedication
For MARCUS and LEO

The Fenians
in Context

Irish Politics and Society 1848-82

R. V. Comerford

Wolfhound Press
HUMANITIES PRESS INC.

First published 1985 by
Wolfhound Press
68 Mountjoy Square
Dublin 1

© 1985 R.V. Comerford

All rights reserved. No part of this book may be reproduced or utilised in
any form or by any means, electronic or mechanical, including photography,
filming, recording or video recording, or by any information storage and
retrieval system, without prior permission in writing from the publisher.

British Library Cataloguing in Publication Data

Comerford, R.V.
    The Fenians in context: Irish politics and society, 1848-82. — (Topics
in Modern Irish History, ISSN 0790-0783; v.3)
    1. Fenian Brotherhood — History
    I. Title
    322.4,2,09415   DA954

    ISBN 0-86327-61-1

Typesetting by Print Prep Ltd.
Printed and bound by Billings & Sons Ltd., England.

Co-published in the United States 1985 by
Humanities Press Inc.,
Atlantic Highland, New Jersey 07716

ISBN 0-391-03312-3

TABLE OF CONTENTS

ACKNOWLEDGEMENTS

This book has to open with an expression of sincerest gratitude to the late T.W. Moody. It was under his guidance that I did much of the research work of which this is an end product. Along the way I have benefited from his abundant kindness, his fastidious insistence on standards, and his willingness to consider new ideas even when they went against the grain. Important encouragement and advice came also from Professor John A. Murphy at a crucial point. Over a number of years I have called from time to time on the expertise of Leon Ó Broin, Marcus Bourke and Hugh Ryan. I am indebted in all the obvious ways and in some less obvious ones to the authors of half-a-dozen major theses on mid-nineteenth-century Ireland completed at Maynooth in recent years: Liam McNiffe, Maurice Johnson, Patrick Brennan, Stephen Stewart, Kevin Quigley and Brian Griffin. I thank Rev. Professor P.J. Corish and my other departmental colleagues for unfailing courtesy and for an atmosphere of scholarly fellowship.

Professor Donal McCartney read the MS and gave very helpful advice. W.E. Vaughan and R.F. Foster each read a number of chapters and made valuable suggestions. I thank them all most sincerely, without holding any of them responsible for what has finally appeared.

In the course of my work I have been facilitated by the staff of many institutions including the National Library of Ireland, Trinity College Library, the State Paper Office (Dublin Castle), the Public Record Office of Ireland, the Royal Irish Academy, the National Gallery of Ireland, Dublin Diocesan Archives, the British Library, the Institute for Historical Research, the Public Record Office (London), the National Register of Archives and the Archives Nationales de France. I owe special thanks to the staff of Maynooth College Library.

Permission to reproduce illustrations has been received from the National Gallery of Ireland, the National Library of Ireland and the State Paper Office, Dublin Castle. The Maynooth Scholastic Trust and Maynooth College Executive Council kindly granted a sum towards the expenses of publication, which, however, fall mainly on the publisher, Seamus Cashman.

Finally, I thank my immediate family for continuing patient support.

R.V. Comerford
Maynooth, 1984

LIST OF ABBREVIATIONS USED IN THE NOTES

C.S.O.:	Chief Secretary's Office, Dublin Castle
C.S.O., R.P.:	Chief Secretary's Office, Registered papers
Clark and Donnelly, *Irish peasants*:	Samuel Clark and J.S. Donnelly, Jr. (ed.), *Irish peasants: violence and political unrest, 1780-1914* (Liverpool, 1983)
D.P.B.:	*Devoy's Post Bag, 1871-1928*, edited by William O'Brien and Desmond Ryan (2 vols., Dublin, 1948 and 1953)
D'Arcy, *Fenian movement*:	William D'Arcy, *The fenian movement in the United States, 1858-86* (Washington, 1947)
Moody, *Davitt*:	T.W. Moody, *Davitt and Irish revolution, 1846-82* (Oxford, 1981)
MS 331 and MS 333:	T.C. Luby's recollections of fenianism and the *Irish People* (N.L.I.)
MS 5964:	[General Millen's] account of fenianism as from April 1865 to April 1866 (N.L.I., S.L. Anderson papers)
Ryan, *Fenian chief*:	Desmond Ryan, *The fenian chief: a biography of James Stephens* (Dublin, 1967)
S.P.O.:	State Paper Office, Dublin Castle
Varieties of tension:	F.S.L. Lyons and R.A.J. Hawkins (ed.), *Ireland under the union: varieties of tension; essays in honour of T.W. Moody* (Oxford, 1980)

PREFACE

There is a widespread and deepseated assumption that Irish history is essentially — and perhaps almost entirely — the story of struggle between the 'Irish' and the 'English' for sovereignty over the island. This is not merely a popular attitude: it flourishes at all levels of educated society and especially among the literary and journalistic élites, of course with individual exceptions.

From this point of view the task of the professional historian is taken to be twofold: that of adding details to a well-established framework, and that of impartiality. The acceptance within the body politic that historians are not required to produce nationalist (or unionist) propaganda is one cf the major advances made by the historical profession in Ireland in recent generations. But the fact that the historian is permitted to speak in dispassionate tones and to paint 'our' warts as well as 'theirs' does not of itself dilute the notion that he (or she) is still telling a story of 'us' versus 'them'.

In fact the preoccupations of most Irish historians comprehend but also transcend that kind of impartiality and embrace a concern to convey a more complex picture of the country's past. In particular there is a desire to have that past appreciated and savoured in its own right and not simply as a prelude to contemporary political dilemmas. The 'us and them' outlook restricts history to the function of explaining the present and imposes on it impoverishing teleological preconceptions.

The work of emancipating Irish history from this is all the more difficult in that its names and terms are loaded with accumulated connotations of national struggle. Thus for anyone even slightly familiar with discourse on Irish affairs the word 'fenian' is redolent of insurgent nationalism. This book

7

is indeed intended to give all due weight to the insurrectionary
activities and separatist aspirations of the early fenians. But it
is also intended to show that the fenians cannot be adequately
understood merely in terms of guns and republicanism. Their
movement was not a manifestation of 'indefeasible nationality'
but rather the product of a range of social, economic and
intellectual-sentimental factors, and of assorted contingencies
of personality, place and time.

For 'us and them' history fenianism is essentially timeless.
The intention here is to explain the fenian movement precisely
as a product of its own time. That entails an examination of
Irish politics and society over a period that has been covered
very unevenly by published work up to now. So, while for the
years 1878-82 the task has been to synthesise and re-interpret
the large body of secondary work on the 'new departure' and
the land war, for other periods, and especially the late 1850s
and most of the 1860s, writing this book has entailed the first
sustained interpretation of many major political and social
developments.

This is not to deny that the story of the fenian movement in
these years has often been told. Indeed the story has been re-
counted so frequently that awareness of its context and significance has been blunted, and it appears to assume a life of
its own. As a consequence other political developments have
been largely ignored, including many that are vital to understanding the fenians; and events with wider ramifications, such
as the funeral of Terence Bellew MacManus, the affair of the
Manchester martyrs, and the 'new departure' have been seriously
misunderstood. Relating the fenians more rigorously to their
time and place may have the effect of seeming to diminish their
importance, but it also makes them more comprehensible and
more interesting.

In the endeavour to reconstruct context, reference is made
at various points in this book to relevant features of the wider
international scene. However, it may also be appropriate here to
recall the general character of the period. The quarter century
between the early 1850s and the late 1870s — bounded at each
end by international economic crisis — constituted an era of
remarkable economic and industrial progress, as rapidly improving communications helped to bring more and more of the world
within the ambit of an international capitalist system centred
on London. Although trailing far behind their commercial
betters, a significant section of the working class in the advanced
countries was now enjoying some of the fruits of the industrial
revolution. As American and Australian farmers had yet to make
their full impact on the European grain and meat markets,

European agriculture enjoyed a boom period, meeting the needs of a growing industrial population.

In retrospect this golden age has sometimes been mistakenly invested with an aura of political stability to match its material prosperity. Germany and Italy were each unified at this time, but only following war. If the empire of Louis Napoleon brought the appearance of tranquillity to France it gave way to the third republic amid trauma and disaster. The unity of the U.S.A. was maintained only at the cost of a civil war of horrific proportions. Britain and the United States appeared on a number of occasions to be on the brink of going to war with one another. Even in Britain the mid-Victorian consensus was not nearly so complete as it is often depicted in retrospect. Because, in the event, there was no sharp break in the political order the very considerable level of discontent in England at this period has been underrated and almost forgotten. The Irish counterpart of this evidence of alienation — the fenian movement — scarcely posed any greater threat to the Pax Britannica but it has been remembered by reason of having been fitted into the 'tradition of resistance' which is so consistently read into the Irish past, and not only by Irish nationalists.

The general economic trends of the mid-Victorian era made a deep impact on Ireland. The country acquired an impressive railway network and became a single market to an extent previously impossible. Agricultural incomes rose very significantly if not uninterruptedly, but more prosperous agriculture entailed a smaller population on the land. Only in the Belfast area was there sufficient industrial development to support a significantly increased urban population. Improved communications facilitated the regular large-scale emigration that now became an established feature of Irish life. Between 1851 and 1881 the population declined by twenty one percent, from six and a half million to something over five million. Average standards of living improved dramatically. Irish society in these decades came to be orientated as never before towards England and North America and much of the material and non-material culture of the society was transformed as a consequence. The fenian movement can legitimately be depicted as a reaction against fundamental social, economic and cultural change. But that is only one side of the story: the fenians can also be seen as people striving to find a place for themselves in the new dispensation.

William Smith O'Brien

Michael Doheny

Charles Gavan Duffy

John Mitchel

Chapter One

ANATOMY LESSONS, 1848-56

As 1848 opened much of western Europe was in the grip of serious social and economic crisis. The previous year had seen the onset of an upheaval in the realms of high finance that was continuing to have baneful effects on trade and industry. This had come on top of an agrarian catastrophe resulting from the effects of poor harvests on heavily-populated countrysides. The crop worst affected was the potato, struck in 1845 and subsequent years by a blight-producing fungus new to Europe. In those parts of the Netherlands, Belgium, the German lands and Switzerland where considerable numbers of people depended on the potato for sustenance, rural distress was particularly acute.[1] In Ireland there was calamity on a scale rarely equalled in Europe in modern times. The extremely high rate of Irish dependency on the potato was compounded by — indeed was intimately linked with — agrarian structures that left a high proportion of the population with scarcely any economic resources to spare, many without even that capacity to buy time that is one of the first benefits of participation in a commercial economy. The industrial revolution in anything like its plenitude was confined to the north-east of the island. Elsewhere in the country it had arrived largely in the form of comparatively inexpensive factory-made English goods, especially cloth, that undermined the old-established trades and domestic industry, thus aggravating the demographic problems of the countryside. The logical exodus to the places of new employment had begun long before 1845 but had not attained the volume that circumstances demanded. And those for whom escape was most urgent were the least likely to have the necessary resources and vision.

By January 1848 the great famine had already wreaked havoc among the poorer sections of rural Irish society through death (from hunger and associated diseases) and panic-stricken emigration, and a few more years of devastation were still to come. The more substantial farmers had their own problems which, if not as grave, were still appalling by normal standards. Nobody was secure from the threat of famine disease; agricultural profits had virtually disappeared and at the same time there was a spectacular rise in the local rates demanded to meet the cost of poor-law relief for the destitute. In the middle of a cataclysm the farmers had no way of knowing that they would as a class profit from it all in due course. Even an intimation of class advantage would have given no reassurance of individual survival in a time of upheaval and calamity. Landlords had a similarly difficult time, and even if many of them were able to remain at some physical distance from the fray that did nothing to prevent the financial collapse which befell many estates as rents went unpaid, poor rates soared, and moneylenders refused to advance any further credit.

The famine put an end to the great popular agitation for repeal of the union with Great Britain that was presided over by Daniel O'Connell and that had flourished from early in the 1840s. After 1845 sustained mobilisation of the masses simply was not feasible. On top of this, the accession of a whig administration in June 1846 evoked O'Connell's old ambivalence on the constitutional question: did he want self-government for Ireland, or did he simply want changes in how Ireland was actually governed that could be achieved through cooperation with the whigs? This ambivalence was unacceptable to the clique of intellectual, romantic nationalists associated with the weekly *Nation* (founded 1842) who had been a source of trouble for O'Connell within the Repeal Association and who had been dubbed, with pejorative intent, as 'Young Ireland'. On 28 July 1846 the leaders of this group seceded from the Repeal Association in a public and dramatic fashion when called upon to reaffirm O'Connell's dictum that the use of physical force to obtain Irish freedom could not be justified. This was a question of temperament and philosophy, not of policy. There were indeed policy differences, but they related to dealings with the government of the day: in 1846 the Young Irelanders had as little intention as O'Connell himself of launching a rebellion. Their alternative organisation, the Irish Confederation (established in January 1847), voted overwhelmingly as late as December 1847 for non-violent political action, thereby rejecting the call of one of their number, John Mitchel, for an uprising of the masses.

Following O'Connell's death in May 1847 the Repeal Association came under the leadership of his son, John, and retained
the support of the preponderance of those priests and other
local leaders who still had any time for politics. The appalling
misery of the times and the inability (or failure) of the government to provide a remedy resulted in the popularity of the whigs
being very low in Ireland at the general election of July-August
1847. The outcome was the return of 36 M.P.s in the repeal interest – a higher number than at any election since 1832 and under
the electoral conditions of the day an impressive proportion of
Ireland's representation of 105.[2] The suggestion of unprecedented
strength was however highly deceptive. The popular mobilisation
that had given the repeal campaign its strength was in abeyance.
Most of the 36 were whigs or Liberals who had flown the flag
of repeal for temporary convenience. And even with the best of
intentions the most they could hope to do about Irish affairs
was to influence the government in small ways.

The surface of Irish politics, darkly quiet as 1848 opened,
was disturbed by a deceptive whirl of activity in the spring and
early summer. The sudden and comparatively bloodless overthrow of King Louis Philippe at the end of February, and the
subsequent inauguration of a French republic, created in Ireland
as elsewhere (at least among those disposed to be so convinced)
the illusion that revolution was easy. With the capitulation of
established authority throughout much of Europe in subsequent
weeks the conviction grew that change was not only comparatively easy but also inevitable. The result was a sense of
expectation that spread right across the spectrum of those
favourably disposed to Irish constitutional change of any kind,
from John Mitchel to John O'Connell. Those with pretensions
to leadership proved quite incapable, individually and collectively, of rising to the occasion, and in any case the opportunity
was more illusory than real.

A politically-frustrated bourgeoisie campaigning under the
banner of liberalism was one of the most powerful elements in
the European revolutions of 1848. In Ireland this factor was
missing. There was no serious constraint on the exercise of the
classical political liberties to be complained of, and the politically
motivated could 'banquet' to their hearts' content. By the
same token the business and entrepreneurial sector, such as it
was, enjoyed all the legal advantages it could hope for anywhere.
In any case the Irish bourgeois and professional groups, like
Irish landowners (though not to fully the same extent) were
predominantly protestant and so preponderantly on the side of
the constitutional status quo which had been challenged during

the decade by a nationalist movement that appeared to be essentially an expression of collective catholic militancy.

Those driven to the brink of economic annihilation but who had not yet gone over provided prime revolutionary material in many countries in the late 1840s. From this point of view Ireland had probably passed its explosive peak sometime in 1847, but there was undoubtedly still much potential of this kind in 1848 in areas of the country at the appropriate point on the scale of misery.

Over much of western Europe the artisans were in the forefront of revolutionary activity and many Irish artisans shared this disposition. In Dublin they had entered the Irish Confederation in considerable force in 1847; indeed, the confederation had been formed largely to harness and control their enthusiasm.[3] They constituted the group most obviously prepared for an Irish rebellion in 1848. The outmanoeuvring by authority and establishment of their English counterparts in the chartist movement in April 1848 does not seem to have seriously dampened the revolutionary ardour of the Dublin artisans. However, even more than the chartists, they were at a loss for leadership.

In his newspaper, the *United Irishman* (launched in February 1848), John Mitchel called repeatedly for instantaneous insurrection, and he did so in most provocative language. On the other hand, William Smith O'Brien M.P., now the acknowledged leader of the Young Ireland group, hoped for a revolution that would be not only peaceful but within the constitution as he understood it. Insofar as a clear purpose can be attributed to him at this time it was the mobilisation of 'national opinion' into an open paramilitary force, something that he believed to be quite legal. By analogy with 1782 and what Young Ireland rhetoric depicted as the concession of 'Grattan's parliament' to the armed Volunteers, Smith O'Brien envisaged the British government of 1848 restoring Ireland's rightful legislative independence within the empire when faced once again in a time of international uncertainty with the marshalled might of the 'nation'. The analogy was imperfect. In 1848 Irish property was almost completely on the side of the status quo. In vain did the Young Irelanders hope that the gentry's dissatisfaction with government handling of the famine crisis would prompt them to declare for repeal of the union. Among the population at large only the artisans displayed any readiness for seizing the opportunity of the hour. The rural masses were in ferment, but could they be mobilised? A sprinkling of young intellectuals offered some local leadership towards that end, but the only serious hope lay in the priests. By early summer priests in some numbers were indeed entering the local clubs of the Irish Confederation where as a matter of course they assumed prominent positions. This trend was formalised on 12 June when the Irish Confederation and the Repeal Association agreed to merge as the Irish League. The moderation of the leading Young Irelanders had made this possible. Smith O'Brien and his henchmen indulged daydreams of riding to glory with swords aloft, but in practice they had no stomach for either futile bloodshed or illegality. They were envisaging a denouement in the autumn — after the harvest — if nothing happened spontaneously in the meantime, but throughout the spring and early summer they discouraged every inclination towards immediate resistance to authority on the part of their urban followers in the clubs. No amount of responsible behaviour by the Young Irelanders would of itself have lured so many priests into the confederate clubs but for the widespread expectation that something was indeed going to happen: they were acting more or less instinctively on the principle that if something was inevitable they had better be part of it.

The sense of riding on the tide of ineluctable epochal change had been emphasised in March when Smith O'Brien led a delegation of Young Irelanders and Dublin artisans to Paris to convey greetings to the new government. The reception was cordial but the republican regime was in no position to offend Britain by offering any help to Irish revolutionaries. In any case Smith O'Brien had grave doubts about the desirability of direct external aid. Eventually his immediate subordinates conspired to seek such aid from France and America, but without fully implicating Smith O'Brien. By April 1848 there was an impressive mobilisation of Irish-American opinion and resources in support of what seemed like the inevitable spread to Ireland of the European political upheaval. Large sums of money were contributed, particularly in New York, for Irish revolutionary purposes, and armed companies of Irish-Americans were drilled with a view to action in Ireland. Smith O'Brien gave verbal sanction to this while at the same time neutralising it through procrastination about discussing arrangements for any practical coordination of effort. For a variety of reasons he had no desire to give Irish-Americans any say in the reshaping of Ireland's political institutions. But the idea that they might exercise such influence was to recur in subsequent decades, with consequences of the kind that repelled Smith O'Brien in 1848.

The government that was so ineffectual in the face of the socio-economic cataclysm gave at least the appearance of competence in dealing with the threat of rebellion. The Treason Felony Act[4] passed in April 1848 was an ingenious measure

that enabled the authorities to strike at the instigators of disaffection, especially in the press, without having to invoke the
charge of treason, with its mandatory death sentence, or sedition,
which carried comparatively minor penalties. John Mitchel was
convicted under the new act on 26 May and sentenced to fourteen
years' transportation. There had been much talk in the Dublin
clubs of not permitting him to be taken from the city in chains,
but he was, on 27 May, on board a government steamer: the
cautious Young Ireland leaders had quelled the clamour for a
rescue attempt.

The *United Irishman* was now succeeded as an organ of
insurrectionary rhetoric by the *Irish Felon* (edited by John
Martin) and the *Irish Tribune* (edited by Kevin Izod O'Doherty
and Richard Dalton Williams) both of which flourished briefly
in June-July 1848. The *Nation*, under the editorship of Charles
Gavan Duffy, remained the mouthpiece of the more circum-
spect of the Young Irelanders. In the wake of unsuccessful
prosecutions for sedition against a number of Young Ireland
leaders, including Smith O'Brien and Gavan Duffy, the government put through parliament a measure (enacted 25 July 1848)
temporarily suspending habeas corpus in Ireland.[5] Troublesome
individuals could then be detained without any need to resort to
the courts. This derogation from liberal principles of jurispru-
dence changed the rules of the game to the serious disadvantage
of the Young Irelanders. They faced a dilemma: to abandon
their hopes (and either take flight or submit meekly to arrest);
or to press ahead with a rising for which they were quite unpre-
pared. Smith O'Brien declared (and the others agreed) that if
honour were to be saved a stand would have to be made. But
who could be expected to stand with them? Potential support
from the artisans of the cities and towns was neutralised by large
and alert military garrisons. That message was brought home to
Smith O'Brien by the middle-class and clerical club leaders as
he moved from Enniscorthy (where he first received news of
the suspension of habeas corpus) to Graiguenamanagh, to Kilkenny, to Callan, to Carrick-on-Suir, to Cashel, in the last week
of July. The artisans were in a fever of enthusiasm, but who
would lead them on to mayhem and slaughter? Not the shopkeepers, not the priests, not the Young Irelanders. This was not
the irresistible revolution that had been expected. Farmers
with crops in the ground who had been hearing talk of a rising
after the harvest were unlikely to favour distractions in late
July, a few weeks before the harvest. Countrymen with little or
no grounds or crops might be more susceptible. Crossing through
the south-east of County Tipperary, the Young Irelanders found
a stratum of the dispossessed, broken smallholders and rural

proletarians on the edge of economic ruin who (together with the labourers of Mullinahone and Killenaule and the colliers of Ballingarry) had been gripped for some weeks with an expectation of imminent insurrectionary relief from their problems. They were dissuaded from flocking en masse to Smith O'Brien by the strenuous admonitions of their priests, most of them leading members of confederate clubs.[6] Nevertheless thousands did at least come out to see Smith O'Brien at one point or another as he moved from village to village (accompanied by an entourage of Young Ireland notables), but he had no idea how he might use their services and he sent most of them back to their homes. Under attack he would assuredly have acted in self-defence, but left to take the initiative he was paralysed by his aversion to bloodshed and to the destruction of property. The charade ended on 29 July near Ballingarry shortly after an undisciplined band of would-be rebels had been scattered by gunfire from a party of constabulary taking refuge in the farmhouse of one Mrs McCormack.

The outcome was admirable from the government's point of view. Not alone had the attempt at rebellion failed, but it had failed ignominiously and the authorities had contributed to this by judicious restraint in the use of force. Indeed, the use of minimal force had been a feature of the administration's handling of disturbances throughout the famine years.[7] Even one serious clash (however unsuccessful) with regular forces could have earned the Young Irelanders heroic stature. Instead of that it now proved possible to ridicule their efforts as 'the affair of the Widow McCormack's cabbage garden'. Even a minor setback for crown forces could have moved the malcontents of half a dozen counties to wild action. A similar effect might have been achieved if Smith O'Brien in the days leading up to Ballingarry had provided his followers with food supplies 'raised on the credit of a provisional government'. There was no possibility whatever that Smith O'Brien could win Irish self-government in July 1848, but he did have the capacity to unleash boundless trouble on the authorities and on the country. True to his profoundly conservative and humanitarian instincts he refused to disturb the peace, even though he consequently appeared to be a kind of Don Quixote. He was strengthened in his caution by the opinions of priests, shopkeepers and farmers, about which he was left in no doubt. In restraining the rush to rebellion the priests were at once both opponents and allies of the Young Irelanders.

If Ballingarry proved that there would be no Young Ireland rising, it did not mark a halt to insurrectionary activity. For a period of up to two months afterwards some hundreds of countrymen, armed mostly with pikes, remained in camp on the hill of Carraigadoon, east of Slievenamon, on the borders of Counties Tipperary and Kilkenny. From the beginning of their adventures in the early summer these people seem to have looked to catholic gentleman-farmers for leadership. A few showed interest, and most notably John O'Mahony of Bally-curkeen House. Probably without his encouragement, 'followers' of his attacked Glenbower constabulary barracks, and a passing stagecoach, on 12 September 1848, in what was probably a much bloodier affray than that at Ballingarry. Most of the blood spilt belonged to the attackers and they dispersed shortly afterwards. A similar group across the Suir in County Waterford scattered at about the same time following an attempted assault on Portlaw barracks.

Disaffection survived much longer among the artisans in Dublin and Cork cities and in the towns of the south-east. Through the Irish Confederation they had had thorough experi-ence of political clubbism and following the disintegration of the confederation in what were now termed 'democratic clubs', that were linked together in an 'Irish Democratic Association'. Meetings of these democratic clubs were reported as late as summer 1850.[8] Before the end of 1848 many of these same artisans were being sworn into secret revolutionary organisations. By mid-1849 a loose but impressive network extended from Dublin to Cork, taking in the principal towns of Counties Kilkenny, Waterford and Limerick, and of south Tipperary. Firearms were procured and ambitious plans for a rising were formulated. There was talk of attempting to kidnap Queen Victoria on her visit to Dublin in early August 1849. However, the tide of opportunity had been missed and the '1849 move-ment' achieved nothing more spectacular than an assault on the constabulary barracks at Cappoquin, County Waterford, on 16 September.[9] After that it declined rapidly, but small frag-ments survived and these provided the nucleus of the fenian organisation almost a decade later. Because of this direct con-nection with the fenians it is important to insist that the 1849 movement was not a link in any chain of 'apostolic' succession between them and the United Irishmen of half a century earlier. The 1849 movement was the product of its own time, and not least of a keen and widespread awareness among Irish radicals of happenings in France, where their counterparts were immersed in clubs and secret political fraternalism. Besides, Irish artisan society had many links with English chartist culture.

The special legislative aids available to the government in dealing with the problems of Ireland in 1848 included not only the Treason Felony Act and the temporary suspension of habeas corpus but also the Crime and Outrage Act of 1847.[10] This empowered the lord lieutenant to proclaim troublesome districts; within these, police powers were much increased, and the right to hold and carry arms severely restricted. This legislation was renewed from time to time until superseded by the milder Peace Preservation Act of 1856.[11] The inhabitants of Ireland in the mid-Victorian period enjoyed the essentials of English legal liberties, but there was vested in the Dublin Castle authorities the power of overriding some of (the less important) of these in places where, and at times when, it was deemed to be necessary. The conferring of such power on the executive in England would have been considered intolerable; in Ireland it was used only reluctantly and judiciously.

One institution as untouchable in Ireland as in England was trial by jury. While this could not be dispensed with, it could be biased to favour the executive because of the sheriff's discretion in drawing up lists of jurors and the prosecution's right to challenge individuals. In any case the high property qualification gave the panel a very marked socio-political bias. In accordance with due process Smith O'Brien, Thomas Francis Meagher, Terence Bellew MacManus and Patrick O'Donoghue were convicted at Clonmel of high treason for their revolutionary endeavours (which had gone far beyond the limits of what was intended to be dealt with as treason felony). Wisely determined not to make martyrs, the government, not without some legal difficulties, commuted their death sentences to transportation. These four, together with John Martin and Kevin Izod O'Doherty (convicted in Dublin for treason felony) joined Mitchel in Van Diemen's Land. Other leading Young Irelanders, notably John Blake Dillon, P.J. Smyth, Thomas Darcy McGee and Michael Doheny, had fled the country in late summer or autumn 1849, as had scores, and perhaps hundreds, of less well-known rebels and would-be rebels. That the jury system was not simply a tool in the hands of Dublin Castle was shown by the experience of Charles Gavan Duffy, who had been arrested on 8 July 1848. Repeated attempts to secure convictions against him failed and he was eventually released in April 1849.

North-east Connacht, south Ulster and north Leinster constituted, in the post-famine years, the homeland of the elusive phenomenon known as ribbonism. Recent work has given us a clear picture of the ribbon society of the 1820s and 1830s as an oathbound, ramified and hierarchical organisation of lower-class (but not impoverished) catholics, with political objectives and colourful rituals.[12] However, the ribbonism of the post-famine years is best thought of as a mode of collective action rather than a coherent association. Accordingly it became a source of much bewilderment to contemporary policemen and later historians, both types in search of a tangible and clearly identifiable entity. The name and some of the conventional paraphernalia of the dilapidated organisation were assumed by localised groupings with diverse functions, such as the offering of catholic counter-provocation to organised protestant militancy, the opposing of tangible and unpopular social or economic change (including evictions), or the provision of an outlet for the 'spirit of faction'. These and similar manifestations, when occurring in the northern half of the country, were frequently dubbed as ribbonism even when the participants did not use the term of themselves. The south, too, had its factions and its *ad hoc* agrarian conspiracies, but these were not given the ribbon label. It is, however, justifiable to recognise the existence of a distinctive 'ribbon' territory broadly defined by certain social characteristics, most obviously the survival of endemic conspiracy not easily amenable to the influence of church or state. And at the heart of the ribbon territory was the area where the size and structure of the rival religious confessions made possible sustained communal rivalry between them, in the 1790s and later. If ribbonism had become largely amorphous by the 1850s, it was not totally so, as organisation appears to have been renewed here and there and from time to time. Besides, the society (with appropriate modifications) had been established for decades among Irish emigrants in America and Britain; from both places there occasionally came missionaries attempting to reconstruct Irish ribbonism in the expatriate image.

In its heyday ribbonism had been something of a mirror image of the orange order. That organisation was re-established in 1846 after a decade of voluntary dissolution. Many of its members would gladly have come to the defence of the constitution in 1848 if there had been a serious nationalist rising. The celebration of 12 July 1849 was marred by a bloody clash with a body of catholics at Dolly's brae in County Down. Early in 1850 parliament passed the Party Processions Act which was intended to eliminate the provocations provided by characteristic orange celebrations.[13] Legislation could not diminish the reality of orange feeling about catholic and nationalist political ambitions.

The widespread support for O'Connell's repeal campaign had rested on a number of assumptions, including a belief that success — and so some form of Irish self-government — was actually attainable, and confidence among various groups and sections of Irish society that this self-government would solve their problems. The death of O'Connell in 1847 and the break up of his organisation in 1848 showed that success would not be easy, but these set backs do not come anywhere near to explaining the profound and widespread lack of interest in the question of repeal in the post-famine years. The famine had done nothing to endear British administration to Irish people of any class or creed; nearly everyone believed that the government could have handled the crisis much better than it did, and there was a consequent rise of anti-English sentiment among those already that way inclined. But it is a serious error to conclude that this dissatisfaction took the form of an increased desire for self-government. John Mitchel and others did proclaim at the time that the famine was the ultimate argument for Irish independence. It was a view that the militant artisans accepted, but it gained more general adherence only among people removed in time or place from the realities of the famine. For most observers, including the great bulk of previously 'repealer' opinion, the famine provided not an argument in favour of self-government, but several devastating arguments against it. At one level it exposed — something that every nationalist movement disguises — the almost total irrelevance of constitutional questions to the basic things of life, such as the provision of food, and economic survival generally. At another level it shattered the confidence of the repealers in the viability of a self-governing Ireland. This was not simply a matter of evident economic insufficiency, strikingly though that was highlighted. The famine had also uncovered an enormous potential for savage conflicts of interest between individuals and classes. The heartless mass-evictions of impoverished smallholders effected by some landlords during the famine years (and continuing as late as 1852) constitute a striking example. But heartlessness was a condition of survival for numerous individuals at every level of society and countless thousands of sub-tenants were forced off the land by farmers, big and small. The dominant feeling left behind by the famine in Ireland was not a desire for self-government but a sense of embarrassment and inadequacy. The self-confidence (or the illusions) essential for a strong nationalist movement would not be evident again for a generation. That did little to inhibit the dreams of a small but significant band of nationalist ideologues, but these people had a very small following in the 1850s.

Charles Gavan Duffy resumed his place in Irish political life in September 1849 with the relaunching of the *Nation*. He made a fresh start with agitation for self-government by founding a new organisation, the Irish Alliance. He soon discovered that the times were inopportune for promoting the nationalist question. In its place he embraced a newly-prospering agitation with more limited aims which was both close to his heart and likely to make sale for newspapers in the period ahead. This was the tenant-right campaign. The stresses of the famine years had moved farmers in the north-east and the south to organise themselves in pursuit of their particular interests. In Ulster their specific demand was for legislative recognition of the customary right of an outgoing tenant to receive compensation. An incipient movement in Counties Tipperary and Cork in 1847 attracted the support of James Fintan Lalor who had an interesting ideological angle on the subject, but who found the farmers unappreciative and drifted into the radical politics of 1848 and 1849.[14]

In the south noteworthy tenant organisation arrived in October 1849 with the founding of the Callan Tenant Protection Society. By mid-summer 1850 a series of similar societies existed throughout Leinster and Munster, with a few in Counties Mayo and Galway.[15] The specific original purpose of the tenant protection societies was simply to compel landlords by means of a united front to accept levels of rent deemed reasonable by the tenants. This superficial difference from the Ulster campaign with its emphasis on winning legislative backing does not take from the basic common essentials. North and south the tenants were making common cause in face of unprecedented uncertainty about their immediate economic and financial future at a time when at every level of agrarian society, from the landlords down, the weak and the unlucky were going to the wall. The change of these years seemed to be unprecedented though in fact it was largely a speeded-up phase of long-term developments. In this process the farmers as a class were growing in strength relative both to those above them and those below them in the agrarian hierarchy. Nevertheless, individual farmers were in economic peril, and this was especially true in the late 1840s and early 1850s as financially embarrassed landlords made exceptional efforts to collect rents, which were often seriously in arrears.

The geographical spread of the tenants' movement was related to its social basis. It flourished in areas where the farming class and its allied interest groups had reached a critical level of prominence *vis-a-vis* landlords on the one hand and the landless or near-landless on the other. North and south, the tenant societies were strongly supported by shopkeepers. Indeed, almost all the societies were based in towns or large villages rather than in purely rural parishes. The interest of the shopkeepers in the economic and financial well-being of the farmers is easily understood. So is the interest of clergymen. The Callan Tenant Protection Society was launched by two curates, Thomas O'Shea and Martin Keeffe. Everywhere else in the south and in a few places in Ulster, priests were central figures. In County Down, and in County Antrim, and here and there in Counties Tyrone and Londonderry, presbyterian ministers filled the same role. This alliance of clergy, shopkeepers and farmers betokens what can fairly be described as the emergence of a new order. It implied the absence or decline of secret agrarian conspiracy in a locality; it also implied a relative, though not necessarily permanent, decline in the local influence of the gentry and of the establishment in general. The landowners as a class had lost esteem in the famine years, because so many of them were seen to be in financial difficulties, and because so few of them had been able to play a beneficial, paternalistic role in the crisis. The encumbered estates acts of 1848 and 1849,[16] making provision for the easy sale of entailed properties, were a source of relief to individual bankrupt landowners but were also a serious blow to the status of Irish landlordism.

In August 1850 the tenants' movement was united in the Irish Tenant League which formulated a three-fold demand (the three Fs): fair (that is, independently fixed) rents; fixity of tenure subject to payment of this rent; and the right of free sale of the tenant's interest in his holding. ('Free sale' implied compensation for improvements.) Guided by Gavan Duffy and other newspaper proprietors, the league determined to seek legislative action on its demands by involving itself in parliamentary politics. It was to support election candidates who pledged themselves to make favourable land legislation a condition of their support for any government. A concurrent political development gave immense plausibility to a campaign of electoral pressure by the tenantry. The Representation of the People (Ireland) Act, 1850 became law on 14 August.[17] The basic voting qualification in the Irish counties would now be the tenure of property valued at twelve pounds or more for the purpose of poor law rates: absolutely no legal estate in the holding would be required, and so there would be an influx of thousands of tenant farmers to the voting lists making them a clear majority in very many constituencies. Following a pet idea of Gavan Duffy's, the league thought in terms of securing a parliamentary party that would exploit the current confusion of parties in the commons to bargain single-mindedly for a new deal for the Irish tenant farmer. This strategy would be supported, like the repeal campaign and the anti-corn-law campaign, by popular demonstrations. In the autumn of 1850 thousands, and in some cases tens of thousands, of farmers and their supporters attended Irish Tenant League gatherings throughout the country.[18] But even tens of thousands did not represent overwhelming support by the standards of the age. Already in 1850 recovery was under way, which must have sapped the enthusiasm of the farmers for protest. The key role of a minority notwithstanding, most priests remained aloof from the league. And if some presbyterian ministers were extremely active, others were strongly opposed to the league or even to the very idea of tenant-right. Significantly, only a few sitting M.P.s committed themselves to the league's policy. Almost by definition, most M.P.s had a vested interest in landlords' rights, but with an eye to the next election, many would undoubtedly have moved to accommodate the Tenant League if it had appeared really formidable in electoral terms. Before the issue could be put to the test of the polls, the picture was complicated by the intrusion of another question.

The Ecclesiastical Titles Act of 1851, provoked by the restoration of the catholic hierarchy in England and Wales, was seen by Irish catholics as an affront to their religion and, if not as actually threatening the reimposition of religious disabilities, then as an attempt to reimpose a badge of inferiority. Protest meetings were held throughout the three southern provinces. There was particular dismay in that the offending measure was the work of a Liberal government. By 1851 more than sixty of the Irish members were Liberals in the rather loose party categorisation of the time. (This included the repealers elected in 1847; they had changed designation with the minimum of difficulty when repeal becamse self-evidently a dead letter.)[19] The great majority of them — either being catholics themselves or being dependent on catholic electoral support — voted against the titles bill. About twenty — undoubtedly with an eye to the electoral potentialities of aroused catholic feeling in Ireland — refused to resume their normal general support for the government afterwards. They adopted a policy of making life as difficult as possible for the ministerial side in the commons until the titles act would be repealed. Their admirers called them the Irish Brigade; others dubbed them the Pope's Brass Band. Their leaders, including G.H. Moore, William Keogh and John Sadleir, won notice and admiration at home. In August 1851 they set up in Dublin the Catholic Defence Association. The association, not surprisingly, adopted the strategy of exhorting voters to support election candidates dedicated to forming a parliamentary group committed to singleminded struggle for the vindication of the civil and religious equality of catholics. Without much delay the Catholic Defence Association and the Irish Tenant League came to an informal working arrangement.[20] This was forced by circumstances on the weaker party — the league — despite the reservations of Gavan Duffy, the pres-

Some economic and social indicators, 1849-82

	Year-on-year percentage change in aggregate Irish Bank deposits	Emigrants per 1000 population	Railway journeys per head of the population	Letters delivered per head of the population	Illiteracy rate Ulster	Illiteracy rate Leinster	Illiteracy rate Munster	Illiteracy rate Connacht	Illiteracy rate Ireland
	%				%	%	%	%	%
1849	+ 6								
1850	+11								
1851	0		0.9	5.5	35	39	56	66	47
1852	+30	30							
1853	+ 1	28							
1854	+ 7	23							
1855	+ 5	15							
1856	+12	15							
1857	− 5	16							
1858	+15	11							
1859	+ 6	14							
1860	− 3	15							
1861	− 4	11	1.8	8.6	30	31	46	57	39
1862	− 4	12							
1863	−10	21							
1864	+21	20							
1865	+19	18							
1866	+13	18							
1867	+ 4	15							
1868	+ 2	11							
1869	+ 2	12							
1870	+ 8	14							
1871	+ 7	13	2.9	13.3	26	27	39	49	33
1872	+ 5	15							
1873	+ 4	17							
1874	+ 6	14							
1875	+ 7	10							
1876	+ 3	7							
1877	0	7							
1878	− 3	8							
1879	− 5	9							
1880	− 3	18							
1881	− 4	15	3.4	15.5	20	20	28	38	25
1882	+ 8	18							

Sources: *Census of Ireland, 1851,...1861,...1871,...1881.*
Thom's Directory, 1850 etc.
W.E. Vaughan and A.J. Fitzpatrick, *Irish historical statistics; population, 1821-1971* (Dublin, 1978).

byterians, and indeed the league priests.

The Liberal government fell in February 1852 and was succeeded by a minority tory administration, there being an understanding that an election would follow in the summer. Immediately before the election Irish religious fury was rekindled by a government proclamation against catholic processions in England and by the anticatholic Stockport riots for which the government was rather unfairly blamed. This helped the cause of those candidates standing on the question of catholic rights. In most constituencies in the three southern provinces catholic electors found themselves being drawn into an enthusiastic crusade — often organised by the priests, with more or less circumspection — on behalf of candidates (many of them former Liberals, others newcomers to electoral politics) who had pledged, or intimated, that they would stand up in parliament for tenant-right and religious liberty. The principal slogan of this campaign was 'tenant-right', although its main inspiration was clearly the assertion of catholic rights and catholic identity. Despite the prominence of religious feeling in the south, many presbyterians in Counties Down, Armagh, Londonderry and Monaghan supported tenant-right candidates.[21]

Many of the new electors had a baptism of fire. Landlords, who were preponderantly Conservatives, tended to assume that they could command the votes of their newly-enfranchised tenants-at-will, so that many an unfortunate voter had to choose between the wrath of his landlord and that of his parish priest (and neighbours). In the event the Conservatives increased their representation from thirty-eight to forty-one. They did well in the north, where even a good showing by William Sharman Crawford in County Down, by Samuel McCurdy Greer in County Londonderry and by Dr John Gray in County Monaghan was not sufficient to win a seat for the tenant-right cause. Elsewhere in the country the tenant-righters and their allies had considerable success. Exactly how much became clear when at one or other of two post-electoral conferences in Dublin a total of forty-eight M.P.s turned up to pledge themselves to remain 'independent of and in opposition to' any government not giving substantial satisfaction on the questions of the land and religious equality.[22] Thanks to both the passion of the campaign and the extension of the franchise under the 1850 act, this number was far ahead of the 36 seats won for repeal in 1847.

This new 'independent opposition' party as it came to be called, acting in accordance with its pledges, used its numerical power to vote down the Conservative government in early December 1852. When a new administration was formed, composed of Liberals and Peelites, the cohesion of the independent oppositionists was put to a severe test. The prime minister was Lord Aberdeen who had opposed the Ecclesiastical Titles Act; with him in office the offending act would be a dead letter. In other ways, too, Aberdeen would be more sensitive to Irish catholic interests than any possible alternative prime minister. In effect — though not in any formal way — the campaign against the titles act and what it was thought to represent had triumphed with Aberdeen's accession. There was no comparable success on the tenant-right question. But many of the forty-eight pledged M.P.s had no real heart for the land issue and knew that it carried little enough weight in most constituencies. Within a short time twenty of them were supporting the new government. Two of them actually accepted office, namely, John Sadleir as a junior lord of the treasury, and William Keogh as solicitor-general for Ireland. The defection of Sadleir and Keogh subsequently became a *cause célèbre* in Irish political discourse, not because it was particularly brazen — which it was — but because it was extensively used for propaganda purposes. The independent oppositionist M.P.s had split into two camps. One set — and this grew gradually over subsequent years — returned to the loosely-knit fellowship of the Liberal--whig party. The other group including Gavan Duffy (new member for New Ross), Frederick Lucas (proprietor of the *Tablet* and new member for County Meath), and G.H. Moore, proclaimed continuing allegiance to 'independent opposition', denounced Sadleir and Keogh as villainous traitors, and continued to demand land legislation, although the tenant-right movement in the country had largely collapsed after 1852. The division partly reflected divergent economic interests within the politicised stratum of Irish catholicism: whigs-in-the-making involved in speculative land-purchase and high finance opposed the self-appointed spokesmen of tenant farmers and shopkeepers. Of course, there was more involved than the rational conflict of class interests. Some ideological nationalists latched on to independent opposition for the connotations of nationality implicit in its rhetoric. The presence of Young Irelanders (and especially of Gavan Duffy) on one side revived the animosities of the previous decade between them and former O'Connellites on the other side, although this division of the 1850s was only marginally comparable with those of the mid- and late-1840s. For one thing, the independent oppositionists unlike the Young Irelanders in 1847-8 had a substantial party in the country, articulated by an able *cadre* of tenant-right priests and 'second generation' Young Irelanders. Their most prominent supporter was Archbishop MacHale of Tuam, who had been a bitter critic of Gavan Duffy and his friends in O'Connell's time. MacHale's adhesion to the independent opposition side was all the more determined because it placed him on the opposite side from Paul Cullen, archbishop of Armagh, 1850-52, and of Dublin from 1852, for whom he had developed an abiding personal antipathy. From the archbishops down, the split quickly became less a matter of objectives, principles or tactics and more a matter of unreasoning 'come-hell-or-highwater' loyalty to one or other of two factions.

The apparently limited political impact of the tenant-right movement of the early 1850s should not be allowed to obscure the importance of the agrarian question in contemporary Irish minds. The campaign for repeal of the union had derived much of its strength from largely unspoken assumptions about changes that would follow in the land laws. (Indeed throughout most of the nineteenth century everyone concerned assumed that some such changes would be an immediate consequence of Irish self-government.) The disappearance of the prospect of repeal did not diminish the underlying drives, and large numbers of Irish people continued to dream of an improvement in their lot through change in the land system. This attitude involved antagonism towards the existing agrarian order, and the strength of this feeling throughout the 1850s, 1860s and 1870s is undeniable. It was reflected in the newspapers, for instance. Those depending to any extent on popular support (whether they were Dublin-based or provincial) displayed an unflagging preoccupation with questions of tenancy, land ownership and landlord-tenant relations. Their reaction to agrarian outrages is very instructive, being marked by large measures of ambivalence.[23]

Just as mid-nineteenth century critics of the English land system found a historicist justification of their position in the baneful impact of the eleventh-century Normans or the sixteenth-century purchasers of monastic land, so many Irish catholics of the nineteenth century were wont to persuade themselves that they had been robbed by Cromwell in the seventeenth. Irish presbyterian tenant-righters had their own distinctive rationalisation; according to this they were the heirs of seventeenth-century settlers who had been given very favourable (and inalienable) status *vis-a-vis* their landlords.[24] Resentment of the existing land system was an integral part of the sense of communal identity of Irish catholics. It was shared by catholic landlords, including those of the 'new breed' of purchasers under the encumbered estates acts who saw themselves challenging the domination of land ownership by the protestant elite. Closely associated with these in interest and attitudes were the catholic graziers — a group of rising significance in the 1850s. Archbishop Cullen saw in such people a major prospect for the advancement of the catholic interest. (His family connections among them undoubtedly had some influence on his attitudes, though this point should not be exaggerated.)

Whenever it was politically expedient catholic whigs could pay lip-service to tenant-right, a policy for which they themselves had little or no liking, but which was seen by an immensely larger number of catholics as the form that the expected beneficial agrarian change would take. 'Tenant-right' was to mid-Victorian Ireland what 'free-trade' was to England in the same era, namely, the catch-cry of an emerging dominant interest. Some of the significance of tenant-right is caught in the recent assertion that 'the Tenant League of the 1850s constituted an ideological alternative to the laissez-faire principles of the landed elite'.[25] But it would be a serious error to see here a philosophical conflict about the nature of property, with Irish landlords as the vanguard of individualistic capitalism being challenged by the shock troops of communalism. The tenant-righters were second to none in their determination to enjoy individual property-owning and accumulation. They simply wished to have a once-off change in the law that would convert their landholding into a form of ownership, at the expense of the landlords. On the other hand, the Irish landlords as a whole are rather implausible pace-setters of either the practice or theory of 'devil-take-the-hindmost' capitalism. They supported the land law as it stood because it favoured them and not because they were imbued with any Manchester-school principles. Like 'Manchester', tenant-righters menaced the 'landocracy', but not for reasons of ideology.

The fundamental flaw in the tenant-right formula was that it envisaged major legal (and social) change stopping short at an arbitrary point. But if the existing ownership of land was to be interfered with by law, what was sacrosanct about existing landholding? Why should there not be a redistribution of occupancy as well as of ownership? It was the threat to their own interests from below (from the smallholders and the landless) that perhaps more than anything else prevented the farmers from driving home their advantage against the landlords. The cottiers and labourers had been decimated in the famine but, as the emigration figures of subsequent years were to show, they were still in surplus in 1851. Significantly, the earliest statement of objectives by the Callan Tenant Protection Society mentioned the labourers, and called for the provision of opportunities for them off the land.[26] The farming classes in western Europe generally had entered the 1850s with a dread of 'communism' haunting their minds, and Ireland was no exception. The fear of opening Pandora's box undoubtedly dissuaded many who sympathised with tenant-right from joining in the political campaign of the Irish Tenant League. Another factor was doubt about the likelihood of success. The evident lack of success of the campaign, together with a sharp rise in agricultural prosperity, sapped the farmers' enthusiasm after 1852.

By 1855 the morale of the independent oppositionists was low. There was no prospect of worthwhile success in parliament. In Ireland they appeared to be losing the propaganda battle with the catholic whigs. Archbishop Cullen of Dublin was becoming more openly and more effectively antagonistic to them. The influential *Freeman's Journal* had ceased to give its valuable support.[27] Against this background Gavan Duffy resigned his seat in parliament, disposed of the *Nation*, and left Ireland in November 1855 to begin a new career in Australia, where in due course his talents received deserved recognition. In a farewell editorial in the *Nation* Duffy declared that there seemed to be 'no more hope for the Irish cause than for the corpse on the dissecting table'.[28] That memorable phrase was seized on subsequently by various fenian apologists and used in two somewhat contradictory senses. It was held forth as evidence that Ireland was indeed moribund until revitalised by fenianism; and it was used as evidence that Duffy and others like him were traitorous traducers of the Irish national spirit, imagining the death of the indestructible. The literal truth underlying Duffy's metaphor was the impossibility of fomenting widespread political agitation during most of the decade. The Party Processions Act of 1850 discouraged the holding of the more spectacular kind of public demonstrations typical of the catholic emancipation and repeal eras, but it merely reinforced more effective inhibitions, above all the lack of any sense of political occasion or opportunity. The absence of political agitation and the lack of interest in self-government that mark most of the 1850s can be taken as evidence that the 'nation' was indeed in ashes, needing the 'spirit' of fenianism to stir it up to a phoenix-like resurrection; that, however, is to accept a pseudo-spiritual concept of nationalism which is no less naïve for being widely entertained, or for having, like all myths, an insidious attraction for the human mind.

The creators and custodians of mainstream Irish mythology have succeeded over a period of generations in blurring recognition of a salient fact about Irish nationalism, namely, that, since the early nineteenth century at least, it has been essentially an expression of the felt needs, social and psychological, of the Irish catholic body, including the apparent need to challenge other Christians on the island in various ways. In the 1850s the catholic church in Ireland was bringing a new thoroughness and efficiency to its institutional life and so was consolidating the sense of catholic identity. This nation-building ecclesiastical development was founded on a firm basis of improving parochial organisation, backed up by growing numbers of religious active in education, and, in the case of the Redemptorist and Vincentian Fathers, giving parish missions which could reinvigorate the religious patterns and sense of identity of an entire locality.[29] All of this had begun long before the famine, but in the 1850s conditions were particularly suitable, not least because Archbishop Cullen had the vision and determination to give countrywide leadership. Cullen's primary preoccupation was to secure the adhesion of the maximum number to the catholic community. There were after the famine many pockets of population still in contention between the catholic and protestant churches. The most spectacular work of the catholic mission movement in the 1850s was a series of assaults — mainly successful — on recently-formed protestant communities along the western seaboard. Even more long-drawn-out was the effort to secure Irish catholicism against 'leakages' caused by the institutional advantages of the established church in schools, workhouses, prisons and so on. This labour not to lose a single soul was at one level a most pressing spiritual obligation for Cullen as a pastor. At the same time it was an assertion of national identity: nobody ever felt more strongly than Cullen the sense of Irish catholic belonging. Besides, he had a clear vision of the institutional changes that he desired for the Irish catholic nation. These included disestablishment of the anglican church in Ireland, the state endowment of a clerically-controlled catholic education system, and the creation of catholic chaplaincies in the public services. He displayed his determination at the synod of Thurles in 1850 when as apostolic delegate he campaigned successfully for rejection by the assembled bishops of the recently-established Queen's colleges because these colleges were not under catholic control.[30] They decided to create their own Catholic University as an alternative.

A 'nationalist' catholic identity was the largest political fact of Irish life in the mid-nineteenth century. The catholics as a body might seek Irish self-government, and so be 'nationalist' in the strictest sense (as happened in the mid-1840s), or they might not (as was the position in the 1850s): the difference between the two was superficial. Archbishop Cullen, whatever he may have thought in the mid-1840s, accepted by 1850 that Irish self-government was not a feasible proposition. He stood for another and less well recognised 'nationalist' policy, namely, an Ireland with its own distinctive life and institutions (radically different in some respects from those of Great Britain) but without benefit of indigenous government. Westminster would have to be pressurised from time to time by popular protests or by parliamentary action to concede desired changes, but in Irish politics for its own sake he saw no benefit. Little wonder, then, that he had mostly difficult relations with Irish popular agitators and politicians, such as Gavan Duffy. The independent opposition so strongly advocated by Duffy meant the abandonment of all prospects of sharing in government patronage. That Cullen was not prepared to sacrifice for any lengthy period: he wished to see as many catholics as possible at all levels of the Irish establishment and he looked to the Irish Liberal M.P.s to seek places for them. Cullen and Duffy shared the same basic sense of Irish catholic belonging but they had rationalised their common atavism by means of two quite different ideologies. Duffy, following his friend Thomas Davis, had a concept of the Irish nation as a secular community in which Irishmen of all religious persuasions might feel at home. This indifference to confessional allegiance was anathema to Cullen. But in one respect at least Cullen's ideology was superior to Duffy's: it corresponded more closely to the confessional reality which so largely determined Irish political allegiances then and later.

John MacHale had been promulgating catholic nationalism and opposing non-denominational education for a generation before Paul Cullen returned from Rome to become an Irish prelate, and both archbishops were agreed on these issues. Apart from an understandable resentment against a newcomer who enjoyed Roman favour, there seemed to be little reason in 1850 for MacHale to be at loggerheads with Cullen. One of the small number of really substantial and basic points of difference to emerge between them in the subsequent decades of near-continuous bitterness concerned the function of the church in popular Irish politics. MacHale never lost his yearning for the national mobilisations of O'Connell's time. In particular he liked the idea of ecclesiastical immersion in popular politics. This Cullen, by contrast, found distasteful: he could tolerate it only on specific occasions and for specific objectives set up by the church. In the 1840s the organisational facilities of the church — and, most importantly, its capacity for fund raising — had been placed at the disposal of a political movement. During the thirty years following the famine this recurred but rarely and briefly. That was how Cullen liked to have things, and he worked to maintain it, but it was not a situation that arose at his behest: the contribution of the church organisation at local level to politics was determined by the reactions of priests and laity rather than those of bishops.

The failure of the independent opposition movement to achieve anything at Westminster was grist to the mill for those other Young Irelanders who, unlike Gavan Duffy, had come to maintain that revolution was the only worthwhile form of endeavour for Irish nationalists. Their *doyen*, John Mitchel, escaped from Van Diemen's Land in 1853 and made his way to New York, where he at once threw himself into propagandist journalism. In his newspaper, the *Citizen*, he serialized his reflections written in captivity, which were subsequently published as the *Jail Journal*. The fiercely intransigent anti-English tone of his prison writings was matched by the leader columns of the *Citizen*. With the outset of the Crimean war Mitchel urged Irishmen to turn the situation to revolutionary advantage. Duffy felt obliged to dissociate himself from this advice in the most unequivocal fashion. (If constitutional nationalism was out of fashion in Ireland revolution was anathema.) There ensued another round of a dispute that had set Mitchel and Duffy against one another in 1847-8. This time the exchanges were less inhibited and the personal bitterness was more pronounced.

Like Mitchel, most of the Young Ireland exiles had gravitated to America. Two of his fellow-prisoners — Thomas Francis Meagher and Terence Bellew MacManus — had escaped and arrived in the U.S.A. before him. Others, such as John Blake Dillon, Richard O'Gorman, and Michael Doheny had fled there directly in 1848-9. More numerous were the many young local confederate leaders who had taken flight in the late summer of 1848. Out of those élites a significant number found profitable employment in promoting Irish revolutionary doctrines among the Irish-American masses. American politicians had begun this work by organising meetings in support of a supposedly-imminent Irish republican rising in 1848. Committees had been formed and fundraising drives launched. Much of the instigation had come from opportunists endeavouring to muster the Irish vote in New York for the 1848 presidential election: the state had been carried by a whisker in 1844. A significant proportion of the Irish immigrant masses found in demonstrative nationalism-in-exile an answer to some of their social and psychological needs in a strange and not very friendly environment. In 1848 and the following years the flexible American state militia system provided a convenient vehicle. Especially in New York, thousands of Irishmen were enlisted into exclusively Irish regiments of militia — such as the New York 69th — where they made believe to be preparing themselves for a war of Irish liberation. At another level various societies — more or less secret — were instituted to encourage and direct revolutionary Irish nationalism in America. These included the Irishmen's Civil and Military Republican Union, the Emmet Monument Association and the

Irish Emigrant Aid Society.[31] There was no united leadership to channel all of this effort. On the contrary, it seems to have been accompanied by a quite extraordinary amount of in-fighting. John Mitchel's arrival gave rise to hopes of unity and effective leadership which were particularly ill-placed.

Mitchel and some other sanguine Irish-Americans saw in the Crimean war (1854-6) a possible opportunity for an effective Irish *emeute*. Mitchel himself negotiated with the Russian Ambassador in the U.S.A. hoping for a supply of arms for Ireland.[32] Nothing came of this, but diplomatic disputes about British recruitment in the U.S.A. raised the prospect of an Anglo-American falling-out and the Emmet Monument Association decided on an armed invasion of Ireland to take place in September 1855. Joseph Denieffe, a Kilkenny-born tailor living in New York has recorded how he was engaged by the association in the most casual fashion to organise preparations in Ireland as he was about to return there on personal business in the summer of 1855. What he did was essentially an attempt to revive secret conspiracy among people whom he knew to have been implicated in it in 1849. His procedure was to seek out suitable individuals, tender an oath, give details of the promised invasion and then arrange means of communication. His most intensive efforts appear to have been made in Kilkenny and Callan. In these towns he recruited John Haltigan, Edward Coyne and James Cody, all subsequently prominent local fenians.[33] There is no way of telling whether or not the nucleus of revolutionary organisation had been preserved in the Kilkenny area between 1849 and 1855. We know for certain that it had survived among a group of artisans and small traders in the Dublin area. Their most substantial structure appears to have been the St Patrick's Society of Kingstown, founded in 1848 and destined to become a registered friendly society, providing at the same time excellent cover for political conspiracy. The identities of some of the Kingstown group have been recorded: the Hickey brothers, the Rochfords, a tailor named Scott, an old-clothes man named Jennings and George Kelly of Dalkey. Together with a group of city men led by one Peter Langan a lath-maker they were accustomed to go on Sunday trips to the Dublin mountains, where they practised military drill under the direction of a sympathetic staff-sergeant of militia. They also collected money for the purchase of rifles.[34] Denieffe contacted Langan in 1855 and enlisted him and an unknown number of his associates. Denieffe and his organisation remained in readiness for the promised invasion throughout the summer and autumn, and they maintained their system of communications even after the uneventful passing of 1855 had shown that their hopes were in vain.

By the mid-1850s the leaders of Young Ireland had come to be highly regarded by many people in Ireland, Australia, America and Britain who did not at all approve of the policies which had brought them exile and fame. Their potential influence over Irish people and Irish opinion was greatly enhanced by their obvious ability and talents and their superiority in intellect to any surviving leaders of 'Old Ireland'. Yet they were to count for comparatively little as a group in subsequent Irish political life. Instead a quite separate élite group was to inherit the political momentum of Young Ireland.

This new breed can be seen at work for the first time in the leadership of the '1849 movement', which was initiated and controlled by Thomas Clarke Luby, James Fintan Lalor, Philip Gray, Joseph Brenan and John O'Leary. Excepting Gray, they conform remarkably well to a stereotype: a man in his twenties or thirties (O'Leary was 19, Lalor 42) from a comfortable family, in the commercial or lower professional bracket; youth spent in leisure or formal education without financial responsibility; an intellectual, highly literate, and well read in literature and acquainted through the journals with 'progressive ideas'; alienated from work — both the family business and the professional career that the parents typically had in mind for him. Comparisons with the Young Ireland élite are obvious (especially the intellectual dimension, and good financial circumstances) but the contrasts are important also.[35] Duffy worked hard and had proved himself as a newspaper man by 1842; Davis and Dillon had qualified as barristers; Mitchel had earned his living as a solicitor; Smith O'Brien and Martin were landed proprietors (though at opposite ends of the landowners' social scale); Terence Bellew MacManus was a businessman. In their distaste for money-making the younger men were more 'gentlemanly', but on the social scale they were a few notches below the original Young Irelanders (other possibly than Michael Doheny). On the other hand they were most definitely located at a level far 'above' their artisan followers in the '49 movement.

These 1849 leaders constituted the tip of an iceberg. Soon to be revealed were dozens of others, all a minor by-product of larger economic and social developments, usually the alienated sons of commercial prosperity. We are concerned here with those of them who discovered a meaning for life in ideological nationalism. In the mid-1840s while the masses were finding in the *Nation* a sense of communal uplift generated by accounts of Daniel O'Connell's political activities, the occasional young man here and there was deriving something extra from the leading articles — a personal devotion to nationality. So, Denis Holland in Cork, Charles J. Kickham in Mullinahone, John O'Leary in Tipperary, A.M. Sullivan in Bantry, and scores of others, underwent an experience that has to be compared to religious conversion. Dedication to any humdrum profession was henceforth impossible. The only avocation that could satisfy was the political and ideological advancement of the national cause. This was particularly realisable through the newspaper press. Indeed, journalism was the one occupation that was totally compatible with the ideal. In most cases family financial support was not available indefinitely, and, if one had to earn an income, journalism was the obvious choice. And so Ireland in the 1850s produced a small army of newspaper people fired with romantic nationalist ideals. It so happened also that during the 1850s the newspaper business in the United Kingdom in general entered an era of unprecedented opportunity and expansion. The economics of journalism were revolutionised by technical and, especially, fiscal factors: in 1853 the tax on advertisements was dropped, to be followed by the abolition in 1855 of the compulsory newspaper stamp, and in 1860 of the tax on paper. Falling costs led to reduced prices, a mushrooming of new publications, and a spectacular expansion of circulation and readership. When the boom reached Ireland towards the end of the decade there was to hand an enthusiastic band of would-be editors and leader writers. This was to be of some considerable importance for the subsequent development of Irish political opinion. Equally important, there was still a considerable surplus of these talented scribes so that many made their way to America and England and found congenial employment in which they influenced the political outlook of Irish exiles to a degree quite out of proportion to their numbers.

In Ireland it was not until 1857 and afterwards that the boom in journalism made entry to the business comparatively easy in the way described. Before that the newspaper ventures of the neo-Young-Irelanders had been limited and unsuccessful. Joseph Brenan edited for some of its short life the Dublin-based *Irishman* which appeared during 1849 and 1850. Fintan Lalor divided his efforts in 1849 between his secret society and an unsuccessful attempt to launch a newspaper. Denis Holland launched the short-lived *Ulsterman* in Belfast in 1852. In early 1855 a host of young enthusiasts surfaced in the management, editing and writing of the *Tipperary Leader* (Thurles). They included T.P. O'Connor (*not* the later M.P. for the Liverpool Scotland Division), C.J. Kickham, William Kenealy and A.M. Sullivan. The *Leader* displayed undisguised expectation of a crisis in British fortunes as a consequence of the Crimean war. Like the war, the *Leader* came to an end early in 1856. The *Tribune* (Dublin) was another newspaper launched in 1855 on the wave of extremist euphoria. It was edited by T.C. Luby until it collapsed, again, early in 1856.

If the new élite was still finding difficulty in the early and mid-1850s in making a breakthrough into journalism, the Irish catholic community did not suffer for want of newspapers. The most important journal in the country was probably the *Freeman's Journal*, owned and managed by a close associate of Daniel O'Connell, Dr John Gray, in partnership with J.M. Cantwell. The *Catholic Telegraph*, founded by John Sadleir, was in the same political camp. John F. Maguire, though no Young Irelander, supported the independent opposition line in the newspaper he had founded and continued to manage, the *Cork Examiner*, and so was to some extent allied with Lucas in the *Tablet* and Duffy in the *Nation*. Before leaving for Australia in 1855, Duffy sold the *Nation* to a partnership dominated by A.M. Sullivan, who, under the persisting influence of the Young Ireland intoxication, had turned his back a few years before on all occupations except nationalist journalism. By early 1858 Sullivan was the sole proprietor of the *Nation* and he was being helped with the editorial work by his brother, Timothy Daniel.[36]

Attempts were made subsequently to show that Duffy was disappointed by his successor's editorial line, but Sullivan obtained his opportunity in 1855 precisely because he was an admirer and supporter of Duffy. Unlike Sullivan, most of the young generation of national-minded journalists were siding against Duffy and with Mitchel in 1855. Their platonic idealism found the latter's rhetoric of revolution and intransigence more congenial than Duffy's compromise with liberal constitutionalism. There was no necessary reason why these products and heirs of Duffy's *Nation* of the 1840s should reject the policies of Duffy's *Nation* in the 1850s, but their intellectual and emotional make-up had a built-in compulsion towards intransigence. When Duffy's practical alternative, independent opposition, proved to be unsuccessful, most of them accepted Mitchel's assertion that it was also demoralising, and the attractions of the extremist stance were enhanced. In Mitchel's polemical work they found a simplistic but brilliantly expressed revolutionary intransigence. Through them Mitchel's cult of violence, his disdain for democratic politics, and his glorification of hatred — especially hatred of all things British — were to make considerable impact on the rhetoric of later nationalism.

James Stephens and John O'Mahony were to become two of the most influential members of the neo-Young-Ireland élite.

Looking at their origins, one might not be immediately certain that they were in the same social band. Stephens was the son of an auctioneer's clerk in Kilkenny city. Despite the efforts of a painstaking biographer there remains a mystery over his background and early years. But we do know that he worked briefly as a railway engineer until, in 1848, just coming to his mid-twenties, he abandoned humdrum existence for the career of romantic commitment, and joined the attempted rising.[37] O'Mahony was the son of a gentleman-farmer from near Mitchelstown. He was a graduate of Trinity College, Dublin, and as a young man he came to live near Carrick-on-Suir on the large farm of a relation, which he was to inherit.[38] There was about O'Mahony's part in 1848 a hint of the chief rallying his men, and O'Mahony displayed at all times an intense family pride which was implicitly explained by reference to his family's alleged connection with the chieftainship of the clan. A biographical study exploring his background would possibly reveal some important elements in O'Mahony's make-up. But both Stephens and O'Mahony can perhaps be understood best if we are aware of some uncertainty on their own parts about where precisely to locate themselves in the social firmament, notwithstanding that the silent classification system observed so faithfully by their contemporaries put them both into the same caste as O'Leary, Luby, and the other neo-Young-Irelanders. However, one gets the feeling that Stephens was there only by the force of his personality, while on the other hand O'Mahony was sufficiently well thought of for some of the Young Ireland élite, and even Archbishop MacHale, to engage in correspondence with him without acting *infra dignitatem*. O'Mahony dropped to within social range of Stephens and company after 1848 because he was by then propertyless, having before his flight into exile made over his holdings and goods to his sister and her husband. Significantly, she was married into one of the most aristocratic families in south County Tipperary, the Mandevilles of Ballydine, who traced their presence in the Suir valley back to the early decades of the Norman invasion in the twelfth century.

Like all the inspired activists we have been talking about, Stephens and O'Mahony were intellectuals. O'Mahony was, in addition, a scholar who more than held his own in the admittedly not very crowded world of mid-century Gaelic scholarship with his translation of *Foras feasa ar Éirinn* by Seathrún Céitinn.

Stephens and O'Mahony were among the dozens of Irish refugees who reached Paris in late 1848. Unlike the majority, they settled down there for a number of years. They lived frugally in squalid lodgings, surviving on meagre and irregular remittances from Ireland and on fees for language lessons. In due course Stephens's command of French was sufficiently good for him to earn some money as an occasional translator of English texts. Much credence has been given to a near-contemporary assertion that they joined one of the Parisian secret societies, rose to prominent positions and 'became pupils of some of the ablest and most profound masters of revolutionary science which the nineteenth century . . . produced'.[39] The extremely general nature of this information suggests that the author was presenting what he thought should have happened rather than anything he had reason to believe did happen. Scarcely anything put on record by Stephens or O'Mahony amounts to convincing evidence that they were initiated into any continental secret society, and even if they were, it is virtually certain that they never advanced beyond the lower ranks. If at this time their companions in the cheapest eating-places of the Latin Quarter included high-ranking revolutionists, Stephens was uncharacteristically reticent on the topic in his egotistical recollections in later life. On the other hand, they could in Paris immerse themselves in the ethos of radicalism and revolution that had already reached out to them in Ireland and which was redolent of oath-taking, conspiracy and secret fraternity. As we have seen, many of their contemporaries had become enamoured of the revolutionary secret-society *à la Française* without ever leaving Ireland. But the Parisian experience enabled Stephens and O'Mahony to carry themselves subsequently as 'past masters' of the subject. In a general way, no appreciative spirit could sojourn at length in Paris without bearing the mark subsequently. But very little happened to the political outlook of Stephens and O'Mahony in Paris that might not have happened if they had been cooped up together for the same period of exile, in straitened circumstances, anywhere else on the globe. Left with nothing to lose, and little to do, both now found themselves to be what O'Mahony called 'ultra-democrats'. Differences in personality meant that while O'Mahony became more and more preoccupied with Ireland's prospects of independence, Stephens saw himself as the potential benefactor of a much larger portion of the human race. Like Garibaldi in this as in a few other characteristics, he would have taken an opportunity to 'liberate' any other country as well as his own. As ultra-democrats, O'Mahony and Stephens regretted the advent of the second empire. Not much more than that is established by O'Mahony's obiter dictum to the effect that they 'proffered' their lives on the occasion of the resistance to Louis Napoleon's *coup d'etat* in December 1851.[40]

O'Mahony left Paris for America in late 1853. Stephens

apparently remained on for nearly two more years. By early 1856 he was back in Ireland. No doubt he came partly because of the expectations associated with the Crimean war. However, he scarcely came to encourage them: T.C. Luby many years later recalled that Stephens in 1856 saw no hope for an Irish revolution prior to a democratic revolution in England.[41] Because Stephens founded the fenian organisation two years later it has been assumed that he had returned to Ireland with plans for organisation in mind. Readers of his own account of this period composed many years later, are given to understand that he came in 1856 to survey the Irish political scene and assess the preparedness of the people for revolutionary conspiracy.[42] In fact he had a rather different preoccupation at this time: like Karl Marx he was engaged in writing a book intended to effect important change. As with all his projects he was wildly optimistic about the outcome: the publication of his work would, he declared, have an incalculable effect on Irish public opinion and would be of great financial benefit to himself. In the meantime he supported himself by giving French lessons to the children of wealthy families in Dublin, including those of the attorney-general, J.D. Fitzgerald, who was so impressed that he found Stephens a position in the customs service. In the event, Stephens, who must have solicited this help in the first place, pleaded preoccupation with his writing and declined the opportunity.[43]

Stephens was frequently absent from his teaching for long periods. During these intervals he went on the travels which he later magnified into his 'three-thousand-mile walk' around Ireland, allegedly undertaken for the purpose of testing the political temperature of the country. It is noteworthy, however, that, apart from revisiting the scenes of his 1848 adventures, he concentrated on places with scenic, romantic and literary associations — such as Killarney, Clonmacnoise and Lissoy (Goldsmith's supposed Auburn).[44] Obviously he was visiting touristic sites with the enthusiasm of the returned exile who has had time abroad to realise what interesting things at home he had never seen. Also, these travels were intended to provide either substance or colour for the great book (which, of course, never reached the printing press). The specific political purpose was a later invention.

On one of his tours Stephens paid a visit to another returned political exile, William Smith O'Brien. It has been well said that Smith O'Brien proved to be 'more of a success as an exile than as a revolutionary'.[45] In 1854 he was granted a partial pardon as were those other Young Ireland transportees who had not absconded from Van Diemen's Land; in 1856 a full pardon permitted them to return to Ireland. The same self-regard that now allowed the Bohemian Stephens to present himself uninvited at the front door of Cahirmoyle House had enabled him in late July 1848 to assume a prominent position in Smith O'Brien's entourage and to speak familiarly across the social gulf that separated him from a scion of the landed nobility. What had been tolerable 'on the barricades' was deeply embarrassing for Smith O'Brien before a disdainful wife and household. Nevertheless, he was apparently tolerant of the visitor, though even Stephens's account does not give the impression that repeat visits were encouraged. Stephens was similarly kept at arm's length by another fellow-veteran of Ballingarry, John Blake Dillon, who had returned from America in 1855 to resume his legal career. Dillon's family was among those to which Stephens gave French lessons at this time, but Stephens was not permitted to approach the head of the household on familiar terms.

In the course of these tours (during the years 1856-7) Stephens traversed County Cork on a number of occasions on his way to Killarney without getting to know the Phoenix National and Literary Society of Skibbereen. The Phoenix Society was a manifestation of something not confined to Skibbereen. Southwest County Cork and south County Kerry had been badly afflicted by the famine, far too badly to have offered serious support to the revolutionary movement in 1848. In the years immediately after the famine the area underwent some rapid 'modernisation' of the economy and population, including large-scale clearances such as that conducted on the Kenmare estate by William Stuart Trench. A more commercialised economy supported a small class of artisans and clerks in modest prosperity in the coastal towns from Clonakilty to Killarney. Prosperity facilitated fraternisation not only within each town but from one town to another. Thus Jeremiah O'Donovan Rossa, a clerk in Mortimer Downing's hardware store in Skibbereen, had a circle of friends among his peers in Bantry and Kenmare, being required to visit these towns frequently because of his employer's workhouse contracts.[46] In Skibbereen this fraternisation was formalised in the Phoenix Society which seems to have emerged late in 1856. Its format was based on an assortment of examples including the Father Mathew temperance society, the repeal reading room, and the confederate club. Essentially its function was social and recreational. Inseparable from that for such people was the assertion of political opinion. The society had an all-important Irish-American dimension. It was but one of a number of Phoenix Societies scattered through the country, all independent of one another, but all of which can be presumed to owe something to an association of the same name founded in New York in 1852,[47] one of the welter of such groups contending for Irish-American support in the 1850s. A founder of the Skibbereen society, Patrick J. Downing, had returned from America in 1856, imbued with strong revolutionary motivation. Because of the famine emigration most of the other members of the society had strong family links with Irish-America, and so with Irish-American nationalism.

In Jeremiah O'Donovan the Phoenix Society possessed an important if not fully typical specimen of the neo-Young-Ireland élite. He had the benefit of high family self-regard based on hereditary claims to long-confiscated lands at a place called Ros Mór (whence the suffix 'Rossa') and on the more recent consideration of commercial success in the linen trade. However, by the time of Jeremiah's birth, in 1831, the domestic linen industry of west Cork was in serious decline. His father worked a small farm near Rosscarbery — a junior's share (soon encumbered by debt) of what remained of the family empire — until his death of famine fever in 1848. Wife and family emigrated, except for Jeremiah, who obtained his clerkship in Skibbereen with Downing, a relation by marriage.[48] This appointment would have been unattainable without a reasonable standard of literacy. Rossa had acquired that in a national school in Rosscarbery along with a taste for reading. Like other keen young readers he was captivated by the ideology of the *Nation*. However, he obviously was not one of those whose family circumstances permitted an extended period of education and youthful leisure. When at the end of his second year as Downing's clerk he received his first pay Rossa by his own account spent half of it — one pound — on a miscellaneous lot of two hundred and forty books offered by a second-hand dealer. He took them up to his garret above Downing's shop and read them at night by precarious candlelight.[49] In 1853 Rossa married a girl with some property and set up his own hardware business, still in Skibbereen. However, like O'Mahony, Stephens, Kickham and Luby, he never could put his heart into earning a living. By 1857 they were all on the eve of an opportunity to practise a congenial *metier*.

Chapter Two

ENGLAND'S ELUSIVE DIFFICULTY, 1857-60

Karl Marx wrote much of *Das Kapital* in the years 1857-8 with his thoughts galvanised by an international economic crisis that he interpreted as a portent of the imminent collapse of capitalism.[1] Numbers of Irish people experienced a similar acute sense of expectation at the end of the 1850s, but the crisis of the time as they perceived it related to international political tensions and British power. Any serious diminution of the latter would threaten the basis of the status quo in Ireland, a fact given expression over some generations by a variety of Irish political malcontents in the sloganised assertion that 'England's difficulty' would provide 'Ireland's opportunity'. British involvement in the Crimean war (1854-6) produced ripples of expectation among some of the more sanguine Irish-American revolutionaries. However, because France was Britain's ally in the Crimea, the illusion of imminent 'English difficulty' was impossible to sustain: it was taken for granted in the mid-nineteenth century that only France (or the U.S.A.) was capable of delivering a serious blow to Britain's might. In the aftermath of the Crimean war however, Anglo-French tensions palpably increased. Napoleon III continued to maintain a large standing army thereby giving support to the fears of some (and the hopes of others) that Bonapartism would inevitably issue in a military challenge to Britain. Suspicion was reinforced when the French embarked on the construction of a 'new generation' of warships. These were steam-propelled ironclads even a few of which might counter-balance British numerical superiority in conventional vessels.[2] For the next few years the fear of a French landing haunted many English minds. Anglo-French relations were complicated further in early 1858 by the attempted assassination of Louis Napoleon in the Orsini plot which had been concocted among continental revolutionaries living in London.[3] From summer 1857 to summer 1858 an extra dimension was added to the apparent insecurity of the British system by the mutiny of the native troops in British service in India, the Sepoys. A protracted war against the Sepoys could require the dispatch of large forces from the United Kingdom, leaving it even more vulnerable to French attack or internal upheaval. Friend and foe understood that the loss of India would shatter the empire.

By July 1858 the Sepoy threat had been scotched but the prospect of a European war loomed even larger and many were convinced that once it began Britain would be drawn in on the anti-French side. When it came, in May 1859, the war was fought in Northern Italy with France and Austria as the main protagonists. It ended quickly with French military might triumphant. The possibility that the victorious Napoleon, having humiliated Austria, would strike next against his other 'natural enemy' promoted widespread war mania in Britain. The summer of 1859 witnessed the rise of a mass volunteering movement throughout England and Scotland, called into being by the spectre of French invasion. Hundreds of thousands up and down the country purchased rifles, joined local volunteer corps and devoted their spare time to drill and arms practice. Not since the era of the first Napoleon had Englishmen been so fearful of war on their own soil.

Behind the scenes, statesmen were working to avoid conflict. The signing of the Cobden-Chevalier free-trade agreement between the two countries in January 1860 was a pointer to a future of peaceful co-existence, and by early 1861 the prospect of an Anglo-French war was rapidly disappearing. Because the threatened upheaval did not come to pass, its reality, and its impact on events in Ireland in the period 1857-60, have often been underestimated or totally missed by later commentators. Yet the contemporary evidence shows that Irish political activists were keenly aware of international tensions and that anticipation of an exciting denouement profoundly influenced much that they said and did at the time. In the heightened Anglo-French tension and in the Indian mutiny many saw the first realistic prospect since 1848 of achieving a change in the constitutional relations of Ireland and Great Britain.

Dr Robert Cane of Kilkenny city was a key figure in the early response to this apparent political fluidity. As a catholic nationalist married to a protestant and with an extensive medical practice among the protestant gentry, and as a repealer who had remained on the best of terms with both O'Connellites and Young Irelanders, he was obviously a man with a talent for bridging gaps. His capacity for crossing barriers was useful in helping him to gather a group of writers of the neo-Young-Ireland type around him in the summer of 1857 to contribute to a new 'journal of national literature', the *Celt*. This coterie included C.J. Kickham, William Kenealy and Robert Dwyer Joyce. The first issue of the *Celt* appeared in August 1857 with its editorial page displaying a real, though vague, sense of anticipation. Early in 1858 the vagueness dissipated and the March issue carried proposals from Cane for a national political organisation embracing 'Old' and 'Young' Ireland. His introduction adverted to English difficulty and Irish opportunity. There ensued a debate in the newspapers, and in private correspondence, on the topic of national organisation among a number of Young Irelanders at home and abroad who had not seriously considered the question since 1848.[4] One of these was William Smith O'Brien. Following his return to Ireland in 1856 he had little to say publicly on political matters until the spring of 1858 when he published a series of ten articles in the *Nation* on the question of what was to be done now that once again 'the days were full of prodigies'.[5] The *Nation*'s leading articles from first news of the Indian mutiny had been brimming over with expectation and during the next few years they constantly raised the topics of international war, French invasion and great changes for Ireland. Provincial newspapers followed suit. The accession to editorial chairs at the time of a collection of journalists of neo-Young-Ireland vintage helped greatly to diffuse the notion of national opportunity in the air. Peter Gill launched the *Tipperary Advocate* (Nenagh) early in 1857; a year later from Clonmel came the *Tipperary Examiner*, which was edited at different times by John F. O'Donnell and A.W. Hartnett; William Kenealy became editor of the *Kilkenny Journal* and Martin A. O'Brennan, editor of the *Connacht Patriot*, both about this time. Even first generation Young Irelanders joined in the trend: John Martin in early 1859 was considering the setting up of a newspaper; in Waterford city a committee headed by the local independent opposition M.P., J.A. Blake, launched the *Citizen* in September 1859 with P.J. Smyth as editor.[6] However, the new journal of this period most singlemindedly devoted to nationalist policies, and that featured most prominently in subsequent years, was the *Irishman*, launched in Belfast on 17 July 1858 with Denis Holland as proprietor and editor. Holland's mentor in undertaking this venture was the Young Irelander John E. Pigot. The unrelated Richard Pigott, son of an employee of the *Nation*, was in charge of the printing. In early 1859 the *Irishman* and its team transferred to Dublin.

In the late summer of 1858 the archbishop of Westminster, Cardinal Wiseman, visited Ireland for the dedication of a church in Ballinasloe. He was conscious of being the first cardinal to set foot on Irish soil for over 200 years. To his surprise and delight the visit turned into a triumphal tour of the country as huge crowds flocked to see and hear him, and his itinerary was expanded in response to urgent requests from various quarters for the honour of a visit.[7] 'His coming was all but the advent of the holy father', John Henry Newman remarked, correctly identifying the specifically ultramontane tone of the catholic identity that was so strikingly asserted.[8] The acclamation of the loyal Cardinal Wiseman could scarcely be represented as evidence of political disaffection, but it did show the strength of an allegiance with most important political implications. And the obvious readiness of large numbers of people for instant mobilisation was a sign of the times: the sense of political occasion was abroad once more in Ireland.

An English correspondent with considerable experience of Ireland, looking at 1858 in retrospect, declared that the year had seen disaffection from British rule reach alarming proportions in the country.[9] He was referring to the palpable expectations aroused by 'England's difficulty' and especially to what was publicly known of a conspiracy to exploit it by armed force — the movement known to history as fenianism. The leaders of the Emmet Monument Association had reacted to the prospect of international trouble for Britain in the autumn of 1857 by dreaming of an Irish-American military expedition to liberate the old country. Again they sought to have appropriate secret military arrangements made beforehand in Ireland. This time they chose James Stephens for the task.[10] Two of them, O'Mahony and Doheny, were old acquaintances of his, and since Stephens's return to Ireland O'Mahony and himself had re-established contact.[11] But the initiative was almost certainly take by Doheny.

The American offer, conveyed across the Atlantic in a letter carried by Owen Considine, reached Stephens towards the end of 1857.[12] It carried the implication of substantial preparations already made on the American side. That, and his perception of the international situation, conjured up for Stephens the vision of a role commensurate with his notions of his own importance and capacity, a role that suited his talents as writing never would. James Stephens the activist, and actor, had been given his cue. He assumed the initiative at once, displaying that talent for leadership and tactics that was to make him an influential personage in Irish politics for the best part of a decade. He not merely undertook to prepare for an invasion, but specified that within a matter of months he would be able to have ten thousand men available for action at any point in the country at twenty four hours' notice. This undertaking however, was conditional on an adequate and regular flow of American money: at least £80 per month was the stipulation. Another condition was that Stephens's efforts should be untrammelled by any check on his authority in the proposed organisation: he used the phrase 'provisional dictator'.[13] Stephens had all of this conveyed to the Emmet Monument Association in a letter carried by Joseph Denieffe. The choice of messenger was tactically inspired. By agreeing to undertake this mission Denieffe implicitly surrendered his own commission of 1855 and handed over to Stephens control of what remained of the organisational network he had set up in that year.

In the opening weeks and months of 1858, as Stephens awaited news from America, the combination of international tensions was at a high peak of intensity. Matters became even more urgent for Stephens in March with the publication in the *Celt* of Dr Cane's plan for a national political organisation on the lines of the Repeal Association. Cane had received Denieffe in 1855, encouraged him in the American-inspired work and promised to help 'in his own way'.[14] In other words, he displayed no objection to the organisation of militant artisans for political purposes, but he envisaged them lining up obediently on the periphery of a more broadly-based movement under the direction of people like himself. Stephens was well acquainted with Cane and his views and was determined not to be subordinate to him or any other rival leader.

Denieffe reached Dublin again on 17 March 1858 bearing a document dated 28 February with the signatures of eighteen Irish-Americans (including Doheny and O'Mahony) styling themselves 'members of the Irish Revolutionary Committee'. They purported to appoint Stephens 'chief executive of the Irish revolutionary movement' and to give him 'supreme control and absolute authority over that movement in Ireland'.[15] Denieffe also brought money. Stephens lost no time: that evening he formally established his organisation by initiating T.C. Luby, Denieffe, Peter Langan, Garret O'Shaughnessy and Owen Considine.[16] Stephens had composed his blueprint by taking ideas from various continental societies. He adopted the cellular principle that had been a feature of the *Société des familles*, which flourished in France in the 1830s.[17] Thus, the new organisation was to consist of circles each headed by a centre, or A, known only to the officers immediately below him, nine

Bs; each B would command nine Cs and would be known to them alone; each C would be responsible for and known only to nine Ds, the rank and file. The *Société des familles*, like so many of the societies, had an awe-inspiring initiation ritual; this Stephens eschewed, tending instead towards the simplicity which was characteristic of Mazzini's Young Italy. Like members of every secret society, Stephens's followers were to be oath-bound, but, again in line with Young Italy, the oath was simple and contained no reference to a death penalty. Stephens gave no name to his movement — this too had precedents on the continent — and the initiated referred to the project among themselves as the organisation, the movement, the brotherhood, and by similar informal designations.[18] Subsequently the terms Irish Revolutionary Brotherhood and Irish Republican Brotherhood ('I.R.B.' in either case), and 'fenians' were adopted or imposed. For convenience we can refer to the organisation from its inception as the I.R.B. and to its members as the fenians, though strictly speaking these terms are anachronistic for the early years.

France and the U.S.A. were both crucial to early fenian strategic assumptions. In the case of the U.S.A. there was an important consideration not applying to France: irrespective of the attitude of the government an Irish revolutionary movement could expect support from a section of the population, the Irish-Americans. During the 1848 crisis, preparations, however ineffective, had been made in New York to send military aid to Ireland for the expected rising.[19] The 1850s was the decade of the American filibuster; it saw Narciso Lopez organising private expeditions to liberate Cuba, William Walker leading private armies against Nicaragua, and John Brown and his men attacking Harper's Ferry. Elsewhere, Garibaldi was perfecting the same mode of warfare. Rapidly improving communications made it possible to envisage the staging of a filibuster across the Atlantic to aid an Irish rebellion. Steamships were improving the speed and reliability of transatlantic journeys. The inception in 1858 of a regular steam packet service between Galway and New York made an immense impression on some minds. (Later in the year companies of Irish-American militia had to be dis-suaded from purchasing tickets for group travel to Galway in their colourful uniforms.)[20] And in the spring of 1858 it was well known that the transatlantic cable — with its terminus at Valentia Island — was nearing completion. Henceforth, news of happenings in Ireland could be conveyed to America in hours instead of weeks. (In the event the cable was completed in August 1858 but it suffered damage shortly afterwards and regular transmission was not achieved until 1866.)

Denieffe's organisation provided Stephens with a nucleus in Dublin, and also in Kilkenny city, to which he travelled immediately after the Dublin launching to enrol John Haltigan and his associates.[21] During the summer of 1858 the new body obtained a firm foothold in the south, predominantly in the places where radical organisation had emerged in 1848-9. Stephens sought out some of the small number of substantial farmers in counties Kilkenny, Tipperary and Waterford who had shown sympathy with the Young Ireland rebels in the summer of 1848.[22] One of them, Denis Mulcahy of Redmondstown, Clonmel was receptive, and his son, Denis Dowling Mulcahy, became a key supporter. Otherwise the farmers were cool and Stephens obtained most of his following in the towns and villages among men of no great social or economic weight.

In May 1858 Stephens arrived in Skibbereen. In short-time he met and swore in O'Donovan Rossa, Dan MacCartie and most of the other Phoenix Society men. The society was transformed into a branch of the new secret body and Rossa's men took to midnight drilling.[23] They also turned missionary. Throughout the high summer and autumn of 1858 they enrolled their social counterparts in large numbers in the towns and villages of south-west Cork and across the county boundary in Kenmare and Killarney. Country people were canvassed in their homes or on coming in for Sunday or fair day and many of them joined in a near-millenarian frenzy. There was talk of one shilling and sixpence per man per day once action began, and of free land. Stephens promoted the enthusiasm by maintaining a discreetly mysterious presence in the area — where he was referred to in Gaelic parlance as 'an seabhac' (the hawk), which was anglicised by monoglots (fenians and others) as Mr Shook or Shooks — and by reiterating the promise of early action. It is abundantly clear that the brotherhood in Kerry and west Cork at this time fully expected invasion, American arms and rebellion before the end of the year.[24]

The local representatives of civil and ecclesiastical authority could not have failed for long to notice that something unusual was afoot. For the priests a secret society could only mean the recrudescence of an old evil, inimical to public order; besides, their theology gave them an aversion to unjustified oath-taking which might bring some of their young parishioners to perdition. Church and state had a common interest in dissolving the conspiracy, but contact between the two was usually at arm's length. Bishop David Moriarty in Killarney, and the parish priest of Kenmare, Archdeacon John O'Sullivan, were less inhibited than average about cooperation with the civil authorities and passed on discreet warnings of what was happening. Priests who did not make direct contact nevertheless confirmed police information and suspicions by preaching sermons against secret societies. From early autumn 1858 Dublin Castle was directing a methodical campaign of observation and infiltration in Cork and Kerry against what it knew as the Phoenix Society, using the local magistrates, the constabulary, plainclothesmen and co-operative citizens including a process-server named Daniel Sullivan Goulah.[25] Between 8 and 15 December a few dozen Phoenix Society suspects were arrested in Skibbereen, Bantry, Kenmare and Killarney. They included O'Donovan Rossa. Magisterial investigations and long drawn out trials followed, in Cork city and Tralee, producing only one conviction. By October 1859 all were free following a bargain, the terms of which included guilty pleas by the prisoners.[26] A half-dozen fenians arrested in Callan, County Kilkenny, on 2 January 1859 — and referred to by extension as Phoenix Society men — were also freed after the ordeal of court appearances.[27]

Stephens had launched his society on the understanding that his sponsors in America would prepare an expeditionary force and that they would supply him with adequate funds. Denieffe's experiences should have inculcated scepticism about American promises. True, he had brought back eighty pounds, but the difficulty with which it had been collected and the obvious lack of any serious activity in New York were ominous. More cash followed only when Denieffe was sent on another begging mission, and when that supply ran out Stephens decided to visit New York himself.[28] He arrived there on 13 October 1858 on a mission which demonstrated both the creative and the destructive sides of his political genius.

He intended to secure a constant and reliable supply of money from America, but he also had his eye on an even bigger prize than anything that could be collected in the short-run among his friends in New York. This was a large sum of money — many thousands of pounds — which had originally been collected in 1848 to support what appeared from America like an imminent Irish bid for self-government. It was now in the hands of a committee, styled a directory, awaiting the emergence of an Irish enterprise qualified to benefit from it. The directory included Thomas Francis Meagher and Richard Gorman, Judge Robert Emmet and Horace Greeley (the proprietor of the New York *Tribune*). John Blake Dillon had belonged to this circle during his sojourn in New York (1848-55) and Stephens had tried very hard, and in vain, to get a letter of recommendation from him before leaving Ireland.[29] He did have a letter of introduction from another Young Irelander, Fr John Kenyon of Temple-derry, County Tipperary, to John Mitchel, who could be expected to carry influence with the directory, though not himself a member. Mitchel's initial response to Stephens's personal approach was encouraging. He wrote in support of Stephens to the directory and gave him some money.[30] Meagher was even more enthusiastic, actually giving Stephens a written undertaking about supporting his claim before a special meeting of the directory.[31] He even joined most of Stephens's original American backers in signing a revised version of Stephens's commission which gave him 'supreme control and absolute authority' over the movement *at home and abroad*.[32] This remarkable document, dated 9 December 1858, is evidence of Stephens's megalomania and also of the impact that he made in the early stages of his American visit with his confident exaggerations about the extent and quality of his organisation in Ireland. That story was ruined a little later by news of the Phoenix Society arrests and of the subsequent judicial proceedings which disclosed facts to suggest that the authorities had the whole business under easy control. That and, perhaps, communications from Dillon and others in Ireland, changed the attitudes of Meagher and Mitchel. On 26 January 1859 Meagher formally withdrew his signature from the document of 9 December and gave as a pretext his conviction of the uselessness of a revolutionary movement under existing circumstances.[33] All hope of success with the directory had vanished.

However, Stephens still had his original New York allies. Early in 1859 they formed what was to be the American wing of the society already existing in Ireland. The generally accepted account is that given by T.C. Luby: 'Stephens — after weeks if not months of embarrassment — founded in America the organisation subsequently known as the Fenian Brotherhood, putting O'Mahony at its head as the subordinate of himself.'[34] O'Mahony has left an account which has some significantly different implications: 'In 1859 ... the small remnant of the Emmet Monument Association then in existence remodelled its organisation and elected me its president. ... The association at my suggestion assumed the title of the Fenian Brotherhood.'[35] The details are of little consequence. What is important is the existence, among those most closely concerned, of seriously divergent views about the position of O'Mahony *vis-a-vis* Stephens. In any case, O'Mahony's assumption of a central position on the American side involved the elbowing sideways of Doheny, with Stephens's assistance. It is no surprise that unrepresentative enthusiasts in a cabal riven by personal jealousies should, in conferring authority on themselves and on one another, create an organisational muddle. Nomenclature was similarly unsettled. There is no doubting that John O'Mahony

Proposed Atlantic harbour at Galway Bay. This drawing, probably from the late 1850s, captures the grand hopes then held out for a regular steam service between Galway and New York. A sense of the new immediacy of transatlantic communications influenced fenian beginnings. (Courtesy of the National Library of Ireland)

introduced the title 'Fenian Brotherhood' for the American organisation (recalling the *Fianna* of Gaelic legend) and it is probable that he did so in April 1859. But for some months before that the term 'Irish Revolutionary Brotherhood' had been used in America to refer to the movement *on both sides* of the Atlantic, though whether as acknowledged title or as simple description it is difficult to say.[36]

Ever ready to turn adversity to profit, Stephens used the Phoenix Society arrests as a pretext for raising money in America. A fair trial fund to aid the Cork and Kerry prisoners had been created in Ireland by A.M. Sullivan and others, and its work had been advertised in Irish papers in New York.[37] Early in 1859 Stephens's New York associates launched the 'Irish patriotic defence fund' which was intended solely for financing Stephens's work but whose ambiguous title enticed contributions from some people who took this to be another fair trial fund. This piece of duplicity, which was apparently Stephens's own idea, backfired embarrassingly when the trick was exposed in June 1859 by the *Irish American* (New York).[38] 'This unlucky name', Luby recalled, 'was in my opinion the pregnant cause of long-lasting misconceptions, of collapse of revenues, almost of the utter breakdown of our movement.'[39] Nevertheless, Stephens had the equivalent of over six hundred pounds to his credit when leaving America in March 1859.[40] He had not left for Ireland, however. References during the Phoenix Society court proceedings to the activities of Mr Shooks had convinced Stephens that he would henceforth be a marked man: 'Of course, I shall be seized as soon as I lay foot on British soil', he confided to his diary in New York on 12 January 1859.[41] So he settled once again in Paris, his old haunt, but also the capital of a nation about to go to war, possibly with Britain. Quite independently, but with the same strategic notions John Mitchel moved to Paris a few weeks later and remained there — with a break of six months — until September 1862. There is documentary evidence that during this period he approached the French government about support for an Irish insurrection.[42]

Stephens was joined in Paris by T.C. Luby, who was to be his *alter ego* for the next six years, and by John O'Leary, who had agreed in late 1858 — rather unenthusiastically — to lend his support. From Paris Stephens, now spending freely, tried to provide for the military education of his followers in Ireland. O'Mahony was instructed to send large numbers of Irish-Americans with army or militia experience home to their native localities where under the guise of 'returned yanks' they could act as drill-masters for the I.R.B. men of their respective districts; they would also reinforce the sense of transatlantic solidarity.

A number of them arrived, but O'Mahony failed to keep up their money supply and they eventually straggled back to America in a demoralised state leaving similar demoralisation behind them.[43] Also at this time Stephens laid plans for a 'school' in Paris to which 'A s' in the Irish organisation could be brought for training. The project never got off the ground and a handful of young cadets who came across from Ireland received no special education apart from an introduction to some of the civilised pleasures of Parisian life.[44] Meanwhile Luby was acting as right-hand man in Ireland for the 'captain' (as he referred to Stephens) and was able to do little more than keep contact with the existing circles. As 1859 passed into 1860 the 'organisation' was in very poor shape indeed.

Early in 1858 Stephens had introduced himself to A.M. Sullivan the proprietor of the *Nation*, hoping to gain the support of this key figure for his new organisation. The meeting was not particularly amicable and support was not forthcoming.[45] However, when some months later the secret society in its Phoenix Society form began to attract attention in West Cork, the promoters were found claiming that Sullivan with many other notables, including Smith O'Brien, was involved in the plot. Sullivan on a visit to his native district in August 1858 discovered that no amount of disclaimer on his part would convince the young 'phoenix men' that he was not a party to the conspiracy.[46] Some time later Bishop Moriarty informed him that the civil authorities knew all about the organisation, and suggested that some public advice in the *Nation* would induce the members to desist before they provoked government retribution. Sullivan sought advice from Smith O'Brien in a letter dated 25 October 1858 in which he outlined his dilemma.[47] The next number of the *Nation* carried a leading article quoting a letter from O'Brien, dated 26 October, denying any connection with secret societies, past or present, and thoroughly repudiating them. The leading article itself adverted unambiguously to the existence of a nationalist secret society in an un-named district in the south (clearly West Cork) and denounced its folly. Care was taken to make the criticism from a popular nationalist point of view and heavy strictures were laid upon parish priests who had denounced the society from a 'loyal whig' stance.[48] Sullivan's leader and O'Brien's letter together constituted a blow to the fenian organisers but they contributed nothing to the exposure of the society to the police. The existence of the conspiracy had been a notorious fact for weeks before the *Nation* made its comment, and it had been referred to in sermons and newspapers, including the *Irishman*.[49] In the weeks and months after the arrests Sullivan was indefatigable in his efforts to provide

succour and support for the prisoners and was the chief pro-
moter of the fair trial fund. When Luby went to France to meet
Stephens in the spring of 1859 he was disposed to speak well of
the editor of the *Nation*. But Stephens would have none of it.
He vehemently denounced Sullivan and declared that he should
henceforth be known as 'Goulah' and so identified with the
informer.[50] Stephens blamed Sullivan's leading article of 30
October for the Phoenix Society arrests and denounced it as
'felon-setting'. John O'Mahony and Michael Doheny subsequently
vied with Stephens in the campaign of vituperation against
Sullivan; the hatred of all three was incubated in New York at
the end of 1858 and the beginning of 1859, with Stephens
seizing on the *Nation* as a scapegoat for the defects in his own
organisation that led to the Phoenix Society arrests and the
near-ruination of his projects.

The international tensions of the late 1850s that spawned
fenianism influenced Irish electoral politics, too, but in an
oblique way. One rather surprising effect was the enhancement
of the popularity and success of the tory party in Ireland. The
general election of March-April 1857 was a low-key affair by
comparison with that of 1852. The Conservatives gained a few
extra seats to bring them comfortably over the forty mark for
Ireland as a whole. Of the sixty or sixty-one Liberals returned,
about a quarter can be classified as independent oppositionists.
The distinctiveness of the group was as strong as ever, even
though some members identified with it only irregularly. That
distinctiveness was highlighted by a willingness to cooperate
with the Conservatives. As early as 1851 Disraeli was set on
wooing Irish catholic support, but his efforts were nullified by
Lord Derby's insensitivity and by the essentially Liberal bias
of many of the leading independent oppositionists elected in
1852.[51] The hard core of oppositionists remaining by the
middle of the decade was determinedly anti-Liberal. It was in
principle also anti-Conservative, but, in practice, keeping up
animosity on both fronts was difficult, and by 1856 co-operation
between independents and tories was influencing Irish by-
election results.[52]

One episode of the international crisis (the defeat in the
house of commons of a bill intended to assuage French resentment over the Orsini affair) gave rise to Palmerston's resignation
in February 1858 and the accession of a Conservative government. It was at once warmly supported by the independent
oppositionists, and with good reason. For, after years of Palmer-
stonian obduracy, concessions were being made to catholic and
popular Irish demands: a new deal for catholic chaplains in the
army; legislation to provide for denominational control of

reformatory schools in Ireland;[53] prospects of government
support and post office business to make the Galway transatlantic packet viable; and progress towards a national gallery
of art in Dublin.[54] International affairs provided a further
pretext for supporting the tories: their stance on the Italian
question could be represented as being less inimical to the
temporal power of the papacy than was Palmerston's attitude.
Disraeli attempted — with some effect as far as Ireland was
concerned — to make of this the basis of a tory-catholic alliance.
However, the unqualified support of the Irish independents
could not be secured without a measure of tenant-right. On 19
June 1858 Disraeli received a deputation of independent
opposition M.P.s and offered to legislate for 'compensation
for disturbance' for Irish agricultural tenants, but without
retrospection.[55] The independents were divided on the pro-
priety of accepting this limited concession. In any event it
had not been introduced before the debate on the reform bill
of 1859 got under way. This was the kind of major measure
on which independent opposition principles should be applied,
if they were ever to be invoked. In fact, in the crucial vote on
31 March 1859 the hard core of independents split: some
voted against the government, and a measure desirable in itself,
on a strict interpretation of the original 1852 pledge; others
supported a government which, while it did not concede tenant
right, seemed more favourable to the Irish interests they represented and to catholic interests in Ireland and Italy, than the
alternative government.[56]

Despite this division among the oppositionists on a fundamental point of policy, and despite the fact that they no longer
possessed even the semblance of central organisation, they did
well in the general election of May 1859. Just how well it is
impossible to say exactly, owing to the continued blurring at
the edges of independent opposition and catholic Liberalism,
especially at election time as candidates endeavoured to head
off competition at the polls by adopting comprehensive platforms. Even the *Nation* was slow to put a figure on the total of
independents returned, but it expressed very great satisfaction
at the results.[57] Seventeen is probably a reasonably accurate
figure though this includes a few M.P.s who became almost at
once supporters of the new Liberal government that came to
office after the election.[58] In Ireland, however, victory had
gone to the tories who won fifty-five seats to give them their
best Irish result for a generation. The extra seats came almost
entirely through co-operation with independent oppositionists,
and an unwonted level of catholic support.[59] This phase of co-
operation between tories, catholics and independents found

most striking embodiment in the flamboyant person of a young catholic graduate of Queen's College Cork named John Pope Hennessy, who was elected M.P. for King's County in 1859 on a tory/independent-opposition ticket.

Neither in 1857 nor 1859 was there a concerted attempt to maximise the independent opposition vote or to mobilise the catholic vote. Individual candidates garnered the popular vote where it was to be had without excessive difficulty. The contrast with 1852 is significant. The electoral effort of that year had caused a considerable amount of unpleasantness for many tenant farmers without producing observable benefits. In the second half of the decade English radicals and Irish independent oppositionists had the same difficulties in utilising parliamentary politics to forward their demands. The independents recognised that electoral reform such as the radicals were seeking would greatly enhance their own prospects.[60] When John Bright returned to English public life in the autumn of 1858 with the launching of a campaign for reform, some of the leading independent oppositionists attempted to set up a supporting movement in Ireland. Bright was invited to come across and help with the work but was unable to oblige.[61] In the spring of 1859 the Tipperary Independent Club, guided by leading independent M.P.s, formed a county committee to campaign for the ballot.[62] The independent oppositionists attached far more importance to the secret ballot than to the extension of the franchise or the redistribution of seats; indeed, they professed to see little benefit in an extension of the franchise unaccompanied by the ballot.[63] The *Nation*, the chief organ of independent opposition by the late 1850s, was eventually characterised, not unfairly, as advocating a policy of doing nothing but sitting back in expectation of the ballot.[64] At least from 1858 onwards it was assumed that the ballot would come eventually. The independent oppositionists of the late 1850s and early 1860s were unenergetic about purely parliamentary politics feeling that it was futile to expend great amounts of effort fighting against obstacles that would soon be swept away by the *deus ex machina* of electoral reform.

By 1859 the recognised leader of the independent oppositionists inside and outside parliament was Daniel O'Donoghue, styled The O'Donoghue, chieftain of the Glens, in recognition of his headship of a Gaelic family that had retained possession of some of its ancestral lands in remote parts of Kerry and West Cork. He was the representative not only of the O'Donoughes but also of the line of MacCarthy More.[65] For good measure he was a grandnephew of Daniel O'Connell. However, when he first appeared on the political scene in 1853, barely aged twenty-one, he was lined up against his O'Connell cousins and alongside

Gavan Duffy and the independent oppositionists. The occasion was the run-up to a by-election in Clonmel. Four years later, supported by G.H. Moore, he contested a by-election in Tipperary county on the independent opposition ticket, and defeated a catholic whig. He retained his seat in the general election of that year. When G.H. Moore shortly afterwards lost his Mayo seat on petition, The O'Donoghue was left as the undeniable leader of the independent oppositionist M.P.s and of a staunch if amorphous party in the county. He had a dashing style and considerable oratorical flair.

The only figure who might have overshadowed The O'Donoghue during this period was William Smith O'Brien. He studiously avoided all public occasions, yet there was undeniable evidence of the existence of a widespread desire to show him honour. This did not imply any widespread re-evaluation of 1848: the events of July in that year were still a source of unmitigated embarrassment; rather, there was a desire to honour the romantic figure from a more colourful era despite his misadventures at Ballingarry. The establishment shunned him for the remainder of his life, but otherwise he evoked respect even from people who had no sympathy with his politics. Members of the neo-Young-Ireland élite were eager to be associated with him, and to carry his lengthy communications in their newspapers. He had a wide circle of nationally-minded correspondents. However, O'Brien refused absolutely to participate in any public movement. He had lost confidence in his own capacity for leadership, and he was keenly aware that the Irish self-government for which he yearned no longer commanded widespread interest. Somewhat more sanguine was his fellow-Young-Irelander and former fellow-exile, John Martin. Martin had none of O'Brien's charismatic appeal, but he, too, commanded widespread respect and ready access to the nationalist press.

In the crisis of the years 1857-60 Smith O'Brien found himself in disagreement with all his closest political friends on the question of possible French intervention in Ireland. While he declared that it would do much more harm than good, they spoke and wrote of it as the answer to the dreams of all believers in Irish self-government.[66] Naturally, the seriousness of the expressed desire for a French invasion varied from one individual to another. Many of them did not truly want it but hoped that the fear of it could act as a lever to win concessions. Most probably did not know exactly what they wanted but could not resist the rhetoric of the 'Shan van vocht'. All found a suitably vague mode of expression in the MacMahon sword project. The victorious French campaign that he directed in northern Italy in summer 1859 won fame and renown for Marshal Patrick

MacMahon, and greatly excited francophile Irish nationalists. MacMahon's 'wild geese' antecedents were proclaimed in the pages of the *Nation* and the *Irishman*. On 2 July 1859 both papers carried leading articles proposing that his Irish admirers should present the marshal with the fashionable symbolic gift of a sword of honour. The *Irishman* of the same day reported a suggestion from a correspondent that Ireland might soon be in need of a monarch, as Belgium had been in 1830, and that MacMahon would be the ideal choice. Subscriptions were forthcoming from around the country and the MacMahon Sword Committee was formed in Dublin during August. The officers included P.J. Smyth, T.D. Sullivan (brother of A.M.), The O'Donoghue M.P., and Patrick MacMahon, independent oppositionist M.P. for County Wexford.[67] The specially designed and manufactured sword, with sheath, was not ready until a year later. The presentation was made in the military camp at Châlons on 9 September 1860 by a delegation consisting of The O'Donoghue, T.D. Sullivan, George Sigerson (medical practitioner and poet), John Mitchel, and J.P. Leonard, an Irish literary man resident in Paris. The marshal received them with warmth and courtesy, but went out of his way to underline that the significance of the occasion was purely sentimental.[68] That was only one of the reasons that made the occasion an anticlimax; more importantly, Magenta and Solferino had in the preceding months become an embarrassment to Irish catholics, as France's Italian ally, Piedmont-Sardinia, turned to menace the papal states.

In the summer of 1859, when it was possible to envisage a new northern Italian state co-existing with the temporal power of the papacy, Irish ideologists of nationality, such as the editors of the *Nation* and the *Irishman*, could enjoy the luxury of supporting both the Piedmontese and the pope. Later in the year, when it became clear that Italian nationalism and the temporal power could not coexist, both papers expressed themselves in favour of the pope, though not without showing an awareness of some inconsistency.[69] These expressions of fealty were in line with an overwhelming wave of public opinion. During the closing months of 1859 and the early part of 1860 large and enthusiastic crowds turned out throughout the country for public meetings in support of the pope. Many of these were organised and addressed by bishops. All the leading popular politicians identified themselves with the movement. As the pope's plight worsened steps were taken to translate sympathy into something more useful. A collection was launched. On Sunday, 25 February 1860 nearly £11,000 was reportedly taken up at church doors in the archdiocese of Dublin, and by the end of the summer nearly £80,000 had been collected countrywide.[70] It is doubtful if any single collection between 1845 and 1882 in aid of any Irish political aim raised a more impressive sum from public subscriptions in Ireland.

The next step was to offer physical support. As early as 15 October 1859 the *Nation* was promoting the idea: 'Let but the slightest arrangement be made, the least facilities be given, and help will flow out from Ireland to maintain against all foes the legitimate and time-honoured rights and possessions of the vicar of Christ'. But not until the first quarter of 1860 did the papal government accept the necessity of calling for volunteers from the catholic nations.[71] Soon after the decision had been taken an Austrian military agent, acting for the papacy, reached Dublin and contacted some key figures including A.M. Sullivan. Contacts, mainly clerical, were set up around the country and arrangements were soon in hand for potential soldiers of the pope to be discreetly recruited and sent to Italy.[72] 'A great enthusiasm to enlist in the pope's brigade took possession of all the youth of the country' wrote a Tipperary parish priest who was approached by no less than sixty volunteers, ten of whom he recommended for enrolment.[73] Archbishop Cullen reported in April that many young men were eager to go fighting for the pope; two months later he described the enthusiasm as 'uncontrollable'.[74] The evidence of support for the papacy pleased Cullen enormously, though he was not completely happy with the military form it was taking. His reservations were not caused by qualms about the recourse to arms, but by fears (which proved to be well-founded) that the business was not sufficiently well organised and that a great deal of the money collected earlier in the year would be expended for a less than satisfactory return.[75] Over one thousand Irish volunteers (vetted by their local priests) made their way in small groups to the papal states where they were constituted as the Battalion of St Patrick. They were a predictable collection of young men of respectable background and adventurous temperament — students of medicine and law, disenchanted policemen, ambitious shop-assistants, and sons of well-to-do farmers. They had no time to learn more than the rudiments of military art before the Papal States were invaded by the Piedmontese in September 1860.[76] In the brief but futile resistance some of the Irish obtained the opportunity to display noteworthy courage and an unknown number (probably a few score) were killed in action.[77] For the survivors the next stage was detention at Genoa by the victorious government of Victor Emmanuel.

Popular opinion in Ireland soon transformed defeat into triumph. The London *Times* provided the stimulus with a taunt

John Martin

John O'Mahony

James Stephens

Thomas Clarke Luby

of cowardice. This was countered with inflated citations of heroism in the *Nation* and elsewhere.[78] By early October Cullen was able to say that the story of Irish bravery had made such an impression that 100,000 men could then be recruited, if it would do any good.[79] Now that the battalion's *raison d'être* had disappeared it could be identified with the 'Irish Brigade' of nationalist rhetoric, and the problems of consistency that it posed for ideological nationalists dissolved. None of these had ever dared to speak a public word against the project; now they could join in the general praise. The *Irishman* carried 'A song for the Irish Brigade' by C.J. Kickham.[80] On their way home the volunteers were greeted in Paris by John Mitchel. Most of them reached Queenstown from Le Harvre, on 3 November 1860. The homecoming celebrations extended over many days.[81]

Archbishop Cullen reported the 'madly enthusiastic' welcome in writing to Rome, but he appeared to be relieved when the whole business was over and done with.[82] The campaign in support of the papacy had demonstrated most convincingly the strength and depth of Irish catholic identity, but it also had some untoward consequences from Cullen's point of view. It helped the tories to their striking success in the 1859 general election in Ireland. When the public meetings in support of the pope were being held in late 1859 and early 1860 the lay public figures who identified with the movement were independent oppositionists — The O'Donoghue, G.H. Moore, John Pope Hennessy and J.F. Maguire. Cullen's catholic whigs, unwilling to criticise the government, were conspicuous by their reticence. Indeed, as the 1850s came to a close, Cullen's policy of supporting the whigs seemed to have been totally unproductive: the few legislative concessions made to Irish catholics during the period had come mainly from a conservative government (February 1858 to June 1859) courting the support of independent opposition members. The general election of 1859 had given the Liberals an overall majority (notwithstanding their losses in Ireland), and had returned Palmerston to office exhibiting the strongest antipathy to the papacy in its hour of danger.

Within a few weeks Cullen and his fellow-bishops had launched an agitation for concessions to the catholic church in the field of education. In a joint pastoral issued in August the bishops called for public meetings and petitions in support of their demands.[83] The general body of Irish M.P.s ignored this campaign just as they ignored the almost contemporaneous popular movement in support of the pope. The only significant response by public representatives to the hierarchy's pastoral was a meeting of support held in Dublin on 15 December 1859.

Fourteen of the sixteen M.P.s who requisitioned this meeting, and at least ten of the eleven who actually attended it, were independent oppositionists.[84] This amounted to a devastating indictment of Cullen's political strategy, and the independent opposition M.P.s must have taken considerable ironic satisfaction in the occasion. The *Freeman's Journal*, which since 1854 had followed Cullen in supporting the whigs and opposing the independent oppositionists, gave its comments in a leading article that attempted most unconvincingly to dissimulate acute embarrassment.[85] But Cullen was quite unmoved by the independents' display of support for the pope and catholic schooling: at the end of 1860 he could still make the following seriously unfair comment (in private) on the same independents: 'Some who abused the bishops in 1854 are now coming out — G.H. Moore etc. — and they are for a repetition of 1848'.[86] Cullen was so attached to the Liberals that in the 1859 election, when they stood for a threat to the papacy, he stayed at home on polling day rather than vote against them.[87] Cullen was never *of* the Liberals or whigs but he sided with them instinctively as the opponents of the tories whom he disliked so intensely as the party of the Irish protestant establishment, and whom he regularly branded with the epithet 'orange'. He would have nothing to do with the tories even when he was pressed by English catholic leaders or by Rome itself.[88]

If fenianism is the best known product of Irish response to the crisis and expectancy of the years 1857-60, that is owing to the accident of survival. At the time a far greater impact was achieved by a petition campaign for a plebiscite on Irish self-determination. Plebiscites were in the news. They were used in the spring of 1860 to give the seal of democracy to the annexation of Tuscany, Parma, Emilia, Modena and the Romagna by the kingdom of Piedmont-Sardinia. British statesmen approved fulsomely. On 14 April the *Nation* proposed that they be challenged by petition to apply the same principle in Ireland. This was the era *par excellence* of the parliamentary petition: thousands upon thousands of them rained down on Westminster by the month. They appealed particularly to those who had attained the proud accomplishment of writing their names but were denied the satisfaction of the franchise. If petitions in general were a substitute for electioneering, the 'national petition' launched in Ireland in 1860 was intended by its proponents as a substitute for the plebiscite they were requesting but well knew they would not get. The *Irishman* at first refused to recommend the petition on the high principle that it amounted to begging for national rights and so was degrading. By the end of June the same paper was attempting to justify a

changeabout to active encouragement of the movement.[89] Without doubt the change of mind was prompted by evidence that
the petition was catching on in the country. A Dublin-based
committee used the newspapers, and especially the *Nation*, to
advertise the text of the petition and the procedures and
practices to be followed by local organisers: only males over
fifteen were to sign; each one should either write his own name
or affix his mark; a house-to-house canvass should be held in
the larger towns.[90] At the first known public meeting to forward the petition, held in Clonmel, it had been decided to seek
support outside the chapel doors; soon signatures in the town
and surrounding countryside were claimed to run to many
thousands. At the end of June 20,000 were said to have signed
in Cork city, 5,000 in Belfast and over 3,600 in Skibbereen and
two neighbouring parishes.[91] 'This new movement reminds me
of old times', wrote the veteran repeal campaigner William J.
O'Neill Daunt after he had signed outside the church door in
Enniskeen, County Cork on 7 June.[92]

The petition campaign did indeed bring O'Neill Daunt back
to active politics. He was one of a mixed collection of platform
figures at a public meeting in support of the petition in the
round room of the Rotunda on 4 December 1860. Pride of place
was given to The O'Donoghue M.P., who rehearsed the infamy
of the act of union at great length and declared that he was
addressing the first demonstration in favour of repeal since
1848.[93] The meeting was told that around 200,000 signatures
had been collected, and it was itself used as the launching point
for a renewed campaign.[94] On 4 January 1861 The O'Donoghue
issued a public statement calling for all outstanding signatures
to be forwarded as soon as possible, as he intended to present
the petition early in February.[95] But with the flow of new
signatures continuing unabated, this deadline was dropped. At
the end of February the Dublin committee was thinking in terms
of presentation by the end of March.[96] The deadline eventually
adhered to was 16 April. Following that date the signatures
were counted and a figure of 423,026 was arrived at. On 8 May
the great mass of manuscripts was transported to London to
be put in the charge of The O'Donoghue.[97] He gained himself
some publicity by seeking permission to present the petition
to the queen in person, before conforming to the normal procedure of submission to the home secretary. The latter wrote
to The O'Donoghue on 4 June that he had duly 'placed the
petition before her majesty'. That, The O'Donoghue ruefully
admitted in a letter to the Irish press, appeared to be that, as
far as the government was concerned.[98]

On the basis of the 1861 census it can be estimated that the population of Ireland included almost one and a half million catholic males over the age of fifteen.[99] The signatures of the national petition fell far short of a majority even of that limited constituency. Furthermore, a considerable though unknown number of the signatures came from Irish people in Great Britain. And it is surely reasonable to have some reservations about the authenticity or voluntariety of some signatures: the temptation to perpetrate a little forgery, or a little intimidation, must have been irresistible on occasion. In any case, the mere signature of a petition provided the lightest possible test of devotion to the cause, namely momentary consent without expenditure of money or energy. If the petition was a revival of the repeal campaign its evidence suggested that repeal, and self-government, were no longer as widely prized as they used to be. The catholic body politic that responded with an impressive near-unanimity of sentiment to the plight of the pope was divided in its attitude towards Irish self-government. While a significant number rallied to the advocates of nationalist ideas, the *maior et sanior pars* was not interested. Even in what were apparently unsettled days only the sanguine could believe Irish independence to be a possibility; and precisely because the days were apparently unsettled those with a stake in the country feared that any political change would be accompanied by social upheaval.

From the organisational point of view the national petition was a notable achievement and that would be true even if most of the four-hundred-thousand-plus signatures were fabricated. Petition-canvassing went with a peculiar style of organisation. No close personal links were necessary between local groups and headquarters: newspapers could fill the gap quite adequately. Besides, for activists enthusiasm was more important than in more conventional political organisation, and social standing and financial resources less important. The petition campaign was mainly in the hands of newcomers to politics who were stronger in literacy than in wealth or social standing. They included (notwithstanding the petition's invocation of the 'queens' most excellent majesty') O'Donovan Rossa and others who already were, or were shortly to become, fenians. The 'national petition' campaign of 1860-61 exemplifies what is probably the most important theme of this book, namely the autonomous exercise of political and social skills (under the banner of nationalism) by groups of young men otherwise condemned to social and political insignificance. That they should choose nationalism for their flag was very predictable under the circumstances; that so many of them eventually adopted the fenian variety of nationalism was largely the product of contingency.

The élite of nationalist ideologues found in the late 1850s that even in a time of international crisis they could evoke no more than very muted political responses from within Irish society. But these were thunderous responses by comparison with the interest evoked at that time by the cultural element in nationalist theory. The Society for the Promotion and Cultivation of the Irish Language was formed in Dublin in the summer of 1858.[100] It provided a course of lessons in Irish in its rooms in Middle Abbey Street, beginning on 10 August 1858. A few months later twenty-seven students were reported to be attending regularly.[101] When the society fell into financial difficulties, A.M. Sullivan came to the rescue by making a room available at the offices of the *Nation*.[102] Though he is alleged not to have known any Irish himself, A.M. Sullivan was an able practitioner of the rhetoric of linguistic nationalism. He affirmed 'the duty of a nation not to lose its language', called for efforts to stem the decline of Irish, and deplored the record of national and convent schools in this regard.[103] Early in 1858 he secured for the *Nation* a fount of Irish type — something it had not possessed since 1858 — and began a regular weekly 'Gaelic department'.[104] Sullivan appears to have been regarded as a patron by the Belfast branch of the Society for the Cultivation and Promotion of the Irish Language, which itself appears to have assumed a much more vigorous life than the Dublin original.[105] In December 1858 it published an address to the young men of Ulster, that in its vehement denunciations of 'West Britons' matches anything produced in later generations.[106]

From the early 1860s there are several recorded instances of nationalists taking up the promotion of Irish through intellectual conviction. At the annual conference of the branch officers of the Catholic Young Men's Society on 26 May 1861 Dean Richard O'Brien advocated in the strongest fashion that they should establish Irish classes wherever possible and promote the use of Irish by members.[107] Two years later William Smith O'Brien, at the age of sixty, was engaged in diligent study of Irish and encouraging its use in a number of primary schools.[108] The story of language revivalism at this time may be taken as an illustration of the impotence of ideology without a supportive social or economic environment. The only social need that Gaelic revivalism filled at this time was the provision of occasions for fraternisation for a few groups of young men. In the years and decades immediately ahead that need was to be met in a far more attractive way by other movements.

Chapter Three

LEADERSHIP MANQUÉ, 1861-3

By the autumn of 1860 James Stephens had been out of Ireland continuously for two years, he was again short of funds, and his Irish organisation was almost moribund. The indications were that it would soon slip into oblivion leaving nothing to attract the attention of later historians except for newspaper reports, and files in Dublin Castle, on the Phoenix Society. The kind of people it attracted would be available for the next more or less ephemeral movement that came their way. In the event, Stephens obtained the motivation and the opportunity to make a fresh start.

The beginning of this revival coincided with a visit from John O'Mahony. He was exasperated by continuous calls for money emanating from Stephens, who himself dallied in Paris. Yet O'Mahony's authority in the American organisation depended on the standing of Stephens: if the Fenian Brotherhood lost faith in Stephens, O'Mahony's authority would drain away. Their dependence on one another was fully acknowledged by a document for American consumption passed around for signature among the Irish circles during 1860 (at the behest of Stephens) declaring confidence in 'John and James'.[1] O'Mahony crossed the Atlantic at the end of 1860 on a rescue mission. He called on Stephens in Paris and then proceeded to Ireland where he met Luby and saw something of the organisation.[2] Returning to Dublin in the spring of 1861 from a stay with his sister in County Tipperary, O'Mahony insisted that Luby write to Stephens asking him to come home at once: if, as seems certain, Stephens was inhibited from coming back for fear of arrest,

67

O'Mahony had put him to shame. Soon the two were conferring together in Dublin. The encounter was an abrasive one, but at least agreement was reached on the important point of what amount of aid from America would be sufficient to justify a fenian rising independent of international complications. The figures agreed were not unrealistic in themselves: five thousand armed and trained soldiers with officers, and fifty thousand rifles or muskets.[3] Less realistic was the implication that an Irish rebellion was imaginable without an international war.

Stephens's organisation had been launched on the assumption that a European war was imminent: a sense of urgency was of its essence. In early 1861 with the prospects of war not only unrealised but palpably receding Stephens and O'Mahony decided to maintain constructive tension (and so keep themselves in business) by agreeing that, failing a general war, there would be a rebellion in Ireland, with aid from the American fenians, when adequate preparations would have been made. This stratagem was at best naïvely optimistic and at worst fraudulent. It made a great man of Stephens for a few years and then ruined him when his bluff was called in 1866. His problem was how to maintain the sense of impending action on which the cohesion and vitality of his organisation depended, and at the same time hold back from a conflict which, without very definite international developments, could only end in disaster, as Stephens fully appreciated. Years earlier he had shown thorough awareness of one of the principal lessons of 1848 and its aftermath for revolutionaries everywhere: that change could not be secured by means of national 'people's war' without appropriate international complications.[4]

The return of Stephens and the new understanding with O'Mahony led to a fresh burst of promotional activity. Stephens and Luby toured the provinces. In Dublin the artisan base of the organisation was extended and supplemented. A significant new source of recruitment had been tapped by Luby at the end of 1860. This was the body of young countrymen employed in Dublin's large, new-style drapery establishments and similar institutions. They were literate, the lived in community over their workplaces, they had some money to spend, and they had free time (at least they were free on Sundays).[5] Popular political activity was an obvious outlet for their talents and energies, and they had found it in the national petition movement before Luby offered them fenianism. A few of them had taken the fenian oath in their native places before coming to Dublin. One of these was James O'Connell O'Callaghan from Kanturk, an employee of Cannock, White and Co. of Mary Street, who joined the Abbey Street classes of the Society for the Preser-

vation of the Irish Language in early 1861 and recruited some
of his fellow-learners for the I.R.B. One of those sworn in by
him there was John Devoy, a brewer's clerk originally from
Kill, County Kildare who had moved to the city with his family.
Devoy the I.R.B. neophyte was simultaneously a national
petition campaigner.[6] One gets the impression that, in Dublin
at least, the petition activists had entered the I.R.B. *en masse*
by the spring of 1861. Luby later wrote enthusiastically of 'the
new Dublin [fenian] organisation' of this time.[7] It is clear that
these new recruits did not accept the I.R.B. as an exclusive
or controlling influence over their political activities. Any congenial society or movement would have their active participation.
The I.R.B. was only one such. Another appeared in March
1861, namely the National Brotherhood of St Patrick.

In 1858 and subsequent years responsibility for efforts to
produce a scheme of national political organisation was assumed
informally by a fairly well-defined group of ideologues and
opportunists. Firstly, there were two of the independent
opposition leaders — G.H. Moore and The O'Donoghue. The
largest element consisted of veterans of the Young Ireland
party such as Robert Cane (until he was removed from the
scene by sudden death in August 1858), P.J. Smyth, John
E. Pigot, John Martin, Fr John Kenyon and William Smith
O'Brien. From the 'Old Ireland' side there was O'Connell's
close ally, William J. O'Neill Daunt. Some newspaper men
were involved, notably A.M. Sullivan. Denis Holland, editor
of the *Irishman* from 1858 to 1863, was on the fringe of this
group, but was never quite fully accorded the standing necessary to gain admittance. John Mitchel, who contributed regularly
to the *Irishman* during his sojourns in Paris, might be described
as an occasional member.

Mitchel's membership was limited by the irregularity of his
contributions to the discussion rather than by his inability to
visit Ireland, for the full group was not accustomed to meet
together. Instead, they wrote to one another, individually made
statements in the *Nation* or *Irishman* or on public platforms,
and commented, either publicly or privately, on each other's
proposals. Inevitably some of them did meet from time to
time, as when a few of them addressed the same banquet or
public gathering. The setting up of a club or private committee
to provide a forum for regular contact was mooted as early as
1858. Two years later the want of it was still being lamented.[8]
A meeting held in Dublin around the beginning of 1860 under
the chairmanship of G.H. Moore decided to call 'a conference
of Irish nationalists', but this does not appear to have materialised.[9] However, there are indications, unfortunately vague,

of smaller gatherings, presumably on an informal basis.[10] Given
the divergent views and personalities of those concerned a full
gathering could scarcely have been a very harmonious affair.
However, there was wide agreement that a beginning should be
made by the establishment of a national council. This was
advocated by Cane in 1858, and suggested over and over again
in subsequent years.[11]

As 1860 drew to a close only two of the leading public mentors
of the national cause had any substantial achievements to
point to for the three preceding years. They were A.M. Sullivan
and The O'Donoghue, who had contributed so much in their
different ways to the MacMahon sword movement and to the
rapidly culminating national petition campaign.[12] The *Nation*
promised that following the rejection of the petition a summons
to form a great new organisation would go forth to all Irish
nationalists.[13] But, while those more obviously qualified to
inspire confidence deliberated and delayed, the initiative was
taken by a comparatively obscure individual named Thomas
Neilson Underwood. A presbyterian from a Strabane family of
substance connected with Thomas Neilson, the United Irishman,
he had been a supporter of the Tenant League in the early
1850s. He had subsequently gone to London to study for the
bar and while there he observed the work of the English free-
hold land societies and took from them certain ideas which he
elaborated into a plan for owner-occupiership published in the
Nation late in 1857.[14] Apart from a marked anti-clerical bias,
Underwood was the least doctrinaire of men, but he had a
weakness for projects of organisation, constantly propounding
them himself or responding to those propounded by others. In
May 1859 he was writing from London proposing a conference
of all the Irish Liberal members to concert action in parliament.[15]
At the end of 1860, about the time of completion of his legal
studies, he was in Dublin, where he threw himself into the
national petition campaign. At the big Rotunda meeting in
favour of the petition on 4 December, he was given the privilege
of proposing one of the motions. In his address to the gathering
he advocated self-government for Ireland within a reformed
imperial system, with Ireland and the other colonies enjoying
parliamentary representation at Westminster.[16] Some weeks
later, writing under the *nom-de-plume* 'Celt' he was airing
another fad in the pages of the *Irishman*. This was the holding
of St Patrick's Day banquets in Ireland and by the Irish in
Britain as was already the custom among Irish-Americans. These
should be temperate and thoroughly national affairs, graced by
the playing of Irish music. All of this might have gone unheeded
like his other projects but for the inclusion of one simple

practical proposal, which was that those interested in attending such a banquet in Dublin should hand in their names at the offices of the *Irishman*. This does not mean that the editor, Denis Holland, was particularly enthusiastic, for his brief footnote merely suggested that what the 'Celt' had to say was 'worthy of consideration'. By 9 February, however, the *Irishman* was reporting that the proposal had been well received and that several 'nationalists' had submitted their names. One week later, with the project obviously gathering momentum, 'Celt' elaborated on his ideas and made clear that he was following the model of the American Friendly Sons of St Patrick. He was also able to report that banquets on the lines suggested would be held in Cork and Belfast as well as Dublin.[17]

The invocation of the Friendly Sons of St Patrick was an implicit indication that an organisation was being formed to coordinate the celebrations. That was confirmed on 2 March by a reference to the admission procedures of the 'Brotherhood of the Friendly Sons'.[18] In the same low-key fashion it emerged that the new body was intended to do much more than arrange banquets, that it was in fact to be the answer to the often-expressed demand for an organisation to co-ordinate the efforts of all advocates of nationalist politics.[19] A.M. Sullivan, who was constantly endeavouring to get widely respected individuals to launch such an organisation, was not happy to see the unlikely figure of Underwood seizing the initiative: at best his manoeuvres might queer the pitch.[20] However, Sullivan could not but go along in public with the idea of the banquets: the *Nation* had actually called two years earlier for 'a simple pledge from a number of nationalists to dine together on the national festival'.[21] On 2 March 1861 the *Nation* acknowledged the value of the forthcoming banquet in a half-hearted way, at the same time warning the committee against attempting too much in the political line in so short a time.

Underwood's embryonic organisation drew heavily on the *ad hoc* framework of the national petition movement in Dublin, and made rapid progress.[22] On 9 March the definitive title was unveiled as the National Brotherhood of St Patrick. The brotherhood had already been formed; the St Patrick's Day banquet was to be the occasion of the formal inauguration, and not just in Dublin but at various locations in Ireland and Britain.[23] The rules and prospectus of the society were available in print, ready for despatch to any centre where a banquet was planned.[24] Approaches to prominent personalities brought expressions of encouragement from The O'Donoghue, G.H. Moore, and John Martin. The banquet was arranged for 18 March because the seventeenth was falling on a Sunday.

A.M. Sullivan was in a difficult position in these weeks. He could not explicitly oppose the formation of the new body, yet he had to do all he could to prevent it from pre-empting a position which could be filled far more effectively by others. The policy adopted in the leading articles of the *Nation* on 9 and 16 March was to insinuate, without mentioning the National Brotherhood by name, that plans were well advanced for a much better organisation to be set up after the presentation of the national petition, and that local groups could even now begin preparing themselves for the work. Sullivan's position in relation to the actual banquet was no less difficult. His absence from such a gathering would be interpreted as an ignominious rout; yet if he attended he could hardly expect to be made very welcome: in fact the committee had decided against asking him to speak to any of the toasts, and such exclusion would be a humiliation for the editor of the *Nation*. The O'Donoghue, at this time all things to all men, intervened at the last minute and succeeded in having Sullivan's name added to the list of speakers.[25]

In the round room of the Rotunda at seven o'clock on 18 March 1861 about four hundred men sat down to dinner at five shillings per person, while a few hundred others, male and female, looked on from the gallery. A small band was at the ready to provide music. Above the platform 'was conspicuously displayed the green flag, resplendent with gold harps and motto "Aid yourselves and God will aid you". At the base of the flag-staff was seen the phoenix arising from its ashes.'[26] The chair was occupied by Underwood who concluded his long, effusive, opening speech by reading the prospectus and proposed con-stitution of the National Brotherhood, thus publicly launching the society. The speakers who followed him — G.H. Moore, The O'Donoghue, John Martin, T.J. Crean, Fr John Kenyon, A.M. Sullivan and Denis Holland — were more or less equally effusive, though none of them referred to the National Brotherhood. Clearly, attendance at the banquet was not synonymous with membership, or even approval, of the organisation, and only about sixty of those present wore in their button-holes the green ribbon which was the badge of the society.[27]

After the St Patrick's Day celebrations, then, the society was firmly established but its future scope was far from certain. Straightaway, A.M. Sullivan, who had been hissed by a section of the audience in the Rotunda, set about cutting the new organisation down to size. In his *Morning News* of the very next day, and in the next number of the *Nation*, he criticised the banquet committee for using the occasion to inaugurate a new political society, thus compromising many of those present, who (it was alleged) knew nothing of the affair beforehand. In view of the extensive publicity which preceded the banquet this was unfair criticism, but it served well enough as an attack on the credibility of the brotherhood. Nothing so crude as an outright assault was attempted, but the society was put in perspective:

> We are no opponents of the Brotherhood of St Patrick which may or may become a very useful and proper organisation in its way; we do not at present know enough of its constitution to reach a verdict. Our countrymen for some time past have been led to believe that a strong political organisation was about to be established in Ireland. We in this journal gave our readers to understand that such an organisation was contemplated by men in whom the people of Ireland have confidence. The Brotherhood of St Patrick is not *that* organisation.[28]

Even as that was being written, the *Irishman*, already the unofficial organ of the N.B.S.P., was conceding the point:

> We have been aware for some weeks that a new political organisation of nationalists is contemplated; and it was explained to Mr Moore, The O'Donoghue, and other gentlemen a fortnight ago, that with such an organisation the brotherhood would not in any way interfere but would on the contrary, give it all possible help.[29]

Nevertheless, the brotherhood made rapid progress. St Patrick's Day banquets had been held in conjunction with the Dublin event in about half-a-dozen other places in Ireland, and in an even greater number of places in Britain.[30] Most of these gatherings made arrangements for the formation of a branch of the National Brotherhood and during subsequent weeks and months these branches established firm contact with the leadership in Dublin. 'This most promising organisation is rising fast into healthy and vigorous life', the *Irishman* announced on 13 April 1861. On 9 May the honorary secretary put the number of fully accredited branches at twenty-three.

The rules, drafted and re-drafted on various occasions, allowed for a fairly loose relationship between the branches and the central association in Dublin. However, each branch was required to make arrangements, in conjunction with the central association, for the proper celebration of the national festival. Every branch should provide itself with a reading room and should supply each member with a membership card which would entitle him to enter any reading room managed by the brotherhood. (The central association was to have a monopoly of the supply of membership cards, for which there was a small charge.) The sole requirement for membership was devotion to Irish nationality, though existing members of an established branch would vote by ballot on whether or not to accept new applicants.[31]

The brotherhood did not profess attachment to any specific political objectives. The only practical task that it set itself was to provide occasions, and locations, for social and intellectual contact between ardent nationalists. Insistence on any particular procedure or form for realising the nationality that was being celebrated would bring the socialising to a speedy and recriminatory conclusion. Underwood and his associates were not in agreement on any political programme. And they were not putting up a front for the I.R.B. or anyone else, though it is easy to see how a secret society might infiltrate and exploit the 'talking-shops' that they were bringing into existence. By 25 May the Dublin reading room had been established and the brotherhood felt sufficiently confident to announce plans for a new daily newspaper that would be the official organ of the N.B.S.P.[32] With the same confidence it embarked just at this time on involvement in the funeral of Terence Bellew MacManus — one of the most written-about and least understood episodes in the history of this period.

MacManus was not one of the more charismatic figures among the exiled 1848 convicts, though his stature was enhanced in 1856 when he was bracketed with John Mitchel and Thomas F. Meagher by being excepted from the free government pardon extended to all the other state prisoners of 1848. The three were denied pardons because they had absconded from Van Diemen's Land. In 1858 J.F. Maguire, M.P. made (in a quiet way) an unsuccessful effort to have the amnesty extended to the three.[33] A campaign with the same objective, but on far more activist lines, was initiated in the autumn of 1859 by P.J. Smyth, who had recently become editor of the Waterford *Citizen*, and was eager for popular agitation.[34] Like so much else in Ireland at the time, this campaign was conducted with an awareness of developments in France, where Louis Napoleon had granted a general amnesty to political prisoners on 15 August.[35] The *Irishman* and the *Nation* gave their support, meetings were held, and some town councils adopted favourable resolutions on the subject.[36] Then, on 8 November, Mitchel wrote from Paris to publicly dissociate himself from the movement, and so effectively killed it.[37] MacManus was equally intransigent; his repudiation of petitioning reached the Irish newspapers from San Francisco in the following April.[38] He would not, he proclaimed, crave any favour from the British government and if he could not return to Ireland without the consent of a foreign ruler he would never do so.[39]

MacManus died on 15 January 1861 and his passing was suitably lamented in the Irish nationalist press.[40] Several months later a decision was taken in America to exhume his remains and transfer them to Ireland for re-burial.[41] The idea is widely believed to have been conceived by Fenian Brotherhood members in California, but John O'Mahony's *Phoenix* (New York) claimed that it was first with the suggestion.[42] And it is by no means certain that all those involved in San Francisco were fenians; one of the most prominent of them was Thomas Mooney, who at an early stage founded a branch of the National Brotherhood of St Patrick in San Francisco.[43] It would, how-ever, be even more interesting to know the exact purpose and vision of the originators. Were they perhaps concerned primarily with making money and propaganda for the Fenian Brother-hood in America with little or no thought for what would happen in Ireland? (Certainly the affair became enmeshed in the intricate web of San Francisco Irish organisational rivalry.)[44] Or was the funeral intended to be the occasion of, and a camou-flage for, an Irish-American filibuster followed by a rising in Ireland? To the very end Michael Doheny, for one, intended to use it for that purpose, and it is quite plausible that others were of a similar mind in the early stages:[45] Doheny's influence over the Fenian Brotherhood and more particularly over the *Phoenix* was obviously enhanced in the early part of 1861 when O'Mahony was in Ireland. The imminence of civil war in the U.S.A. very probably influenced the decision to disinter MacManus; even if it did not, the actual outbreak of war in early April 1861, by raising the level of volatility all round, enhanced the potential of the MacManus affair.

Whoever the originators and whatever their motives, we can be sure that in the initiation of the MacManus funeral there was no co-ordination of purpose with the fenians (or with anyone else) in Ireland. There was nevertheless, one organisation in Ireland ready for participation in this affair — the National Brotherhood of St Patrick. News of what was afoot reached Ireland in the second half of May 1861.[46] The *Irishman* of 25 May carried a declaration by the secretary of the brotherhood 'that it is proposed that the members should attend in pro-cession at the funeral of T.B. MacManus when his remains are brought to Ireland'. And the committee of the central associ-ation called a meeting for 3 June at its rooms, where members and others interested could consider the best means of doing honour to the patriot's remains. Over four hundred attended and the MacManus funeral committee was formed.[47] This committee was in time dominated by a group of young men from Dublin city who had been involved in the MacMahon sword and national petition movements, and who at the end of 1860 or early 1861 had been attracted to the fenian organisation by Luby. As committees were formed in the various places in Munster and Leinster at which it was thought the *cortège* might halt, it almost invariably emerged that the dominant members were also prominent local I.R.B. men of the kind who had been active in the petition campaign.[48] Luby, recalling fenian involvement in the funeral, felt that 'Stephens might have discouraged it if he thought that course safe';[49] and we know that as a rule Stephens discountenanced involvement by his followers in public demonstrations. He did not have sufficient control over his men to prevent them from participating, but he could influence their participation; so, turning necessity to advantage, he used them to manipulate the committees, and so the funeral, to his own advantage, or at least so as to deny advantage to anyone else.

Word came from New York in July that it was planned there to put the remains on a steamer for Cork and a circuitous route from that to Dublin with numerous stopping points was suggested; burial should be at Bodenstown, County Kildare, near the grave of Wolfe Tone. On the advice of the Cork committee, the national committee opted instead for a direct and almost uninterrupted journey from Cork to Dublin, with burial at Glasnevin.[50] Whatever reservations they may have had about the good sense of the whole business, once it was certain to take place the former Young Ireland leaders had no choice but to give their support; to do otherwise would have amounted to disowning their own past. Smith O'Brien, John B. Dillon, Fr John Kenyon and John Martin all indicated a warm interest.[51] Similarly, Sullivan in the *Nation* encouraged a big turn-out.[52] In the normal course of events some or all of these, through deference on the part of the committee, would have become prominent in the plans and preparations. If anyone could hope to bask in glory on the occasion it would surely be MacManus's colleagues of 1848. Yet, as Martin complained later, they found themselves 'in danger of being repulsed from following their old comrade's hearse unless they followed as satellites of someone in a mask'.[53] Stephens had instructed his men on the committee to ensure that the '48 men would not be able to use the funeral as a platform or as a means of acquiring publicity. The dispute which arose between the committee and Archbishop Cullen made this task much easier by inducing the moderates to remain at arm's length from the committee.

Those concerned assumed at the beginning that catholic

services would be an integral part of the funeral with mass being celebrated at various stages.[54] In New York there was mass in St Patrick's Cathedral, with Archbishop Hughes in attendance and preaching. Early in October the Dublin committee wrote to Cullen requesting in a formal but rather peremptory manner that 'a solemn funeral service' should be held 'in the cathedral' when the remains arrived. Cullen replied with a demand to know on what grounds such a request was based.[55] This was not a refusal, but within a short time the committee was acting as if he had refused, and it was going ahead with plans that would not involve any church services in Dublin.[56] A.M. Sullivan took on the task of mediator, and both publicly — in the *Nation* — and privately — in conversation with members of the committee — he explained that MacManus could have the ordinary funeral rites available to every catholic without the archbishop being in any way involved; if, however, something special was to be provided that would implicate the archbishop and so he would first have to have guarantees that the entire affair was something with which he could happily be associated.[57]

Though it was not stated explicitly, in effect an essential first step towards the provision of the guarantees would be the removal of the committee from the control of the clique of unknowns who dominated it, and their replacement by men of recognised responsibility; and even then it would probably have required a very diplomatic statement of purpose to reconcile Cullen to conferring special honours on an unrepentent Young Irelander. It is the effort to bring all of this about which lies behind the struggle in, and on the fringes of, the committee, which provided some high drama on the eve of the procession in Dublin, particularly in the conflict between Luby and Kenyon.[58] Guided by Stephens, the extremists controlling the committee held out, and moderate, respected men had to take part in a demonstration managed by unknowns. At least Dillon, Martin, Kenyon, O'Brien and The O'Donoghue did; three days beforehand A.M. Sullivan was 'attacked by a serious illness' from which however, he had 'considerably recovered' a week later.[59]

The remains arrived in Dublin on 4 November and were at once installed in the Mechanics' Institute, Lower Abbey Street, and put lying in state. During the week a total of about 30,000 people filed past to pay their respects.[60] Reports of the arrangements at the lying-in-state would surely have confirmed Cullen's worst suspicions: for example, incense was burned near the catafalque.[61] However, the ordinary religious ministrations at the graveside were still on offer until shortly before the final procession to Glasnevin on 10 November. The chaplains of the cemetery wrote to the committee indicating that their services would be available, but only on condition that there would not be any graveside oration.[62] This move must have been inspired by Cullen; in any case it shows the oversimplicity of the notion that the archbishop had from the outset placed a ban on all ecclesiastical involvement in the MacManus obsequies. Father Patrick Lavelle was at hand to assure the committee that he would supply whatever he could in the way of prayers for the departed, and at Glasnevin he was joined by another priest. The latter recited the *De profundis*, before Lavelle delivered a short and very political harangue which was followed by another recital of the *De profundis*.[63]

Beyond any doubt the MacManus funeral procession was an impressive demonstration. Estimates of its size have naturally varied. Writing over forty years later, Joseph Denieffe contended that the cortège had been about seven miles long. A police witness writing on the day after the procession estimated that it was about one mile in length and contained between seven and eight thousand people.[64] These included large delegations from about twenty Dublin trades. However, those actually in the procession were far outnumbered by the on-lookers. Early in the day about forty thousand had assembled outside the Mechanics' Institute, and the entire route was lined with people.[65] The impression made by the funeral procession was not due entirely to its size. It was a masterpiece of organisation and decorum. The great majority of the processionists wore black armbands with white ribbons, achieving thereby a strong visual impact. Horsemen, strikingly attired, marshalled the pedestrian participants, who move with something like military precision.[66]

However, the significance of the MacManus funeral has too often been exaggerated by historians, largely because it is not seen in its context. Phrases such as 'turning point in Irish history' have been freely used of it. Almost the only incontrovertible interpretation that can be put on the affair is that large numbers of people were in the mood for a public spectacle in Dublin on 10 November 1861. Getting large crowds together was now easier than in the 1840s owing to the railways and their cheap Sunday excursion fares. On the other hand there had been since 1850 a legal constraint on public demonstrations in Ireland, the Party Processions Act of 1850 having been reinforced in 1860 (*23 & 24 Vict.*, c.141). The MacManus funeral, precisely because it was a funeral, avoided the strictures of the act. The paucity of regular opportunities for public processions goes a long way to explain the spectacular turnout on 10 November 1861. It would be a grave error to assume that the crowd was giving assent to MacManus's political doctrines: retrospective approval of rebels is always an ambiguous business. The crowds were out not because the funeral was MacManus's, but because it was a spectacle and an excuse for ovating. Of course any Irish catholic crowd would respond to invocations of nationality. That was a far cry from understanding, much less embracing, the full-blooded separatist republicanism of a handful of the organisers of the MacManus funeral. The visit of the queen to Ireland in late August 1861 proved that there was nothing republican about the popular propensity for flocking to spectacles. The cheering crowds on that occasion had been headed by the establishment and the gentry but were so numerous that they must have included large numbers of the plain people of Ireland. Certainly the *Freeman's Journal* declared that to have been the case. However, the royal visit was officially private and no attempt had been made by the authorities to encourage or facilitate popular participation. Thus, for example, the timing and route of the queen's coach tour of Dublin were not announced in advance.[67] Very impressive participation would have been forthcoming for formalised demonstrations in honour of the queen, above all if they included some minimal rhetorical invocations of 'the green'. Interestingly, when the royal train on its way to Killarney halted in a packed Thurles station the decorations in the building consisted of a profusion of 'evergreens'.[68]

The most comprehensive comment on the MacManus funeral came from Archbishop Cullen, in the form of an equally impressive demonstration staged in Dublin less than nine months later. The occasion was the laying of the foundation stone of a new building for the Catholic University, at Drumcondra. As it was technically a religious rather than a political affair, the Party Processions Act could not be invoked. In every way the MacManus funeral was matched if not outdone. Decorations, delegations, onlookers and bands left nothing to be desired. Purple-robed ecclesiastics and surpliced seminarians took the place of arm-banded mourners. The police estimated that there were one hundred thousand people in the grounds at Drumcondra for the ceremony,[69] and the long route of the procession from the pro-cathedral had been lined with onlookers. The thoroughness of the *riposte* was complete: Cullen ensured that the trade unions marched, as they had for MacManus; and even Archbishop Hughes of New York was present, to make implicit amends for his involvement in the MacManus funeral in America.[70] When the various features of the two affairs have been cancelled off against one another the most significant point remaining is that the MacManus funeral highlighted what had already been revealed by the national petition about the existence (especially in Dublin) of able, active, and independent cadres of the propertyless who were readily available for congenial political purposes.

Close observers could see that the MacManus funeral committee in Dublin had been in the control of a conspiratorial group; more generally, the presence of the I.R.B. was palpable, especially in Dublin, from the spring of 1861. Because of Stephens's policy of keeping his organisation anonymous most contemporaries did not see any link with the 'Phoenix Society' of 1858. And for the same reason many identified the unnamed society with the National Brotherhood of St Patrick. Two years later the catholic bishops were still condemning the N.B.S.P. by name on the ground that it administered an oath in favour of an Irish republic.[71] Despite this misapprehension, episcopal hostility was well founded, for the brotherhood, despite having no agreed policy, was a rallying point for radicals and revolutionists. It was not by any means a secret society, but there was about it from the beginning a certain unspoken assumption concerning the use of physical force. When, eventually, the definitive version of the rules appeared, a maxim adapted from the volunteers of 1782 was appended in a rather heavy-handed attempt at subtlety: 'A member of the National Brotherhood of St Patrick by learning the use of arms does not forego any of his social rights.'[72]

Catholic churchmen detected an air of anti-clericalism about the brotherhood, and they were worried by the presence of an inordinate proportion of protestants in the leading ranks.[73] The efforts of the brotherhood to assert that a healthy independence of churches did not amount to irreligion were seriously undermined by an indiscretion on the part of the San Francisco branch in an address to their Dublin brethren on 7 January 1862. This address was published in a newspaper, *Mooney's San Francisco Express*, managed by the secretary of the brotherhood in those parts, Thomas J. Mooney. By March 1862 the text was available in Dublin, where it was seized upon eagerly, and publicised, by opponents of the National Brotherhood, who revelled in quoting its shocking sentiments. They lighted particularly on a passage which chided the Irish for having spent so much money during the preceding decades on churches and cathedrals: the resources expended on these 'expensive piles', it declared, could more profitably have been devoted to military preparations. The Dublin members rushed to disown these and other disastrously undiplomatic expression, but irreparable damage had been done.[74]

From beginning to end the greatest weakness of the National Brotherhood was the poor quality of its leadership. Underwood appears to have been a rather comic figure, and, although he was president for a short time, either his colleagues or himself decided that the vice-presidency was as high an office as he could permanently adorn in the brotherhood. The other vice-president from March 1862 onwards was Fr Lavelle, a spirited and indefatigable protagonist and a valuable acquisition for the brotherhood, but disqualified on a number of counts from national leadership.[75] On 1 January 1862 Underwood had written to William Smith O'Brien vainly trying to persuade him to accept the presidency and the position was subsequently left vacant in expectation of a suitable occupant. The O'Donoghue was by this time by far the most prestigious supporter remaining to the brotherhood and clearly he could have assumed the leadership if he so desired, but he probably feared that close identification with this particular organisation would have weakened his position with other groups.[76] A number of able young men came forward to work for the society at a lower level. They included Charles Guilfoyle Doran and Joseph Patrick MacDonnell. For want of opposition such people eventually acquired control of the central body in Dublin and subsequent pronouncements often had a distinctly Chartist flavour.

Extant records of the National Brotherhood are very scanty and no complete list of branches is available. Underwood, when endeavouring to impress Smith O'Brien, claimed one hundred and sixty branches.[77] Whatever of the precise number, there can be no doubt about the high concentration of branches in Britain. Examination of the numerous weekly reports in the *Irishman* from 1861 to 1864 would suggest that there were about three branches among the Irish in England and Scotland for every one in Ireland itself. This reflects the readiness of the Irish in Britain at this time for social and political organisation, and also their relative lack of discrimination in the matter of nationalist societies: throughout the 1860s and 1870s they tended to flock to the support of any movement which appealed to them as Irishmen or as catholics much more readily than the Irish at home, and with very little regard for questions of political doctrine. They had played a part in the national petition movement, which in all probability provided the basic organisation for the National Brotherhood in Britain as in Ireland. Even before that they had responded to the new international situation by launching in 1858 the Irish Protective Association, whose objects were 'Mutual instruction and information, and a close and continual watchfulness, when united in one great brotherhood all over England and Scotland, to serve the land of our fathers by every means in our power'.[78]

The celebration of St Patrick's day in the style of the National Brotherhood took place in 1862, 1863 and 1864.[79] By then, however, the fortunes of the society were on the wane. The decline was not unrelated to the expansion of the I.R.B. Initially there was nothing Stephens could do to prevent an overlapping of membership, but when the time was ripe and the leadership of the National Brotherhood wilted, he appears to have embarked on a deliberate policy of suppression of the rival organisation. [80] Whereas in Ireland branches simply withered away, in Britain it appears that branches of the National Brotherhood went over wholesale to the I.R.B., as the latest and most attractive movement available. There are indications that the changeover was sometimes resisted; but that seems to have been the exception rather than the rule. The National Brotherhood of St Patrick is an excellent example of the vulnerability of an open organisation in competition with a secret conspiracy.

Plans for a comprehensive nationalist organisation were set back by the launching of the National Brotherhood in the early months of 1861, but the *Nation* persisted: 'We think we can promise our fellow-countrymen that they shall soon have it in their power to join an organisation which will be founded and fitted for practical purposes.'[81] The promise was renewed and put in perspective on 25 May:

> With the signing of the national petition has commenced a course of well-considered practical action suited to the circumstances in which the state of political affairs in Europe does now, and may at a future time, place us. We, who have had the honour of initiating that movement in this journal, have pledged ourselves to our countrymen that other measures, carrying us on, would in good time be submitted for their approval. At present we shall not say more than that the matter is not being neglected. . . . To existing patriotic organisations, now before the public, no hostility whatever is felt or will be offered . . . but we believe it is not too much to say that men who are willing to serve Ireland, will soon have the opportunity of joining the ranks of an organisation eminently practical in its nature, intelligible in its aims, and having at its head men who will be recognised by Irishmen all the world over as worthy of their confidence. Such is the organisation now needed.[82]

As weeks passed without any such organisation being launched, the *Nation* was plied with indignant queries and felt obliged to offer some excuse.[83] The explanation given was reasonably satisfactory, and it throws some light on an otherwise obscure development. They had, the editor admitted, given an undertaking to follow up the anticipated rejection of the national petition with the unveiling of plans for an 'enduring and effective' national organisation. This work, however, had been taken over by 'men whom the country will regard as trustworthy leaders', who (it was implied) were to be held responsible for the delay.[84]

A month later further explanation was forthcoming. When the *Nation* promised that the petition would only open the way for another movement something definite was in mind; but to their great satisfaction they found that the spirit evoked by the campaign 'rekindled hope' in the hearts of some eminent patriots who had been despairing. 'These men — of names and fames well known to Ireland — met to deliberate on the best form of organisation, the best course of action for the Irish people.' The *Nation* had waited patiently and then had written twice to the gentlemen concerned indicating that 'the people' were eager for some useful organisation, before commencing to appeal publicly to them to make a move. Could all of this, the editor asked, be construed as abandonment of his promises?[85]

The 'eminent patriots' meeting to deliberate on national organisation must have included The O'Donoghue: his omission from such company at this juncture would have been unthinkable. At the same time it seems certain that he had been fully involved in the *Nation*'s scheme of action which was dropped in deference to the wishes of other 'eminent patriots'; this is implied in the *Nation* editorial of 17 August, and in any case seems inevitable in view of his prominence in the national petition movement and his close association with A.M. Sullivan. The paradox can be explained as follows. Sullivan and The O'Donoghue had agreed on a programme of action, of which The O'Donoghue would be leader and director, but, before the time to implement it had arrived, the 'chieftain' had been inveigled into discussions with other prominent nationalists whose support he would dearly love to have but who, as events were to prove, would have great difficulty agreeing on any set of concrete proposals. Throughout the early 'sixties The O'Donoghue displayed an impressive talent for retaining the confidence of opposing sections of his potential grand party — one of the essential traits of successful leadership. However, he seems to have lacked the equally important knack of knowing when to terminate consultation and initiate action.

The scope and importance of The O'Donoghue's apparent leadership potential at this time is illustrated strikingly by his relationship with John Mitchel. As Parnell was to do for Devoy eighteen years later, The O'Donoghue crossed the channel to confer with Mitchel at Boulogne early in May 1861, shortly before the presentation of the national petition. (Significantly, it was also shortly after the beginning of the American civil war.) Mitchel was captivated by the attitudes and policies of his visitor, and gave him an endorsement such as he gave to no other Irish politician between 1848 and his death in 1875. He wrote to John O'Mahony, who he thought was still in Ireland,

urging him to meet The O'Donoghue (who was 'honest, determined and thoroughgoing') and suggesting that the fenians
should be prepared to co-operate with him.[86] The O'Donoghue
had unveiled for Mitchel a radical plan of action:

> He is to attempt in a day or two to present the national
> petition to the queen (it will be refused; that is, the home
> secretary will not even allow him an audience to present it);
> then he will present the city of Dublin petition in the house
> of commons. It will be met, as he expects, with shrieks,
> coughs, sneezes. Then he will quit parliament and go home to
> Ireland, where it is probable he will ask the people to join
> in some organisation for further measures.[87]

This plan was probably a version of the one agreed with A.M.
Sullivan, and deferred under pressure from other prominent
nationalists. No doubt they had qualms about the proposed
withdrawal. That, however, was precisely what would appeal
to Mitchel. The O'Donoghue had begun to use abstentionist
rhetoric at least as early as 4 December 1860, when, at the
national petition meeting in the Rotundo, he declared that
'three years of parliamentary experience, short though it may
appear, have convinced me that an Irishman has no business
in the English house of commons'.[88] At the time Mitchel had
quickly seized upon the logic of that remark, suggesting that
The O'Donoghue should tell his constituents that if he was
elected again it would be to an Irish parliament, and that pend-
ing its assembly he would remain at home.[89]

Quitting parliament would not involve the abandonment of
constitutional processes; elections could still be contested, thus
satisfying the insistence of the *Nation* (in an editorial comment
on parliamentary politics made a few months earlier) that the
electoral battle-ground should not be surrendered to 'the
enemies of nationalism', even though victory might not be
possible through effort on that front alone.[90] In fact, a policy
of constitutional abstentionism was being explicitly promoted
at this time by P.J. Smyth, who advocated the return at elections
of members pledged to refuse the oath in the same manner as
O'Connell had in 1828, but on the grounds, this time, that the
power of the British parliament in Ireland was an usurpation.[91]

At Boulogne The O'Donoghue had discussed with Mitchel
the kind of national organisation that it was hoped to establish
as a follow-up to the withdrawal from parliament. It was to be
within the law, which would please constitutionalists and those
eager for a revival of the Repeal Association.[92] At the same
time it would co-operate with all other nationalist movements,
including underground ones. That pleased Mitchel, because of

the hint of illegality:

> Though ostensibly legal and open it will, and must, naturally seek to connect itself with whatsoever secret machinations may be going on. That is to say, in other words, it will be an organisation looking to revolution, foreign aid and more or less directly preparing for that, though for the moment within the forms of the law.[93]

By comparison with The O'Donoghue, Underwood was a political lightweight, yet he stole some of the young chieftain's thunder by the setting up of the National Brotherhood. The O'Donoghue could not discountenance this attempt to organise national opinion without contradicting his own rhetoric and alienating an important section of activists whose support he needed; so he gave at least tacit approval to its foundation. Once it was in being he genuinely wished it well, being aware that, whatever its deficiencies, its collapse would be interpreted as proof that any attempt at national organisation was futile. Nevertheless, it must have interfered seriously enough with his plans. The MacManus funeral was an even more serious upset and causing that upset was the highest purpose of Stephens's manipulation of the affair. If the Young Irelanders could not control and shine forth at the funeral of a colleague in Dublin city, how could they hope to manage a national organisation? Stephens had embarked on the line of activity that may have been his most effective contribution to the history of his time, namely the sabotaging of nationalist movements not amenable to his own control. However, the first obstacle in the way of The O'Donoghue's hopes was the inability of himself and his would-be collaborators to come to any agreement among themselves. By the autumn John Mitchel was announcing that negotiations for a new national movement had reached the stage of failure or postponement.[94]

On 14 September 1861 a leading article in the *Irishman* considered the question of 'Why political life is paralysed in Ireland' and concluded that the weakness was at the top. In the wake of the MacManus funeral the *Nation* appealed to the recognised leaders of the popular cause: 'We now ask how long more they will leave the bravest people and the best cause in Europe without that leadership which they are the men to supply.' There followed a warning of the consequences of their continued inaction, a warning that proved to be an outstandingly perceptive forecast of the progress of Irish politics in the subsequent four or five years. Anonymous bodies will spring up, the writer declared, and earnest but inexperienced men will join them, seeing nothing better to be had; violent men will dominate them; the rudest-mannered man will set up for being the best patriot; men who do not approve of this order of things will either retire in disgust or be expelled; internal and external quarrels will soon develop themselves, the societies will alarm orders and interests that should be conciliated and that are naturally friendly to Ireland; the government will know all about their doings; it will not interfere while damage so great is being done to the Irish cause, but, when the worst in that way has been accomplished, then it will pounce on them; a jail or two will be filled with the bodies of young men who meant patriotism but did not act it wisely. . . . These things will, we think, come to pass if men whose position, abilities and services constitute them the natural leaders of the Irish people do not speedily place themselves in the van of the national force and organise the struggle for Ireland's independence.[95]

In conclusion the international perspective was sketched: 'The time is growing critical; Europe is on the brink of convulsion; England is in expectation of war; not a day is to be lost.' The prospect of a European war was to reappear again and again during the 1860s. But in late 1861 a different international threat loomed that was to have an even more telling impact on Irish affairs for much of the decade. That was the spectre of Anglo-American war. It caused the most intense excitement in Ireland, highlighted again the potential for national organisation, and provided an admirable occasion for a fresh start on the work of launching one.

In the third week of November news broke that earlier in the month a federal American man-of-war had stopped a British mail steamer, the *Trent*, on the high seas and removed there-from two envoys of the rebellious confederate states bound for England. This insult to the flag aroused intense indignation in England, and, with both governments exchanging bellicose notes in subsequent weeks, war seemed to be the likely outcome. In Dublin A.M. Sullivan convened a meeting of prominent advocates of self-government and sympathetic journalists resident in the city, at the European Hotel on 29 November.[96] This gathering made arrangements for a public meeting in the Rotundo on 5 December 'to take into consideration the position of Irish national affairs at the present momentous crisis'. It was also decided that, after an appropriate amount of oratory, a resolu-tion should be proposed calling on the chairman and secretary of the meeting, together with the proposers and seconders of motions, to summon a conference of nationalists which would in turn draw up a plan of national organisation to be subsequently submitted to a public meeting for approval.[97] At last, it seemed, a start was about to be made; but the opposition of James Stephens was to intervene decisively.

It was a case of 'standing room only' when the public meeting convened on 5 December with The O'Donoghue, inevitably, in the chair. While the crowded Rotundo was resounding to pro-testations of affection for, and gratitude to, America, and promises that Ireland would never follow England to war against 'the great benefactor of her exiled children', Stephens's counter-attack began. His right-hand-man, Luby, slipped onto the plat-form and informed Sullivan, The O'Donoghue, and others that if their motion on organisation was brought forward a substantive amendment in the I.R.B. interest would be moved from the body of the hall; if, on the other hand, the motion was not proceeded with, the amendment would itself be proposed as a substantive resolution.[98] Luby left the platform party in no doubt that I.R.B. strength was so disposed in the auditorium that their amendment or resolution, as the case might be, could be opposed only at the risk of a disorderly end to the meeting; and that would be a disastrous setback for the organisers. The platform motion on organisation was not proposed. As the meeting was nearing conclusion, one of the Californian delegates to the MacManus funeral, Jeremiah Kavanagh, rose to speak and was greeted by rounds of applause and cheering led by fenians acting according to a preconcerted plan.[99] Kavanagh moved 'that a chairman, two secretaries and a committee of twenty-one members — each having been duly and separately proposed and seconded — be chosen by a majority of voices at this mass meeting to take into consideration the advisability of carrying out an organisation in the present state of affairs at home and abroad'. This resolution seemed perfectly innocent of subterfuge to the great body of the meeting and was carried by acclamation. The nomination of the committee members came next, and Stephens's agents were fully prepared for that too. The naming of The O'Donoghue, G.H. Moore and P.J. Smyth disarmed suspicion and distracted attention from the fact that most of the others were comparatively unknown; a clear majority were I.R.B. sympathisers. The meeting had indeed produced a committee to deliberate on national organi-sation, but it was controlled by James Stephens. And the great crowd dispersed with the unsuspecting majority convinced that the gathering had been 'a most harmonious affair' and 'a model of united action'.[100]

The O'Donoghue had once again been thwarted but his position with the public and his pre-eminence among the active public men on the popular side were unimpaired. There is some irony in the fact that the Rotundo meeting at which his plans for national agitation were upset by the I.R.B. caused The O'Donoghue to fall foul of Dublin Castle. Some of his Rotundo statements on the Irish attitude to Anglo-American relations gave rise to a correspondence with the lord chancellor of Ireland which concluded with the announcement that the member for Tipperary was being removed from the commission for the peace in Counties Cork and Kerry. This further enhanced his popularity. Soon a movement was afoot, on the suggestion of Smith O'Brien, to organise demonstrations of support in The O'Donoghue's constituency, County Tipperary; the first of these was held at Templederry on 9 February 1862. Next, a county banquet in his honour was being planned for Thurles, under the direction of a committee of the catholic clergy and middle class of Tipperary.[101]

The list of those invited to attend gives an indication of the high ambitions of the organisers. Included were eight catholic bishops (headed by MacHale of Tuam and Leahy of Cashel), Smith O'Brien, John Martin, G.H. Moore, four or five independent opposition M.P.s, and the former Callan curates, Keeffe and O'Shea, pioneers of the tenant-right movement in the 1850s.[102] On this list interests were represented which, since 1857, A.M. Sullivan, The O'Donoghue, and others had dreamt of aligning in a comprehensive national movement. The organisers of the Thurles banquet clearly had very high ambitions. Operating away from Dublin brought certain advantages. For example, church dignitaries could be invited without reference to Archbishop Cullen. Apart from the invited guests the banquet would be confined to citizens of County Tipperary, so the whole affair would be secure from interference by James Stephens's Dublin activists.

But the reliance of these advantages of location served only to highlight the basic flaw in what was being attempted. For there was no formula that would satisfy all the elements of the 'national party', and any effort to please some sections would inevitably alienate others. Smith O'Brien drew up resolutions for the banquet which suggests that alone of all the organisational ventures of these years it had his unreserved approval. He called for a campaign of parliamentary agitation and condemned secret societies.[103] Such a programme would be immediately rejected by, among others, John Mitchel and P.J. Smyth. In fact, the banquet was likely to alienate the entire 'radical' wing of the hoped-for coalition. Thus, the *Irishman* began to complain early in May about the 'exclusive' tactics of the committee, citing the raising of the ticket price to a prohibitive ten shillings, and the omission from the programme of a toast to the press, allegedly because the person with first claim to reply to this would be Peter E. Gill of the *Tipperary Advocate*, a man given to the expression of 'advanced' views.[104] The banquet never took place, The O'Donoghue being struck by sudden illness shortly before the appointed date.[105] It is difficult to avoid the suspicion that this illness was of the diplomatic variety. Throughout the remainder of 1862 and all of 1863 the nationalist journals continued to publicise the need for a grand national organisation.[106] There are references, some of them vague, to consultative meetings of leading nationalists during this period, but there was no substantial progress to be reported.

This frustration, in the early 1860s, of plans for a public nationalist movement owed much to the opposition of James Stephens. However, the struggle between Stephens and the would-be leaders of public agitation was not the straightforward and inevitable conflict of opposing principles which I.R.B. apologists liked to portray. At first Stephens had been in friendly contact with many of his later antagonists. In the period from 1856 to late 1858 he had met Smith O'Brien, John B. Dillon, Fr Kenyon and, of course, A.M. Sullivan.[107] All of these, and many other respected nationalists both in Ireland and America, decided to have nothing to do with Stephens's organisation. This general refusal by the Young Irelanders needs to be explored to achieve an understanding of the nationalist politics of the period and of Stephens's destructive role therein.

In the attempt to impose some meaningful pattern of this episode it is tempting to represent the conflict between the Young Irelanders (especially A.M. Sullivan) and Stephens as one phase of a long drawn out struggle between constitutional and physical-force policies. But, in fact, Sullivan at this period was an ardent advocate of the principle of physical force, as is evident from the leader pages of the *Nation*. The paper's response to the invasion panic of 1859 was particularly revealing in this regard. On 7 May 1859 it exhorted the population to procure arms, used the term 'national defences and patriot army', and declared that 'in Ireland from September to April the climate would be on the side of the people'. A similar tone was struck over and over again during the remainder of the year, though usually with more circumspection.[108] Whenever the subject of physical force was mentioned by the *Nation* in subsequent years there was no rejection on principle. Thus, in a statement of policy to mark the beginning of the paper's twentieth volume it was declared that the *Nation* would not renounce the country's right to use force when the time was ripe.[109] An article in 1864 provoked by I.R.B. criticism was similarly explicit:

For our own part we have frequently recommended 'preparation' in this journal and made very intelligible what we meant
thereby. We have advised Irish patriots to procure arms and
to learn the use of them as far as that might be done without
incurring legal penalties. . . . We have always believed, and
stated our belief, that the fullness of Ireland's political rights
will never be conceded but by English fear of the strength of
the people of Ireland. Holding this opinion we have coun-
selled the friends of Ireland to make themselves strong, by
the possession of arms, for in arms and opinion combined
is the true power of a nation.[110]

Smith O'Brien, during one of his many repudiations of a
possible French invasion, after having declared that reliance
should be placed instead on the public opinion of the Irish
nation, added in parenthesis that 'their opinion would, of
course, be backed up by their physical force'.[111] John Blake
Dillon was even more outspoken; writing to Smith O'Brien
in 1864 he declared: 'For my own part I don't believe in
the possibility of repealing the union by anything else other
than round shot and rifle bullets, and therefore I cannot
honestly encourage the people to expect it by an appeal to
public opinion'.[112] Quite obviously these men were not turning
away from the I.R.B. because of principled revulsion against
physical force.

If, then, the *Nation* and its allies were not opponents on
principle of a military policy, what was their objection to
fenianism? Many of them expressed qualms about its secrecy.
They made no serious effort to prove that secret association was
morally reprehensible — that was left to the clergy, although
Smith O'Brien did manage to sound as if a definitive interpretation of the moral law were being made whenever he announced
that *he* had always opposed it.[113] When they did give reasons
for their opposition they almost invariably cited the inexpedi-
ency of secret societies, either in general, or under actual Irish
conditions. O'Brien argued that the existence of a secret society
discouraged others from working openly for a cause. In any case
he was sure that the Irish government was fully informed of the
doings of all secret societies in the country.[114] This point about
government infiltration was frequently made, as for example in
the *Nation*'s denunciation on 16 November 1861. The assertion
in the same article that secret conspiracy would 'alarm orders
and interests which should be conciliated' probably touches on
A.M. Sullivan's most basic objection to fenianism — the conviction that it would turn the clergy against joining in a new
national movement as they had joined in support of the Repeal

Association.

Another line of opposition to fenianism held that, while there was a definite place for conspiracy in a national movement, the I.R.B. had gone beyond its proper subordinate role and was attempting to monopolise the action to the exclusion of all other elements. This view was perhaps propounded most coherently by P.J. Smyth, writing pseudonymously in the *Irishman* in 1865. Conspiracy, he wrote, is indeed an essential ingredient of revolution (and should have been used by O'Connell in 1843 and by Young Ireland in 1848), but it is only one ingredient.[115] This serves as a reminder that there was no essential incompatibility between a nationalist secret and a public national movement, even one engaged in parliamentary agitation. But there was no possibility of co-operation between the leader of this particular secret society and the particular men who aspired to leadership of nationalist public opinion at this time.

However, for a few days in December 1861 it seemed as if an attempt would be made to form an alliance. Predictably, The O'Donoghue was at the centre of the affair. On the night of the Rotundo gathering in connection with the 'Trent' crisis, when the fenian-dominated committee on organisation was formed, Luby arranged for The O'Donoghue to meet James Stephens next day at the latter's lodgings in Charlemont Street. There was no third party at the meeting and Stephens's version of the outcome as recalled much later by Luby was that The O'Donoghue agreed 'while still operating on his own hook, to afford us outside and parallel, so to speak, co-operation'.[116] And in furtherance of this co-operation he would act on the new committee. Referring to The O'Donoghue many years later, A.M. Sullivan wrote that 'once or twice in the course of the war between the fenian and non-fenian nationalists I trembled for him',[117] meaning that he feared he would compromise in the struggle. Clearly this was one of the occasions, but Sullivan himself played his cards cautiously at the time, at least in so far as editorial comment in the *Nation* was concerned.

The next issue, that of 7 December 1861, referred approvingly, if unenthusiastically, to the new committee, even though there is no doubt that Sullivan disliked it intensely. It was, however, Smith O'Brien who sabotaged this particular 'new departure', by a public exhortation to The O'Donoghue to withdraw from the committee. O'Brien was the ally that the young chieftain least wanted to lose, so within a few days The O'Donoghue returned to Stephens to call off their deal, he and his supporters withdrawing from the committee at the same time.[118] Indicative of the changed situation, the *Nation* of 14 December carried a detailed *exposé* of the machinations behind the formation of the committee, knowledge which could easily have been imparted a week earlier if Sullivan had thought well of it; instead, in the issue of 7 December he had kept his options open.

The question remains: why this unbridgeable gulf? Why did the fenian and non-fenian nationalists fail so utterly to co-operate? The best answer is the one suggested by P.J. Smyth — that it was because the fenians insisted on obtaining a monopoly — but it needs to be teased out. The secret *hetairia* (which had the phoenix as its symbol) had monopolised Greek preparations for revolution but that was in a country subject to despotic rule. Ireland in the mid-nineteenth century, on the other hand, enjoyed virtually the full range of British civil and political liberties. Over a number of decades there had been built up complex systems of political relationships and many of the typical power structures of liberal-democratic society — admittedly with some local variations. In such a situation a secret society could find itself a niche but it could not reasonably hope to achieve dominance. The example of France in 1848 should have been a lesson to Stephens; even there, the secret societies had constituted only a small (if important) minority of the disaffected who launched the revolution.

The futile attempt to impose the exclusive hegemony of fenianism over the entire nationalist movement owed everything to James Stephens. He was incapable of voluntarily sharing authority or power with anyone else. People in Kilkenny could recall him announcing when he was a boy that he was going to be a king when he grew up.[119] His youthful veneration for royalty obviously underwent a change, but the conviction that he ought to be an untrammelled autocrat did not. The *rapprochement* with The O'Donoghue on 5 December 1861 might at first sight seem to be an indication of a willingness on Stephens's part to reach some accommodation, but that was not the case. Then and on a few other occasions he feigned an interest in compromise for tactical reasons. Stephens never was at the head of a cohesive, disciplined body of zealots. Rather, he was struggling to retain — and eventually make exclusive — his influence over an amorphous mass of non-ideological young activists, the great majority of whom would attach themselves to any attractive public movement on offer. This meant not only that Stephens was eager to nip new movements in the bud, but also that he had betimes to give the appearance of being co-operative.

Advocates of self-government, be they Young Irelanders or neo-Young-Irelanders, did not have a monopoly of attempts to generate nation-wide public movements in Ireland of the early

1860s. Some of the prime participants in the Catholic University demonstration of 20 July 1862 met the very next evening in euphoric mood and set up an association 'to proclaim Ireland's grievances'.[120] The *Nation* offered a word of welcome, while at the same time making it abundantly clear that this was by no means the comprehensive national organisation so ardently desired: 'Its programme is far short of ours, but it goes to a certain extent on the same way with us, and so far it can be made to serve our cause'.[121] But, of course, the most potent source of dispute among the warring élites was not how far anyone was going, nor along which route, but, who should lead the way. The group formed in July 1862 found a congenial symbolic project a few months later. This was the scheme for a monument in Dublin's main thoroughfare in honour of Daniel O'Connell, as launched by the *Freeman's Journal* in September. Here was an astute political ploy, for nobody who hoped for a consensus within Irish catholic and nationalist circles could refuse to pay lip-service (and a little purse-service) to the memory of the liberator, however much they might dislike supporting anything managed by Sir John Gray. So, the *Nation* and the *Irishman* expressed approval with as much grace as they could muster, and Smith O'Brien subscribed five pounds.[122] At a meeting in a Dublin hotel on 14 October 1862 A.M. Sullivan was given a place on the committee forwarding the project, but Dublin Liberals predominated.[123] The attendance of a number of parish priests from the city was a sure indication of Cullen's approval. The controlling group made a point of recalling O'Connell the winner of catholic emancipation rather than O'Connell the repealer, a presentation which, predictably, provoked some protests. John Blake Dillon indicated in a quiet, dignified manner that, although he supported the plans for a memorial, nothing about O'Connell was more important to him than the great man's devotion to national independence.[124] P.J. Smyth got himself appointed to the committee and with assistance from A.M. Sullivan he fought tenaciously to give a more explicitly nationalist tone to the entire project, even to the extent of attempting to engineer MacHale's adoption as a trustee. But he failed to change the political complexion of the movement.

The efforts of would-be national leadership élites to acquire followers were inseparable from the efforts of proprietors of national newspapers to acquire adequate circulation. There were two theatres of journalistic combat, that of the weeklies and that of the dailies. 'It is all the go now, even the farmers buy the daily papers', a County Westmeath observer commented, writing in 1863.[125] In response to this demand A.M. Sullivan, early in

The O'Donoghue of the Glens in 1880, after he had lost some of the dash that distinguished him twenty years earlier. (Artist: L. M. Ward; courtesy of the National Gallery of Ireland)

James Creedon of Bantry, draper's assistant (top) and Michael Cosgrave at Waterford, iron moulder. Two typical urban fenians of the mid-1860s. (Fenian photographs, State Paper Office, Dublin Castle)

John Blake Dillon in 1865 (from C. G. Duffy, *Young Ireland*)

Edward Duffy (from J. Denieffe, *A personal narrative of the Irish Revolutionary Brotherhood*)

1859, using the resources of the *Nation* office, had produced the *Evening News* and subsequently the *Morning News*. By so doing he entered into direct competition with the *Freeman's Journal*. The *Morning News* was a penny daily. In a very short time the *Freeman's Journal* struck back with a price reduction from twopence halfpenny to a penny. Nevertheless, the *News* held on, and it was a viable concern when in 1862 Sullivan handed it over for an unstated consideration to the Irish Catholic Publishing Company.[126] Conveniently, the new directors hired Sullivan as editor. Less happily, they embarked on some expensive projects of expansion thereby incurring debts which eventually forced the discontinuation of the *News* as from the end of 1864. In its flush of early success in 1861 the National Brotherhood of St Patrick had proposed to establish its own daily organ.[127] In 1862 there appeared a prospectus for an 'Irish National Newspaper and Publishing Company' that aimed to collect £20,000 in shares and publish an independent daily newspaper with a circulation of from fifteen to thirty thousand.[128] But it was only to be another prospectus, and the first great impetus for daily newspaper publishing resulted in the emergence in 1865 of a revitalised *Freeman's Journal* as the unchallenged leading daily on the catholic-popular side in Irish politics. The battle of the weeklies was more drawn-out and far more exciting.

As between the *Nation* and the *Irishman* the only policy difference of any significance was on the issue of parliamentary agitation, which the *Nation* advocated in independent opposition form and which the *Irishman* rejected in every form. (Here again it must be emphasised that there was no clash on the physical force question.) However, the contest between the two national weeklies was a struggle between rival commercial enterprises rather than an ideological conflict, and it was enlivened by the development of a bitter personal antagonism between A.M. Sullivan and Denis Holland. For the most part this antagonism was comparatively well veiled until May 1860. Then there were bitter editorial exchanges on aspects of recruitment for the papal brigade;[129] at the end of the year the *Irishman* joined whole-heartedly in a new phase of the verbal warfare between Sullivan and the American fenians.[130]

Holland suffered a disastrous blow in 1861 when he unsuccessfully contested a libel case at Armagh assizes. The aggrieved party was a landowner and magistrate of the county, William Jones Armstrong, who had been accused of injustice to tenants in an article copied by the *Irishman* from the *Dundalk Democrat*. Armstrong was awarded fifty pounds compensation and all costs. To meet these crushing expenses Holland borrowed a large sum from his father-in-law, William Watson, and made

over to him as security the property of the *Irishman*.[131] When
A.M. Sullivan in April 1862, began a meticulous and lengthy
rebuttal of the Stephens-inspired allegations made against him
in connection with the Phoenix Society arrests of 1858, the
Irishman immediately provided his accusers with a platform
from which to reply. In fact the charges were repeated in an
open letter to Sullivan from O'Donovan Rossa carried by the
very next issue of the *Irishman*.[132] Sullivan responded by
bringing a civil action for libel against Holland. The outcome
was virtually a tie as far as point-scoring went: the jury found
in favour of Sullivan, which allowed him to proclaim the
vindication of his integrity; but the damages amounted to
a mere sixpence, which gave the *Irishman* great scope for
ridicule.[133] However, as Holland had to meet the full costs
of the case — about two hundred and fifty pounds — the last
laugh was with Sullivan. Once again Watson came to the rescue.
Holland now owed a large sum to his father-in-law, and despite
attempts to get financial support from his friends he was unable
to resolve his debt. Before the end of 1862 he had opened
negotiations with P.J. Smyth for the sale of his newspaper and
in April of the following year Smyth became proprietor and
editor of the *Irishman*.[134] Sullivan had disposed of Holland,
but he had not got rid of the *Irishman*. However, for the next
few years differences could be aired without stirring up bitter
personal animosity, something which only returned when
Richard Pigott succeeded Smyth as proprietor of the *Irishman*
in 1865.

For a few years the fenians had a convenient working relationship with the *Irishman*. In 1861 Charles Kickham was assured
by John O'Mahony and by 'another patriot' (obviously Stephens
or Luby) that Holland's paper 'could not afford' to oppose
fenianism.[135] If this had any financial connotations, which is
unlikely, they refer to the purchase of the paper by individual
fenian sympathisers. Stephens never had the *Irishman* 'in his
pocket'. Holland might refuse to condemn nationalist secret
societies, and he might join whole-heartedly in the fenian vendetta against A.M. Sullivan, but the *Irishman* was in the early
1860s the organ of a clique which was by no means of one
mind on the usefulness of conspiracy in general and of the I.R.B.
in particular. It carried a regular weekly letter from John
Mitchel when he was in Paris during the period 1859-62, and he
was no uncritical supporter of James Stephens. Neither was
John E. Pigot, another very important contributor. Neither was
Holland himself, while editor of the *Irishman*. His personal
attitudes were best represented by the National Brotherhood
of St Patrick.

The brotherhood certainly experienced a sense of loss when Holland ceded control of the *Irishman* to P.J. Smyth; the central association at once issued a circular to all branches announcing in panic-stricken tones that the new proprietorship 'could not be relied upon for one issue'.[136] The changeover provided the stimulus for the National Brotherhood to go ahead after long threatening with efforts to publish its own newspaper. However, the best that could be managed was an arrangement with James Roche, proprietor of an existing journal, the *Galway American*. From 25 July 1863 this appeared as the *United Irishman and Galway American*, combining the advocacy of the northern cause in the American civil war with that of the National Brotherhood of St Patrick. This together with Holland's departure from the *Irishman* also prepared the way for the I.R.B. to launch a paper of its own. With the able and independent Smyth in control, the *Irishman* was no longer susceptible to fenian pressures. (He set the tone of his editorship with a note to the effect that he was not connected with any existing political organisation in Ireland.) Nevertheless it seems likely that it was not the changes at the *Irishman* office so much as the fear that Roche and the National Brotherhood would make an impact with their new weekly that convinced James Stephens in the summer of 1863 that he should have his own newspaper.[137]

The *Irish People* was intended by Stephens to be a money-making proposition, as is well known. He first told Luby of his decision to start a newspaper just after the latter had returned from a trip to America with a disappointingly small sum of money.[138] To Luby at least, Stephens made no secret of the great hopes which he reposed in this new source of wealth: receipts from O'Mahony had not amounted to £250 per year but, he calculated, the newspaper once established would bring five or six times that amount, and maybe fifteen or eighteen times.[139] Nevertheless, to see the *Irish People* merely as a device for filling the fenian coffers would be to accept a superficial understanding of the workings of fenianism in the summer and autumn of 1863. On Luby's return from America on the occasion mentioned he found Stephens's organisation suffering from troubles much more serious than scarcity of finance. Stephens himself was in an uncharacteristically diffident mood and even momentarily expressed a wish to be finished with the business altogether. The Dublin centres were growing dissatisfied with the captain's leadership.[140] At the same time a radical (but non-fenian) nationalist element — closely connected with the leadership of the National Brotherhood — was posing a threat to the allegiance and stability of Stephens's organisation.

Peter E. Gill of the *Tipperary Advocate*, a colourful character, active in politics at county level, and a member of the National Brotherhood, began during the summer of 1863, in co-operation with some like-minded individuals, to lay plans for a series of great outdoor 'patriotic' meetings at various evocative locations throughout County Tipperary.[141] These gatherings were calculated to prove irresistible to the classes who comprised the ranks of fenianism. And, if successfully carried through, they would place the organisers in that position of leadership of the local malcontents which Stephens hoped to achieve through the I.R.B. Besides, the government might be moved to take drastic countermeasures which would seriously inconvenience the I.R.B. It was precisely because he had a newspaper at his command that Gill was able to promote his project. The editor of the *Nation*, who undoubtedly appreciated every move in the game, had no hesitation in lending his influential voice to augment the advance publicity, assuredly not from sympathy with the eccentric Gill but in the full awareness that his scheme would seriously undermine the I.R.B.[142] Stephens headed off this challenge by utilising the local influence of C.J. Kickham, but the episode shows that he needed a newspaper of his own for even more serious reasons than the raising of money.

The decision to start the *Irish People* was taken in late July 1863; just four months later the first issue appeared. In the meantime Stephens adroitly utilised the preparations as a means to amuse and thereby discipline the organisation in the south; there were funds to be collected, subscribers to be canvassed and local promotion committees to be established. Stephens spent the early autumn supervising this work and planning the detailed arrangements for the newspaper itself. John O'Leary was summoned home from London to assume a major part in the direction of the journal.[143] From around the country Stephens gathered fenians with different talents, including C.J. Kickham, John Haltigan, O'Donovan Rossa, Denis Dowling Mulcahy, and James O'Connor. Talent may not have been the only criterion. All five mentioned here carried very considerable weight locally and had far more personal influence than Stephens wished any of his subordinates to enjoy. By taking them from their own localities and putting them on his payroll in Dublin he was bringing them more securely under his own wing. In a wider context the founding of the *Irish People* was an eloquent comment on the political realities of Ireland at the time. It amounted to an admission by Stephens that the political context in which he was functioning was too sophisticated for the unaugmented efforts of a secret society to hold sway. It also bears out the point that the I.R.B. was something more than a secret society.

While The O'Donoghue, James Stephens and others were contending for national leadership in the early 1860s the agrarian economy was in deep trouble. The agricultural prosperity of the period from 1853 to 1859 began to decline in the latter year owing to severe drought and then turned to near-disaster caused by three successive years of excessive rainfall. Crop yields declined spectacularly and large numbers of cattle and sheep were lost through hunger and disease. J.S. Donnelly, in the standard account of this depression, argues cogently that in many ways it was worse than the crisis of the late 1870s that occasioned the land war.[144] Yet the amount of agrarian agitation in the early 1860s was minimal. There was a definite but unspectacular rise in the agrarian crime figures. The priests of Meath diocese did form county tenant-right committees in Meath and Westmeath in early 1863. These issued denunciations of alleged abuses of landlord power and called for changes in the law. This all amounted to little enough and the contrast with the period of the land war would seem to need some explanation. We should, however, beware of viewing the quiet of the early 1860s as an anomaly and the agitation of the late 1870s as a norm. The roles might just as well be reversed, depending on one's standpoint. In both cases objective assessment would probably indicate that agitation was more likely to add to the sum total of suffering than to reduce it. In the early 1860s the known form of the prime minister, Viscount Palmerston, was such that no campaign for a major change in land law stood any hope of success; the certainty of ignominious failure discouraged speculative agitations.

Moreover, the general sense of international crisis which moved some to action simply induced caution in others. Sudden political change still had overtones of social upheaval, and accordingly the farmers were disposed to leave well enough alone. It is not without significance that the Tenant League which had lingered on through the prosperity of the 1850s — that undermined it without killing it — suddenly and finally collapsed in 1858 just after the onset of apprehension about the international situation. If the tenants were wary about agitating on the land question there was little hope that they would join in any other campaign. It was this absence of interest by the farmers that doomed The O'Donoghue's schemes to failure; given any swell of support from that direction he would have had every chance of bringing his disparate associates into line, and even of overcoming the obstructiveness of James Stephens.

Chapter Four

THE TRIUMPH OF JAMES STEPHENS, 1864-5

The Irish National League was founded in Dublin on 21 January 1864. It was a product of the deliberations of the preceding years about a new all-embracing nationalist movement, but it was evidence of failure, not of achievement. John Martin was one of the most disingenuous of men and, having grown impatient with the lack of progress, he had written a series of letters to the nationalist press in the summer of 1863 on the subject of Irish national fortunes and organisation. In the course of five rambling epistles from his home at Kilbroney, Rostrevor, County Down, he had talked (or written) himself into having to do something.[1] 'I have been provoked into committing myself to an attempt at a renewed national agitation of repeal by a public association', he wrote to Smith O'Brien.[2] The sense of honour that requires a gentleman to keep his commitments pushed Martin towards the initiation of a new association, despite serious discouragements. He understood politics much better than he could practice them, and he had no prospect of success where more worldly men were failing. Throughout the second half of 1863 he worked over his plans in a leisurely fashion, writing several more letters to the papers from Kilbroney, and not getting around to any lengthy period of work in Dublin until late October.[3] His efforts down to the 21 January 1864 produced an attendance of about forty people at the meeting in the European Hotel, Bolton Street, at which his National League was launched.[4] The declared aim and object of the league was simply 'the restoration of a separate and independent Irish legislature', and membership was open for a small fee to anyone supporting this objective.[5] The rules further set out that the league intended no antagonism to any other association but that it itself 'should be free to advocate self-government by any and every means which it may deem to be righteous, honourable, prudent and expedient'. There were expressions of good-will and welcome in the *Irishman* and *Nation*, but nobody displayed very much confidence or enthusiasm.[6] James Stephens naturally disapproved of the league, but he had little to fear from it and felt no need to choke it at birth. Not alone was it no threat: it had the positive advantage for the fenians that it could be cited as an object lesson in the futility of open political movements. The principal function of the National League was to provide a platform for harangues on the national question. An entry in O'Neill Daunt's diary paints the picture with a few strokes: on a visit to Dublin he went to 'John Martin's monthly meeting of the repeal league, where some Dublin artisans and shopkeepers had assembled to keep alive the old political faith till better times'.[7] In due course the National League published a handful of pamphlets including one by Daunt entitled *The financial grievances of Ireland*. While the league's impact lived down to everyone's expectations, it survived longer than predicted and was still meeting in 1868.[8]

The O'Donoghue was one of the few prominent figures to join Martin in the National League. His inclination was to join any new organisation unless he would thereby lose too many friends in other quarters. Nevertheless, he could not avoid seeing that the coming into existence of something as jejune as the league was an adverse verdict on his efforts as a would-be political leader, and that it militated against the possible future success of these efforts, far though this result was from the intentions of honest John Martin. Within a month of the launching of the National League The O'Donoghue and A.M. Sullivan found an opportunity to resume play for higher stakes. Dublin city council on 15 February 1864 allocated a site on College Green for a statue of the recently-deceased husband of the queen, Prince Albert. The same spot had been previously designated for a statue of Henry Grattan which had not materialised. A.M. Sullivan, by this time a member of the city council, proclaimed that a great Irishman had been slighted and called for public protests to force a reversal of the decision. He arranged a mass meeting for 22 February in the Rotundo. The O'Donoghue and himself would once more have a platform and an audience that might match their ambitions. Once more they were thwarted by the fenians and this time with a display of open violence. The fenians could not object to the formal purpose of the meeting, but that did not deter them. A.M. Sullivan's alleged treachery in the Phoenix affair was used as a pretext for causing disruption; when The O'Donoghue, from the chair, made a complimentary reference to Sullivan the strategically located fenians in the auditorium reacted. Rising from their seats in noisy protest, they threw the assembly into confusion. Numbers of them advanced purposefully towards the front of the hall whereupon the platform party fled through an ante-room to the safety of the street. Inside something like a pitched battle developed as outraged non-fenians recovered from their surprise and turned on the disrupters.[9] Sullivan and The O'Donoghue recovered some ground by holding a successful meeting on the same subject, and in the same location, exactly a week later. This, however, was achieved only by resorting to admission by tickets (previously distributed through safe channels) and other security measures. With Stephens directing operations from a nearby public house, his followers endeavoured to repeat the disruption of the previous week, but they were denied admittance. The fenians were excluded but only after some vicious melées with ticket-checkers.[10] Sullivan succeeded in his campaign to have Grattan rather than Prince Albert given space on College Green, for in early May the city council reversed its decision of three months earlier.[11] But on the front that mattered most Sullivan had lost to Stephens, who had shown once again his capacity for stymying the efforts of rivals. The violence of 22 February may have been an expression of Stephens's policy that he himself had not intended but, it followed all too easily from the disruption he had planned.

William Smith O'Brien died suddenly on 18 June 1864. His family prevented his funeral from becoming the great public demonstration that it could have been. The loss of O'Brien's counsel and encouragement was a further blow to The O'Donoghue's prospects. His personal financial circumstances were emerging as another constraint. Elections in a constituency as large as County Tipperary cost a great deal of money, and he claimed to have spent £10,000 of his own money to secure election in 1857 and 1859. By mid-1864 another election was looming. The O'Donoghue could not himself afford the costs of contesting Tipperary and he had failed to create the kind of political organisation that might have financed his campaign. He began to think of finding a smaller, and less expensive, constituency. Then in January 1865 the borough of Tralee became vacant with the elevation to the bench of the sitting member, Thomas O'Hagan. Family connections and local loyalty would favour The O'Donoghue in Tralee, but of course the member returned at a by-election might be difficult to dislodge at the next general election. In a rare display of ruthlessness The O'Donoghue resigned his Tipperary seat and announced his candidature for the Tralee by-election. He was not put off by the fact that another candidate, Joseph Neale McKenna, had already declared himself and was standing on 'independent, catholic and national principles'.[12] McKenna refused to give way and a sharp contest ensued, but O'Donoghue had a clear victory on polling day, 14 February. There was much popular rejoicing:

> His progress through the country on his way to Dublin was such an ovation as Kerry had not seen since the days of the Liberator. Triumphal arches were raised across the roads and streets, the cottages by the wayside were decked with evergreens, and portraits of the young chieftain were hung on their fronts. A procession, which at one time reached a length of four miles, accompanied him on his way, every man of that vast body wearing evergreens in his hat or dress.[13]

Whatever about the local reasons for adulation of 'the chieftain of the Glens', there was little for him to rejoice about on the wider front. The move to Tralee was a spectacular act of retreat. The vote of the member for Tralee was of equal value in the commons with the vote of a member for Tipperary, but the stature of the two in Irish political life was quite different. The O'Donoghue had had to retire from one of the largest constituencies in the country and had taken refuge in a small borough controlled by family interests. He was to hold the Tralee seat for twenty years, but his move there in 1865 marked the end of his once-promising career as potential national leader. In 1865 he was thirty-two — the same age as Daniel O'Connell in 1807, Isaac Butt in 1845, and C.S. Parnell in 1878.

As The O'Donoghue moved from centre-stage the neo-O'Connellite Dublin Liberals were putting their ventures to the public test. The foundation stone of the O'Connell monument was laid on 8 August 1864 with what may have been the most numerously supported public demonstration in the city in the nineteenth century: the police estimated that half-a-million people were in attendance.[14] The procession through the city to the chosen site was almost certainly the most impressive that Dublin had ever witnessed, not excluding O'Connell's funeral seventeen years earlier. More than 40,000 men — trades, societies, confraternities, schools, town-councillors and bishops — proceeded on foot, on horseback and in carriages.[15] The speeches acknowledged that the day belonged, above all, to Sir John Gray and in general it was a triumph for moderate Liberal advocates of popular causes. Archbishop MacHale spared himself the embarrassment of the occasion, pleading a prior commitment to administer confirmation on Achill and Boffin.[16] Bishop

Dorrian of Down and Connor stayed away because, he claimed, some of the organisers were too much infected by 'whiggery'.[17] But most bishops found the tone of the movement congenial and no fewer than ten of them took part in the procession. At a banquet that evening Archbishop Leahy of Cashel lauded O'Connell's union of liberty and religion, in a speech that at least hinted at the desirability of bishops, priests and laity joining in another concerted public agitation.[18] The leaders of the O'Connell monument movement took the hint, but their experience was to illustrate once again that a great public demonstration was no guarantee of the existence of a concerted popular attachment to the specific policies of the organisers.

When the Dublin-based Liberal clique behind the O'Connell monument procession moved on in search of some wider political project it was strengthened by the adhesion of John Blake Dillon. His professional standing made him a match for the others socially and he had recently joined most of them in membership of Dublin city council. His Young Irelandism was a major difference and he still had passionate ideas about the vindication of the idealised nationality that himself, Duffy and Davis had formulated in the 1840s. While asserting that this was now unrealisable he nevertheless re-entered the political arena after a long absence because he believed that something else was attainable or would shortly be so. An even more important recruit, initially, was O'Neill Daunt. He too was becoming politically active because he had reason to hope for some success. O'Neill Daunt had been in contact for some years with the radical-liberal English Liberation Society and had been aware of the subterranean rumblings within the world of British liberalism that might provide Irish catholics with certain opportunities. Further encouragement had come on 11 May 1864 when Gladstone in an important speech on the extension of democratic principles distanced himself from the increasingly rigid policies of Palmerston and set himself up as the spokesman for the many and varied interests within the United Kingdom who felt that in one way or another they had been shortchanged of 'liberty'. Gladstone was tacitly presenting himself as the leader of a coalition of such interests. Politically aware Irish nationalists of many hues saw much local significance in this and the *Nation* straightaway identified Gladstone as a future prime minister.[19] This is not to say that what came to pass four or five years later was ineluctable by 1864; but it could be seen as a definite possibility.

The English Liberation Society had agreed with Daunt on the feasibility of a joint campaign by itself and an Irish catholic party for the disestablishment of the state church in Ireland.[20]

Here was a ready-made campaign which appealed at once to
Gray, McSwiney, Dillon and the others. Part of its appeal was
the obvious attraction it would have for the bishops, whose
power and influence the group intended to tap. O'Neill Daunt
had already started work on the hierarchy, having convinced
Archbishop Patrick Leahy of Cashel as early as June 1863 of
the feasibility of agitation on the church question. From early
1864 Leahy had been promoting parochial petitions in his own
archdiocese and encouraging his suffragans in the province of
Cashel to follow his example.[21] Archbishop Cullen, whose
influence with the general episcopal body would be vital, proved
less easy to convince. He was unhappy about fomenting a
political campaign and personally disliked making platform
appearances. He stayed away from the O'Connell monument
banquet — at which Leahy made his important speech — because
he feared it might be the occasion of what he called a 'row'.[22]
Above all, Cullen must have been wary of the theological
implications; this, after all, was the year of the *Syllabus of errors*
in which Pius IX anathematised the notion of 'a free church in a
free state'. And apart from its willingness to attack the established
church, everything else about the English Liberation Society
was uncongenial to Cullen's taste.

Persuading Cullen to give open support to a new political
movement was not easy, and it appears to have been largely
Dillon's achievement. This movement was embodied by the
National Association of Ireland as launched at an 'aggregate
meeting' in the Rotundo on 29 December 1864. The requisition
for the meeting had been signed by more than twenty bishops,
and Cullen was one of the principal speakers. Mindful, no doubt,
of the experiences of A.M. Sullivan and his friends earlier in the
year, the organisers had taken elaborate security precautions
and the occasion was a model of public decorum. A letter from
John Bright, who had been invited to attend, spelled out quite
explicitly the strategy of a coalition of popular interests on
both sides of the Irish Sea in support of, among other things,
the policy of a 'free church'.[23]

The objectives of the new association — as formally adopted
by the aggregate meeting — were not confined to disestablishment. There was added the not unrelated demand for state
financing of church-controlled education (dressed up as 'freedom and equality of education for the several denominations
and classes in Ireland').[24] However, the first item on the list
referred to a quite different aspect of Irish life: 'to secure by
law to occupiers of land in Ireland compensation for all valuable
improvements effected by them'. Whatever the preoccupations
of churchmen might be, there was no mistaking the primary

concern of the class on whom they mainly relied. Leahy had
acknowledged this from the beginning, circulating petitions on
the land question along with those on the church, and in the
course of preparations for the launching of the National Association it became clear that the prospect of widespread support,
even among the clergy, depended on the interests of the tenant
farmers being kept in the forefront. There was an added political
significance to this emphasis on the land question, for the rift
of the 1850s was still a very important fact of Irish catholic
political life and 'tenant-right' was the watchword of one of the
factions in question, the independent oppositionists. Even with
the emphasis on the land question, which was intended to placate
them, many of the independent oppositionists were unenthusiastic in their responses. Various 'tenant-right' priests refused to
sign petitions supporting the association. A co-ordinated group
of Meath priests joined, but in a truculent mood and insisting
on the priority of the tenant issue.[25]

Paragraph three of the 'fundamental rules' adopted by the
National Association at the meeting of 29 December 1864 read
as follows:

> The association will not support any political party which
> shall not in good faith co-operate with it in establishing by
> law the tenant's right to compensation, or in procuring the
> disendowment of the Established church. Neither will it
> recommend nor assist in the election of, any candidate who
> will not pledge himself to act on the same principle.[26]

This was the independent opposition formula of 1852 without
the name, and its acceptance by Gray, Cullen and the others
was a tacit acknowledgement that a decade of reliance on the
whigs had failed. If nothing had divided them except policy and
tactics the two factions from the 1850s would have readily
reunited in the National Association. In the manner of factions,
they were simply driven farther apart. With the exception of
J.F. Maguire none of the sitting independent opposition M.P.s
gave their support. Archbishop MacHale replied to an invitation
to support the association with a stinging attack on those who
had betrayed the similar movement of 1852 — obviously referring to Cullen — and a bitter refusal to co-operate with such
people in the new venture.[27] George Henry Moore took almost
exactly the same line, and both rejected repeated overtures
from would-be reconcilers, including O'Neill Daunt. They might
have come in if they could have done so in triumph, and this
would be the case if the association explicitly adopted the term
'independent opposition'. That would have amounted to a
bowing of the knee by Cullen and Gray, and Cullen in particular

had no intention of doing that. For much of 1865 the association's time and energy were taken up with a dispute about a proposal to rephrase rule three. An endeavour was being made — in vain as it turned out — to find a formula that would satisfy both cliques. There was very little principle of any kind at stake but there was much personal and group antagonism and much concern with face-saving. The failure to find a compromise effectively emasculated the association. Not only did MacHale and Moore refuse to join, the Meath clergy left to cultivate their own local tenant-right movement, and on the other wing, Cullen lost much of his interest. Although he subscribed to a new version of the independent opposition formula (but still without the contentious term itself), his heart was scarcely in the business. The sitting Irish Liberal members had almost totally ignored the National Association and Cullen was uneasy about cutting links with them, as the policy of the association required; his inclination was to use them to extract as many concessions as possible, great or small, whenever opportunity afforded.

The National Association of Ireland survived until the 1870s but from an early point its function and effectiveness were as limited as those of the Irish National League, namely the provision of a platform for politicians of a particular tendency. The National Association as such made scarcely any impact on the general election of 1865. Three prominent members of the association were, indeed, elected to parliament: John Blake Dillon for County Tipperary, Edward Synan for County Limerick and Sir John Gray for Kilkenny city; but both Dillon and Synan had the words 'independent opposition' emblazoned on their election addresses. Overall, the oppositionists fared well: after a careful reckoning the *Nation* concluded that they had gained eight seats for the loss of three, leaving them with a total of eighteen.[28]

When the initiators of the National Association took thoroughgoing precautions against the possibility of violent interruption of the aggregate meeting of 29 December 1864 they were thinking not just of the fenians but also of the orangemen. For that year had seen sectarian violence take on renewed intensity. By playing down repeal and emphasising 'civil and religious liberty' the organisers of the O'Connell monument demonstration had disarmed the suspicions of the Conservative representatives on the city council; these raised no objection to the project and some of them may have actually supported it. More militant protestants saw the matter in a different light and in particular they were incensed that while their 12 July processions were proscribed under the party processions legislation, the memory of O'Connell could be celebrated in the centre of Dublin by scores of thousands of marchers. The backlash came in Belfast, where O'Connell was burned in effigy. Belfast catholics retaliated and the city descended into a three-week period of ferocious sectarian rioting in which seven were killed and hundreds injured. As a consequence tensions rose throughout the country and there were minor disturbances as far south as Cork city. Sectarian feelings were still hot during the following months as preparations for the launching of the National Association were being made. Indeed the first public announcement of the association was made by John Blake Dillon in the course of a speech that heaped denunciation on the church establishment and proselytism.[29] When McSwiney as outgoing mayor was handing over the chain of office to his successor on 1 January 1865 ten protestant members of the city council formally opposed the routine vote of thanks to him because of his part in the launching of the National Association a few days previously.

Writing to Monsignor Barnabó of the Congregation of Propaganda Fide in early January 1865 Archbishop Cullen represented the National Association as a necessary alternative to fenianism, and no doubt this kind of consideration carried much weight with the primate in deciding to go along with the plans of Gray and Dillon.[30] That is somewhat removed from suggesting that the association was founded solely, or even primarily, to counteract the attractions of fenianism for young Irishmen. But it was a line of explanation that Cullen may have felt to be particularly suitable for the ears and eyes of Roman officials who might have difficulty in understanding how he came to be having dealings — within a few weeks of the publication of the *Syllabus of errors* — with a radical-liberal political campaign. From all that we know of Cullen it is certain that the spread of fenianism would also have aroused in him a contrary emotion, namely revived doubt about (not to say abhorrence of) popular politics of any kind. This reaction is undoubtedly part of the explanation for the obvious lack of enthusiasm with which he was treating the National Association even within weeks of its foundation.[31]

Even before this fenianism may have been having the effect of rendering a large proportion of the population wary of politics. The *Irish People* liked to claim that people had lost faith in elections, parliaments and petitions and that this had happened because of widespread acceptance of fenian ideas. Notwithstanding the obvious popular enthusiasm for the O'Connell monument demonstration in August, even Archbishop Leahy admitted on a few occasions during 1864 that it was nearly impossible to arouse interest in his petition campaigns on current issues.[32] This tendency was accentuated during 1865. Fenianism was at the root of it, but not for the reason that the *Irish People* advanced. Throughout most of 1864 and all of 1865 normal political activity was paralysed by fenianism as by a spectre. The belief that they had in their midst a secret revolutionary army of unknown strength (with powerful allies across the Atlantic) about to throw the country into indescribable turmoil left most of the inhabitants of Ireland without any stomach for politics.

James Stephens had a mind stocked with clichés — ideological, literary, strategic and tactical — but his strength was that he never allowed them to get in his way. He was an unashamed improvisor. At the beginning his organisation was not even allowed to have a name, so strong was his emphasis on secrecy. Six years later, while secrecy was still formally enjoined on all concerned, fenianism was identified with a weekly newspaper published within a stone's throw of Dublin Castle from an office manned by his principal followers. The *Irish People* was no mere adjunct: it was largely responsible for transforming Stephens's movement into a major phenomenon in Irish public life in the mid-1860s. The file of the *Irish People* is rightly regarded as a goldmine of separatist declamation, containing as it does three (and sometimes four) leading articles per issue from O'Leary, Luby, Kickham or (in the very early weeks) Stephens himself. The arguments on the leader page may have made a few conversions but it was not by argument that the *Irish People* conquered. The regular weekly arrival of their own 'in-house' journal gave fenians an enhanced sense of solidarity; it was taken as visible evidence of an extensive movement under able leadership. Even the propaganda activity preparatory to publication seems to have drummed up extra support in Munster. It was apparently at this stage that serious progress was first made in Limerick city, which was later to be a stronghold.[33] T.C. Luby, who was in as good a position as anyone to know, firmly linked the *Irish People* with the progress of the I.R.B. everywhere in Ireland but especially in Connaught and Ulster where it had previously made very little headway. On the link between the newspaper and the progress of fenianism in Britain Luby is even more definitie. 'We had', he wrote later, 'no movement in England and Scotland until after the *Irish People* had appeared'.[34] A.M. Sullivan, too, from his own unwelcome experience, could testify to the success of the *Irish People* across the Irish Sea: 'It swept all before it amongst the Irish in England and Scotland, almost annihilating the circulation of the *Nation* in many places north and south of the Tweed.'[35] The *Irishman* had brought the National Brotherhood to the Irish in Britain; the *Irish People* brought them fenianism. As with the National Brotherhood, and later the home rule movement, thousands of them flocked into the I.R.B. as the leading Irish activist organisation of the moment, without giving very much consideration to points of policy, strategy or tactics. So, when Luby toured Britain in 1865, following earlier visits by O'Donovan Rossa and Stephens, he found himself being obliged to speak from platforms to halls full of fenians who obviously had no appreciation of fenianism's distinctive policy of secrecy.[36]

As it was acquiring a newspaper at the end of 1865 Stephens's organisation was simultaneously about to acquire a name. That too proved to be a boon, though an uncovenanted one, for the name was imposed by outsiders and was eventually accepted, according to Luby, only as a schoolboy accepts a nickname. Nobody had ever seen any advantages in acting anonymously in America and when the Emmet Monument Association was reconstituted in 1859 John O'Mahony had chosen the title 'Fenian Brotherhood', in evocation of the *Fianna*. However, this rather esoteric allusion was lost on most contemporaries. Many interested Irish people — such as John Mitchel and A.M. Sullivan — assumed that 'fenian' was in some way cognate to 'phoenix' and so was related to the name misleadingly given to the sections of Stephens's movement uncovered in Cork, Kerry and Kilkenny in 1858 and early 1859. During the next few years the terms 'fenian' and 'phoenix' were applied occasionally (and interchangeably) to the Irish organisation by some of the small number of outsiders who were aware of it as existing separately from the National Brotherhood. During these years the title 'Irish Revolutionary Brotherhood' was applied by the Fenian Brotherhood to its sister organisation but was apparently not taken up in Ireland by friend or foe.

In October 1863 the New York *Mercury* published a sensationally-pitched *exposé* of the Fenian Brotherhood, which was taken up by papers in Britain and Ireland, and created the impression of a very powerful Irish-American enterprise geared to winning Irish independence, and ready to roll.[37] Awareness was further heightened in November 1863 when the Fenian Brotherhood held its first convention, at Chicago. For its own (American) reasons this assembly proclaimed from the house-tops the existence of a formidable allied organisation in Ireland. By early 1864 authorities in Ireland, and the writers of newspapers, and then the readers of newspapers, were on the look-out for 'the fenians' in their midst. Armed with a name they discovered a society that actually existed, but the name in a sense led to the recreation of the society. Throughout the following twenty months the *Irish People* probably made less editorial use of the word 'fenian' than any other national newspaper in Ireland or England, and, when it did, that was usually in the context of a disclaimer: 'we who are not fenians' served on one occasion; on another occasion there was a declaration that the Fenian Brotherhood was an exclusively American business: and yet again a dismissive reference to 'that imaginary body, the fenian society in Ireland.'[38] None of this was likely to deceive anyone: the leader pages acknowledged at the same time that certain Irishmen were preparing for rebellion and that the purpose of the Fenian Brotherhood was to give them aid. The *Irish People* avoided explicitly identifying itself with the conspiracy, but by the spring of 1864 nobody was being deceived.

Armies, secret or otherwise, exist in a socio-economic context and this is exceptionally important for an understanding of the fenians. A number of efforts have been made to determine the social profile of the fenians in the mid-1860s on the basis of police records — the only extensive set of relevant data available.[39] The most striking finding in every case has been the remarkably high proportion (from a third to a half) of artisans and tradesmen, and the very low proportion of propertied people of any kind, including farmers. When the shop assistants and the national teachers are added to the artisans and tradesmen one has a fraternity of young, unpropertied, educated, urban-dwellers (distinctly beneath the social level of the neo-Young-Ireland élite in the *Irish People* office). These constituted a section of society that was in need of social and recreational outlets. In post-famine Ireland the clergy, the constabulary and the landowners had combined to achieve a fairly rigid form of social control. Many young men in the towns and villages found in fenianism a mechanism for autonomous self-assertion and for the defiance of social restraints. Looking back many decades later at his early fenian years, John Devoy recalled that 'touching elbows with fellow-members at public demonstrations and having a "pint" with others was a great factor' in the appeal of the movement. There is voluminous evidence of a more contemporary vintage that fraternisation in a recreational setting was at the heart of fenianism in the early and middle 1860s. Fenians enjoyed one another's company not only in public houses but as participants or spectators in a wide variety of sports and pastimes. The only serious military activity experienced by most fenians — drill — became their mode of pastime *par excellence*. Learning (under the cover of a Sunday excursion, or the darkness of night) how to step in line and manoeuvre in unison at the command of a militiaman or, more rarely, an Irish-American officer, was the most characteristic of all fenian activities and it was a social rather than purely military business. Drill facilitated the change in physical demeanour that was frequently part of the social dimension of fenianism. The well-turned-out fenian was a bearded young man with a confident step and an independent air who refused to avert his eyes from the gaze of policeman or priest. The conspiratorial aspect of fenianism suited its social role in the mid-1860s very well indeed, but the pretence of full secrecy was hilariously inappropriate given that membership resulted, typically, in a change to a distinctive physical appearance. Fenianism found a following not because there were tens of thousands of Irishmen eager to 'take up the gun' for an Irish republic, but because there were tens of thousands of young Irishmen in search of self-realisation through appropriate social outlets.

This perspective on the fenians helps to put them in their contemporary European social context. In Britain this was the era of colliery brass bands and the beginnings of association football. Much of this was autonomous but much of it also was under the patronage of benevolent squires, parsons and factory-owners. In Ireland, especially catholic Ireland, patronage was much less prevalent. The post-famine clergy had little appreciation of team sports which had become synonomous with disorder, violence and drunkenness, exactly the evils that the priests hoped to eradicate. Even the confraternities in Ireland appear to have been weak in the social dimension that they so frequently possessed on the continent. This is not to discount the many semi-religious mortality societies, temperance societies, mutual-aid societies and so forth that prospered on a moderate scale in many towns. But these were not vehicles for youthful energy. Dean Richard O'Brien of Limerick made the only large-scale attempt to answer this need along the lines of a contemporary French-style confraternity with his Catholic Young Men's Society, founded in 1849. By the early 1860s it seems to have existed in a score or so of towns in Munster and Leinster, and in at least as many centres in the north of England. Members socialised in the society's reading rooms and marched to church on Sundays with flags and banners flying. The overlapping in function with fenianism is clear, and a number of priests appear to have made a rush to set up branches of the C.Y.M.S. when they became aware of fenianism in their parishes. But, overall, branches were scarce and the priests unenthusiastic. Fenianism filled the vacuum. It also served a function performed in Britain by the volunteers when, after the early 1860s, their originally middle-class membership was swamped by artisans and clerks who delighted in the opportunity to drill, march, and feel important.

The autonomous fraternisation enjoyed by the fenians is strongly reminiscent of the 'alternative socialisation' in eighteenth-and nineteenth-century France — that of the 'cafe set' as opposed to the 'church set' — that provided the basis of French anti-clericalism.[40] We have already seen how strong was the instinctive reaction of the priests against fenianism at their first sighting of it in the guise of the Phoenix Society in 1858. It was not simply that they resented 'alternative socialisation' among their flocks (which they did) but that they identified secret association with the social disorders of pre-famine Ireland. When fenianism became better known in the mid-1860s as an apparently serious revolutionary movement, a new intensity was added to clerical opposition. Together with the other dominant sections of Irish catholic opinion the priests — with very rare exceptions — regarded revolution as madness. The apparent threat to the stability of property they particularly disliked. Churchmen, then, did not need spiritual and theological reasons to render them opposed to fenianism, but these too were available. Archbishop Cullen, who denounced fenianism in a series of pastorals, was particularly anxious to establish that the organisation, in both its form and its object, was contrary to catholic doctrine and morality, and he earnestly desired Rome to back him up with an explicit condemnation of fenianism by name. Leahy of Cashel advised against explicit papal denunciation and his advice prevailed until 1870: he was as opposed as Cullen to the fenian society which he described as 'the worst . . . ever to exist in Ireland', but he was a shrewder politician than the Archbishop of Dublin.[41] Appealing to the *magisterium* and to theological argument was the mark of the schoolman. The authority of the clergy in their parishes was based on less remote and less cerebral foundations. Whatever ultramontanism amounted to in practice, it did not mean that papal condemnation of a movement like fenianism would carry much weight except with those already opposed to it for other reasons. (In later years John O'Leary used to point out sardonically, and with great justice, that the papal condemnation of the anti-landlord plan of campaign of 1887 had been blithely ignored by priests and bishops such as had denounced the fenians for impiety.) On the contrary, high-powered ecclesiastical denunciation simply encouraged the kind of public challenge to clerical authority that flourished in the leader page of the *Irish People*. The repeated attacks by C.J. Kickham against priestly interference in politics on the 'anti-national' side are not likely to have won many new adherents for fenianism by the mere force of their logic, but they clearly were very important in building up and maintaining the sense of fellowship that enabled fenians to withstand local clerical pressure.[42] The futility of Cullen's approach was painfully illustrated by his inability to rout or effectively to silence the one priest who supported fenian policies with theological arguments, Patrick Lavelle.[43] MacHale who was Lavelle's bishop, refused to join in the condemnation of fenianism. By this time he tended to be reserved — to say the least — about any cause embraced by Cullen. But it has to be borne in mind, too, that in the mid-1860s the challenge of fenianism in Connacht was not sufficiently strong to make Mac-Hale or his clergy feel that their social influence was threatened. In Cullen's eyes the fenian defiance was a local manifestation of continental anti-clericalism, and it was true that Stephens and O'Leary and Luby were imbued with an ideological dislike of the church, *a la française*. But for the non-ideological rank and file rejection of catholicism was literally unthinkable. It was the essential element in their sense of identity, and there the resemblance to the 'cafe set' breaks down.

The years from 1863 to 1866 when fenianism was at its greatest numerical strength in Ireland were also years of excep-tinally heavy emigration from the country.[44] No doubt the agricultural depression was an important contributory factor, through its effects on the farming population and on those townspeople dependent on farmer spending. At the same time the U.S. civil war was creating an exceptional demand for man-power and various U.S. agencies were working assiduously, with the encouragement of the federal government, to promote immigration. A rise in the numbers actually emigrating from Ireland was undoubtedly accompanied by a rise in the numbers still in the country but seriously contemplating emigration, and all the signs are that fenianism was particularly congenial to young men in this position. The fenian leadership on both sides of the Atlantic displayed an inordinately intense desire to dis-courage the exodus to the federal army.[45] The explanation is not to be found in antipathy to the northern cause but in the fear that emigration would decimate the ranks of Irish fenianism. 'Remember we are running a race against emigration' an American fenian agent warned, reporting from Ireland in the summer of 1865.[46] For the individual young Irishman fenianism could be at once a protest against the prospect of emigration and a preparation for going. For many fenians in the mid-1860s the movement was an ante-chamber to the new world. Their per-ceptions of the U.S.A. included the notion of social liberty and equality and they practised hard at the kind of *insouciance* and impudence towards the 'respectable' classes that they believed to be part of the American way of life. It was well known among the Irish police that fenians had an 'independent look' about them. Because of their consciousness of America as an easily accessible refuge, because mentally so many of them were already on their way there, they could dare to run the risks inherent in 'cocking a snook' at priests, policemen and magistrates in the cities, towns and villages of authoritarian, post-famine Ireland.

A secondary but nonetheless important aspect of the appeal of fenianism in the 1860s was the prospect of material reward, essentially in the form of land. There was a virtually universal assumption at the time that a successful political revolution would result in the redivision of Irish land. Like the shadow of international crisis, the related threat of a revolutionary re-allocation of land is a forgotten aspect of the early and middle 1860s in Ireland, a missing key to the understanding of the politics of the period. There was nothing exclusively fenian about this, but it was something about which the fenians had no choice. Criticism of the fenian leadership along the lines that it was too engrossed in doctrinaire republicanism to formulate an agrarian policy and attract the hard-pressed tenant farmers is, therefore, both mistaken and seriously misconceived. The attitudes and statements of John O'Leary in later life have done much to propagate the notion that fenianism of the old vintage was in some way too pure or high-principled to be seriously concerned with anything as meretricious as land-ownership while it had a country's soul to save and a nationality to vindicate. That reflected the truth about himself and one or two others. In fact the *Irish People* had much to say about the land question, but what it said or did not say mattered little. Like it or not (and most of the fenian élite did like it) the fenians in the eyes of friend and foe stood for both expropriation of the landlords and for a redistribution of land. Hence it was by its nature anathema not only to the landlords but to the generality of farmers.

Talk of Irish-American ships on the sea conjured up images of returning exiles claiming back the holdings abandoned by their families in bad times and snapped up by more fortunate neighbours: the *Irish People* declared on one occasion that 'the exiles would return to the home of their affections, to raise new homesteads on the grass-covered sites of the cabins of their murdered kindred'.[47] With rather less enthusiasm the *Nation* had raised the subject years earlier: 'We may argue as to whether the return of the Irish exiles from America is desirable or not, but it is inevitable as soon as a war between England and America begins'.[48] There was an assumption in the 1860s that the 'soldiers of liberty' whether home-based or from across the Atlantic would be rewarded appropriately. A document of the central council of the National Brotherhood of St Patrick dated September 1863 suggested the figure of fifty acres as appropriate (together with a house erected by the state).[49] Notions of this kind far transcended fenianism. Writing in the *Irishman* of

25 April 1863 J.E. Pigot (the Young Irelander) visualised an Anglo-American war leading to an invasion of Ireland and the return of what he referred to as 'the exiled millions'. In 1864 a prominent rabble-rouser among the Irish in Glasgow denounced the landlords of Ireland and expressed the hope that the men of '48 and the famine exiles would be able to return; he expected this to be a bloody business.[50] The *Liberator*, a radical newspaper published in 1863 for the Irish in London regaled its readers with the prospect of an escape from the dingy world of commerce to the green fields of Erin.

It would be a serious error to minimise the importance of all of this in its time, simply because the return *en masse* never materialised. The thought that it might come to pass constituted one of those largely unspoken assumptions that are fully as important for the understanding of an age as political policies or socio-economic statistics. Recent research has shown that about ten per cent of Irish emigrants to America in the second half of the century actually did return, and even this figure was low by the standards of other national groups in the U.S.A.[51] We can be certain that the percentage who indulged in dreams of returning was much larger and that in the 1850s and 1860s many of them were susceptible to near-millenarian notions on the subject. American fenian leaders, such as John O'Mahony and Michael Doheny traded in radical ideas about Irish land which usually came across as verbal assault on 'landlordism', but which were equally a threat to the security of comfortable farmers. Thus Doheny could write as follows to Smith O'Brien in 1858: 'I favour the abolition of Irish landlordism, and I would put a limit on the amount of land one person can hold, so that the land would be brought within the reach of all.'[52]

It is unlikely that the fenian tradesmen of Dublin were moved by any strong inclinations to become cultivators of the soil; it is less easy to be certain about the clerks and the shop assistants, many of them younger sons of farmers. What is certain is that artisans in provincial towns and villages would have had a strong desire for possession of land, especially as the gradual decline of the old crafts rendered their circumstances constantly more precarious. If the threat to landholding frightened many farmers it did not worry all of them. Smallholders might reasonably expect that a redistribution would leave them better off, and, in any case, whenever the subject was broached expectations outran reason. The Phoenix Society was promoted among the small farmers of south-west Cork in the autumn of 1858 by means of explicit promises about land. In the early and middle 1860s the same desire was used to win recruits from among the same kind of people in Connacht and south Ulster.[53]

A picnic party in pleasant surroundings near Enniskerry, Co. Wicklow, in the 1860s or 1870s. Fenians on both sides of the Atlantic participated enthusiastically in this fashionable pastime. (From a stereo negative in the National Library of Ireland).

The initiator of fenian organisation in those parts was Edward Duffy, who had himself been recruited while serving in Cannock and White's of Dublin. Fenianism was spread in many parts of the country by members of the 'new Dublin organisation' of 1861 returning to their native areas, and Duffy is the most striking example of this. By 1862 he was foreman of a hardware store in Castlerea. His initial fenian missionary efforts were stymied by the resistance of a prior organisation in the locality. The fact that this has been described then and later as 'ribbonism' tells us little enough about it. We may, however, assume that the agricultural recession had given a fillip to endemic agrarian conspiracy among the smallholders of the region. With the help of a national teacher and former 'ribbonman', James Hyland of Ballymote, Duffy began to make gradual headway. We may be certain that this did not mean winning intellectual conversions to republicanism. Instead it meant convincing 'ribbonmen' that despite its new-fangled trappings Duffy's organisation served the same purposes as the ones they already belonged to. In other words, Duffy built up a faction for himself in a faction-ridden milieu. Through him his followers were linked to a larger outside organisation, but the consequences, if any, of this fact remained to be seen. Stephens soon gave Duffy responsibility for all of Connacht as well as the 'ribbon' counties of Longford, Cavan and Westmeath. Duffy extended his efforts to part of County Donegal in 1865. In 1863 Stephens had instructed him to resign from his employment and devote himself full-time to organisation. (Apart from the obvious gain for Stephens there was the more subtle one that this influential regional fenian leader was now dependent on the 'captain' for personal income. Duffy's fenian organisation, like the movement elsewhere, prospered in 1864 and 1865, but Connacht and south Ulster were still far behind Leinster and Munster. In the west the I.R.B. remained a minority interest among the factions. Stephens, Luby and O'Donovan Rossa came on mission to Duffy's territories in these years but they do not seem to have added very much to his efforts. Rossa could at least communicate with the locals, in terms that they understood (and where necessary in the Irish language). But Stephens, who went down so well with urban artisans, could apparently establish no rapport with the denizens of Connacht. He never dealt directly with local leaders in Duffy's area but only through Duffy himself.[54]

The fenian organisation in the north-east had a rather similar palatine independence. Here the key organiser was yet another Dublin draper's assistant recruited in 1860-61, John Nolan, a native of County Carlow. Nolan went to the north in 1862 as a travelling salesman based in Belfast. He attempted to spread fenianism in Counties Armagh, Monaghan, Tyrone, Down and Fermanagh, by winning over ribbonmen, but with less success than Duffy enjoyed. One gets the impression that he endeavoured to win over faction leaders rather than creating his own faction, and so brought even less change to the pre-existing system than Duffy did in his territory.[55] Belfast was a different proposition again. Fenianism flourished there among catholics in the mid-1860s, benefiting both from the urban factor and from the ribbon factor imported from the Ulster countryside.

The pattern of arrests of fenian suspects in 1866 bears out the impression given by the sources in general that fenian organisation in the mid-1860s extended to every county in Ireland but in a very uneven fashion.[56] It was strongest in Munster and Leinster. In Connacht it was weaker but nonetheless well established. It had made only a slight impact in Ulster outside of Belfast. Among the catholics of that city fenian organisation (on its own or in conjunction with other organisations that were indistinguishable to the police) was as strong as in Dublin or Cork.

If under one aspect fenianism was a mode of pastime, under another it was a business enterprise — a consortium of Stephens and Company Ltd. and O'Mahony Inc. There was inexorable pressure on the executives to maximise the number of customers, and O'Mahony in particular had to worry about officious shareholders and ambitious subordinates who would punish any failure of his in the market-place. As in any free-market selling operation customer attraction was largely a function of plausible promises and confidence in the product. The one genuine basis of credibility available to fenianism was the prospect of Britain being embroiled in a major war. We have seen how, when this dissolved, Stephens and O'Mahony, early in 1861, unveiled the deceptive undertaking of action irrespective of international complications. The outbreak of the American civil-war a few weeks later introduced new complications. The 'Trent' affair in November 1861 raised the spectre of Anglo-American conflict and it became an article of faith in some Irish and Irish-American circles that the Washington government would want to go to war with Britain as soon as it had crushed the confederates. That belief was nurtured by American officials intent on encouraging recruitment of Irish-Americans to fight for the union.[57] For this and other (more compelling) reasons the hosts of the Fenian Brotherhood flocked into the union army and soon there was rhetoric about tens of thousands of Irishmen learning the arts of war, and bearing arms that they would not lay down again without striking a blow 'to right Ireland's wrongs'. Up to 150,000 Irish-born may have served in the northern armies and up to 40,000 in those of the south.[58] However, the drift to the American ranks had left the Fenian Brotherhood in a weak condition and John O'Mahony settled down to an anxious wait for the end of the civil war.

With the war dragging on the Fenian Brotherhood languished. Following the inexorable laws of free enterprise O'Mahony came under pressure from ambitious men within the brotherhood who had schemes for improving business, and thereby increasing their own influence. In response to persistent demands from a group of such people in the mid-west O'Mahony had summoned the convention of November 1863. The convening of a representative body was in itself a diminution of the dictatorship which O'Mahony had hitherto exercised on the American side. Nevertheless, he managed to avert the placing by the convention of any serious constraints on his authority. On the contrary, it adopted a very American-centred platform which implied the subordination of Irish fenianism to the U.S. firm and so of James Stephens to John O'Mahony. The second of three secret resolutions passed at Chicago declared Stephens to be the representative of the Fenian Brotherhood for Europe and chief organiser of the Irish people; the obvious intent of this was to proclaim the subordination of the Irish leadership to the American — something that O'Mahony had been determined to procure.[59] Stephens would not take this humiliation lightly.

The 'men of action' had failed at Chicago to make any dramatic headway at O'Mahony's expense, but they were not beaten. They were determined to make the Fenian Brotherhood more of a 'going concern' by giving it some immediate objectives and preoccupations. James Stephens encouraged them, thereby getting his revenge on O'Mahony. He had a further reason, namely, the prospect of an improved flow of cash. The first major venture of the 'men of action' was the so-called Chicago fair, running for a week from 28 March 1864, at which Irish-Americans paid over good money for a bizarre assortment of ethnic junk ranging from memorabilia of 'Fionn MacCumhail' to 'a toothpick belonging to Daniel O'Connell'. Much of this was shipped out from the *Irish People* office in Dublin, and Stephens himself followed on to see the dollars roll in at the fair. The takings may have come to 50,000 dollars altogether. Stephens and the 'men of action' had struck up a working relationship: he was just what they needed, the super salesman. They sent him on an extensive tour taking in Illinois, Ohio, Kentucky and Missouri, an area left almost untouched by the New York-centred O'Mahony. Stephens's tour revitalised the Fenian Brotherhood and got the finances flowing. He was particularly successful in his visits to Irish soldiers in the union armies. They had left fenianism behind to serve the U.S.A.; it now followed them to the camps in James Stephens's carpet-bag.[60]

The tour was an outstanding success largely because the product had been brazenly re-packaged. The definite prospect of action was the open sesame to American purses and Stephens promised just that. Ireland, he declared, would rise in 1864 if England became embroiled in the European war threatening over Schleswig-Holstein; but otherwise Ireland would rise in 1865, irrespective of the international situation. It was the reckless promise of a gambler, and in the short term it paid handsome dividends. Stephens returned to Ireland in August 1864 with his biggest financial haul to date. The successful American tour had been undertaken in consultation with John O'Mahony and ostensibly with his blessing, but it was really calculated to undermine his authority within the brotherhood. Before returning to Ireland Stephens obtained O'Mahony's acceptance of a document providing for the institution of a deputy head-centre who would be a full-time organiser (and of course a serious embarrassment to Head Centre O'Mahony), and who would have the assistance of similar full-time organisers at state level. There were henceforth to be direct communications between American local centres and Ireland (O'Mahony thus being by-passed) even in the matter of transmitting money.[61] O'Mahony was able to prevent the enforcement of most of these arrangements, but the very fact that he had to agree to them initially shows what an impact Stephens had made on the Fenian Brotherhood with his 1864 tour.

O'Mahony assented at the same time to the promise of action before the end of 1865: he did so very reluctantly, because he realised what a foolhardy undertaking it was. Back in Ireland the promise of imminent action had predictable consequences, one being a rise in the numbers and morale of the organisation, which was facilitated by the unprecedentedly large amount of money now at Stephens's disposal. With the ending of the civil war in the spring of 1865 the promise of early action acquired enhanced plausibility for the Irish fenians: the long-awaited demobilisation of the Irish-American veterans was at hand. But the expectation of war in 1865 was not confined to over-enthusiastic fenians. Relations between Washington and Westminster were so poor for a few years that Anglo-American war was a credible prospect in many eyes. Fenianism itself became a further bone of contention between the two powers.[62] Within a few weeks of the ending of the civil war there was a realisation in British diplomatic circles that behind the threatening bellicosity of the Americans there was no intention of going to war.[63] But this was not evident to less skilled observers, especially the Irish-American masses, who were deceived by politicians wishing to exploit their prejudices for the sake of internal American electioneering purposes.[64] As late as December 1867 the British foreign secretary, Lord Stanley, confided to his diary that no aspect of foreign affairs was causing him serious concern except for the still-continuing negotiations with the U.S.A. about the problems that had arisen in Anglo-American relationships during the civil war. He continued:

> It is impossible to say what may happen in that country where the Irish vote is powerful and parties are utterly reckless of consequences if they can secure a momentary advantage.[65]

There was nothing exceptionally naïve in the fenian hope of Anglo-American war.

In Ireland the fenian sense of impending international crisis combined with the reiteration of Stephens's assurances that 1865 would be the year of action to create a widespread expectation of aid from across the Atlantic, usually predicted for harvest-time.[66] Stephens continued to act as though confident that the course of history could not fail to live up to his promises. Reassurance was added to reassurance and the appearance — at least — of preparations was intensified. In compliance with Stephens's wishes, O'Mahony began to send over experienced military men to officer the army of Irish fenians about to take the field. One hundred and twenty arrived during June and the three following months.[67] In early 1865 money began to flow from America regularly and in large amounts. The solidifying conviction of the fenians that a day of reckoning was at hand communicated itself to others. Those who did not want rebellion — the vast majority of those of every religious creed who had any opinion on such matters — held their collective breath.

The euphoria of the fenians in Ireland was based on assumptions about aid from the brotherhood in America. In turn, enthusiasm there depended on the impression that Ireland was about to rise. This left O'Mahony in an unenviable position. For four years he had invoked the civil war as an excuse for inaction. If an Irish adventure were not forthcoming soon, he would be pushed aside by the 'men of action'. But he knew that nothing (except a disaster) was possible in the Irish theatre without prior international complications. O'Mahony was riding a particularly unpredictable tiger. Partly through a genuine desire for accurate information, and partly as a delaying tactic, O'Mahony had despatched to Ireland shortly after Stephens's return an envoy named Philip Coyne who was commissioned to investigate and report on the state of the Irish organisation. (O'Mahony had in fact been sending such envoys for years). He returned in December 1864 with a written report in Stephens's own hand: the captain had ways of handling such investigations. Naturally the report painted a glowing picture of Irish preparedness and solemnly adjured the Irish-Americans to respond appropriately. It was considered by the second convention of the Fenian Brotherhood held at Cincinnati in January 1865 and it was sufficient to prolong enthusiasm for war in Ireland, and so to prolong O'Mahony's leadership. The head centre was instructed to make all necessary preparations and was empowered to proclaim 'the final call' and to issue bonds of the Irish republic as soon as the time was ripe. In these matters, however, O'Mahony was to act with the hitherto shadowy central council which was increased in membership from five to ten.[68] In the following months O'Mahony and his council sent a series of envoys to Ireland — Captain Thomas J. Kelly, General Francis F. Millen, General William G. Halpin and, finally, P.W. Dunne and P.J. Meehan together. Stephens used all his wiles to ensure that they reported favourably, putting each newcomer on the defensive in the first instance by feigning extreme indignation at this latest intrusion. The final reports of both Kelly and Millen were brought to New York together by O'Donovan Rossa in July 1865, a circumstance which scarcely favoured impartial verdicts.[69]

As the American organisation looked more and more closely at Irish fenianism unease was felt about the lack of governing structures in the Irish body. Irish-Americans would have more confidence in some form of committee than in Stephens's irresponsible autocracy. They would also have liked to deal with more prestigious and socially-elevated people than Stephens. The two problems were related. Stephens wished to be an untrammelled dictator and to that end he was determinedly opposed to sharing power with committees and was prepared to sacrifice even the most desirable support. However, pressures from home and abroad forced him to make tactical concessions in the summer of 1865. In compliance with an American demand he appointed an advisory committee in July 1865 consisting of O'Leary, Kickham, David Bell, O'Donovan Rossa and General Millen. In September he set up a military council largely, it would seem, as a device to control the large number of increasingly restless Irish-American officers scattered throughout Dublin awaiting action. To neither of these bodies did he allow any real power or influence. There was also pressure both from America and from within the home organisation for committee structures at provincial and local level in Ireland. Luby commented on a scheme along these lines drawn up by Stephens under pressure as early as 1861, that it reminded him of a well-known patent brand of razor designed not to shave but to sell.[70]

Imperfect though it is, the information transmitted back by the American envoys can help us to solve the riddle they were sent to explore. 'Was fenianism ever formidable?', was how William O'Brien put the same question in 1897 in the title of a magazine article that purported to provide the answer.[71] O'Brien's reply to his own question laid much emphasis on the numerical strength of the organisation and implied that at peak the I.R.B. may have contained at least 100,000 men. Of course, he had no hard statistical evidence on which to base a definite figure and neither have we. Yet, there are some indications, including the reports of the Fenian Brotherhood's various emissaries, that make an approximate estimation possible. The I.R.B. in the mid-1860s was not the kind of organisation that could distinguish clearly between members and all non-members, a fact which makes too much straining after accurate statistics rather pointless. When Philip Coyne was in Ireland in the autumn of 1864 he was 'shown through' the I.R.B. by Stephens, a process that involved meeting individually with fenian centres and organisers, as arranged by Stephens, and hearing from each, under oath, a report on the number of men under his command. After this fashion Coyne received evidence for a total of just over 54,000 fenians in Ireland. However, Stephens claimed that he could have shown Coyne 70,000 and that he himself answered for yet another 15,000. Three months later in a further dispatch to America Stephens claimed a following of 112,000.[72] In the meantime a local leader with whom the captain vouchsafed to share some confidences picked up the figure of 129,000.[73] Clearly Stephens was selecting the highest number that he thought might be believed by any particular listener or correspondent. Captain Kelly was not 'shown through' the organisation but in July 1865 General Millen was. He obtained in this way sworn evidence for the existence of something in excess of 50,000 fenians and that figure included a number of English circles.[74] Yet in May he had heard Stephens claim that 140,000 men had been sworn into the I.R.B. in Ireland. Obviously there were difficulties in bringing all the centres from their respective localities to one or more places of rendezvous, even in small numbers at the time; but making a good impression on the Americans was of such vital importance to Stephens that we must assume he spared no effort at the task. Accordingly, if Coyne and Millen got evidence for little more than 50,000 I.R.B.

men we can be reasonably sure that the true figure did not greatly exceed that. Indeed we must be prepared to allow for the possibility that even though oathbound some of the witnesses may have exaggerated the numbers under their command.

In addition to the ordinary membership, the numbers of fenian recruits in the British army in Ireland and among the Irish militia have often been cited as evidence of the strength of fenianism in Ireland. Canvassing of soldiers in an organised fashion had been initiated in late 1863 or early 1864 by Patrick ('Pagan') O'Leary, an Irish-American with military experience who took up this project in spite of the strong opposition of Stephens. The wisdom of Stephens's objection was demonstrated when, in November 1864, O'Leary was arrested in Athlone on the evidence of some members of the local garrison whom he had attempted to seduce from their allegiance.[75] Nevertheless, O'Leary had had some success — or at least numbers of (Irish-born) soldiers with an eye to free drinks had taken the fenian oath in public houses — and Stephens appointed another organiser, William F. Roantree, to continue O'Leary's work. Roantree was arrested in his turn and was succeeded as fenian organiser of the army by John Devoy, who held the position from October 1865 to February 1866 when he was arrested. Devoy's published recollections of this fenian infiltration suggest that during his period in charge 8,000 of the regular soldiers in Ireland were fenians.[76] However, recent research suggests that independent evidence will support no statement more definite than that there were 'some hundreds or thousands' of fenians in the army.[77] It is likewise impossible to discover how many of the militia were infected by fenianism, but official concern on the subject is clearly shown by the fact that the annual training sessions were cancelled in 1866 and 1867.[78] In any event it would be a mistake to assess the significance of fenian infiltration of the forces in terms of the numbers apparently implicated. Devoy in effect claimed that almost one third of the regular soldiers in British service in Ireland were fenians. However, an unofficered third of the rank and file does not constitute one third of an army, and the only officers of her majesty's forces who took the fenian oath were a handful of N.C.O.s. To make an impact as a fighting force the fenians were going to need a corps of experienced officers. They were also going to need arms and ammunition.

Outside of a few proclaimed districts there was, in the early and middle 1860s, no legal barrier to prevent a fenian or anyone else, as an individual citizen, from acquiring a gun and ammunition. However, the open purchase of guns on a large scale by people at this level of society would certainly have provoked counter-measures. In any case the fenians, though not from the poorest strata, were far removed from the financial self-sufficiency that permitted the English volunteers to arm themselves with Enfield rifles' (and bayonets) that, in 1861, could cost up to 5 pounds and 10 shillings each. From the beginning it was part of Stephens's scheme that his American backers would provide the funds to purchase military supplies for the Irish fenians, who in fact, appear to have done little about arming themselves in the early years. There were some exceptions: Hugh Brophy, centre of a large circle composed mostly of employees of the Dublin building trade, insisted that his men make regular subscriptions to an arms fund, from the proceeds of which weapons were bought for allocation to individual members by ballot.[79] Stephens appears to have actively discouraged the purchase, or at least the importation, of arms until 1864, when a change becomes evident, apparently as a consequence of demand within the organisation. Here we have another one of the many issues on which the motivation of the fenian chief appears decidedly devious. It seems likely that he was initially opposed to arms acquisition because it might alarm the authorities, but also because he could not himself conveniently take full charge of the matter. And it also seems clear that he consented to a change of policy – in 1864 – because it was necessary to forestall complaints from within the I.R.B. about lack of preparations.

The most complete account of the system that actually operated comes from Millen. Stephens, inevitably, was in overall control. Under him Brophy was given responsibility for fire arms; Stephens was essentially taking charge of what he could not suppress. Responsibility for ammunition was entrusted to a young Trinity student with a flair for experimentation, Edmund O'Donovan, son of the celebrated Gaelic scholar. Denis Cromien, another Dublin centre, had charge of a machine for the manufacture of percussion caps. A fourth appointment encourages the suspicion that the entire business should not be taken too seriously: Michael Moore, a blacksmith with a workshop near the centre of Dublin city, was commissioned to produce pike-heads. This in the age of the Enfield rifle. But Enfield rifles were indeed procured in some quantity. They were purchased discreetly, and quite legally, in various English cities, and transferred with similar discretion in 'knocked-down' form to Dublin usually labelled as 'nail-rod iron'. The guns (as also the pikes) were passed on to circles that had paid in advance, usually after a representative had been interviewed by Stephens, who had himself clearly seen as the dispenser of armaments. By early 1865 Stephens had given at least some of his provincial supporters the impression that he had sufficient rifles to arm the entire organisation stored away in Dublin timber yards.[80]

The end of the American civil war in April 1865 caused a depression in the arms market with the result that it was eventually possible to buy a rifle and bayonet at 25 shillings — excellent vallue by comparison with Moore's pike-heads at two and sixpence (5 shillings with a handle). The centres who answered to Millen under oath for 50,000 men in the summer of 1865 swore to a total of approximately 6,000 stands of arms. It was a figure which would have included all the rifles supplied by Stephens to that date, and probably a much larger number of other weapons, many of them no doubt of antique vintage. Six thousand assorted arms with very little ammunition patently would not suffice for the work ahead, and accordingly Millen suggested that the fenians should concentrate all their resources for a surprise seizure of the military arsenals in Dublin city, which would, he reckoned, yield arms for 100,000 men. Stephens rejected the suggestion with the barbed remark that he could arm that many in three weeks if he had the money (that is, as promised by Millen's American friends).

Taken on its own, then, the I.R.B. at the peak of its strength in 1865 was not a very formidable military threat to British power in Ireland. It was a loose, undisciplined social organisation rather than a tight military one, it had a totally inadequate command structure, and it was very poorly armed. Nevertheless, it did embrace some tens of thousands — at least — of young men and it had the potential of assuming strategic importance in the event of British involvement in a foreign war. Divorced from the possibility of such a war, military fenianism was nothing but a charade. What exactly the fenians might do in the event of 'England's difficulty' coming to pass would obviously depend on the course of events, but it is easy to conjure up some of the possibilities. They could, for example, have prepared the way for a foreign invasion, as the Italian secret societies in the papal states had done by demoralising the forces of authority there during the summer of 1860. Disruption which in peace time might be easily dealt with could assume crucial importance at a time of international military fluidity. The potentialities of fenianism in such circumstances would be all the greater because in Ireland paramilitary organisation of the propertied and middle class — on the lines of the English volunteers — was not allowed for by law (for the very good reason that it would give rise to sectarian or other conflicts). Accordingly there was no readily-available stabilising agent apart from the government's security forces. One does not need to have James Stephens's powers of imagination to visualise how even a loosely-disciplined band of enthusiasts, such as the fenians were, might have been used to exploit a major challenge to British military power. But they could never create such a challenge on their own.

The Irish authorities never doubted the capacity of the crown forces to deal effectively with any threat that fenianism might pose, so long as there was no international war. The military threat might be checkmated, but Dublin Castle was still at a loss about the handling of fenianism — precisely because it was more than a military phenomenon. Groups of fenians found drilling might be hauled before the courts, but not even the most ill-disposed magistrate could make this into a serious charge in the absence of more weighty evidence. Even a ringleader, caught red-handed, could be difficult to convict as was shown in the case of Pagan O'Leary, arrested in Athlone in November 1864 for suborning soldiers, but not convicted until eight months later and then only after appearing before two sessions of the County Westmeath assizes in Mullingar. Since March 1864 Detective Superintendent Daniel Ryan had been receiving information from a disillusioned fenian, Pierce Nagle, who had regular, if limited, access to the *Irish People* office. Information, however, did not constitute evidence that would stand up in court, and so James Stephens could operate freely under the noses of policemen who knew him to be the chief motivator of the threatened revolution which held the country in a kind of mesmeric state.

This principled adherence to due process of law, even in the face of subversion, was very important to the liberal British politicians of the age — of every party — and they were reluctant to make an exception even in the case of Ireland. This was not through any unwillingness to admit that Ireland was different from the rest of the United Kingdom, but because they felt instinctively that liberal principles would prove themselves universally. The consequences of this stance became more worrying as the summer of 1865 progressed and the 'fenian fever' mounted. On 5 August John O'Mahony, at Stephens's insistence, had proclaimed the 'final call' which involved announcing the sale of bonds of the 'Irish Republic' and brought the sense of imminent action to a new level on both sides of the Atlantic.[81] Later that month Dublin Castle came into possession of secret documents carried from America by P.J. Meehan and lost by him in Bray. In the second week of September Ryan received from Nagle a note in Stephens's own hand addressed to the local fenian leaders in Clonmel reiterating the promise of action before the end of 1865.[82] This would be a prize exhibit in a prosecutor's brief. Might more like it be available? After intensive discussion at the highest levels Dublin Castle moved against the fenian leadership on the evening of 15 September. The office of the *Irish People* was forcibly entered, the few people found there were arrested, and every scrap of paper in the place was seized; all those associated with the newspaper were arrested wherever they could be found. The law had not been changed but it had been strained in a few respects by the authorities: they subsequently made very heavy weather of defending their seizure of property in the *Irish People* office in a little-remembered case brought against them by T.C. Luby. But crown prosecutors found among the seizures a wealth of documentary evidence to support criminal charges. Preparing cases would take time. In the interim there were appearances before police magistrates for formal charges — of high treason — and for remand. Those arrested included O'Donovan Rossa, Luby and O'Leary. Kickham and Stephens had not been apprehended and they went to live in hiding at a large house in Sandymount previously rented by Stephens (in the guise of a gentleman of substance) for just such an eventuality.

On 17 September Stephens wrote to O'Mahony from his hiding place, demanding more money and indicating that the arrests had changed nothing. However, dog in the manger as always, he added that if word of his own arrest were received no more money should be sent from America.[83] He was eventually arrested on 11 November. At once the military council moved to fill the leadership vacuum (for which absolutely no provision had been made), appointing General Millen provisional head of the organisation. Word of this was sent to Stephens in Richmond prison through his sister-in-law; on her next visit she received from Stephens a pencilled note ordering Millen to proceed at once to the United States and to return with the first expeditionary force but not a moment sooner.[84] Before Millen had his trunks packed Stephens had been rescued from prison — with the aid of fenians in the prison service — on the night of 23 November 1865. He went into hiding in Dublin and all the efforts of the police to recapture him were in vain. From his safe houses he resumed direction of the organisation. Much as he undoubtedly appreciated his freedom, it had the disadvantage of depriving him of the most plausible of all excuses for not honouring his promise of action before the end of 1865. For with five weeks of the year remaining the great majority of the leading activists in the country, and of the Irish-American officers in Dublin, confidently expected a rising. Now that the captain had demonstrated his invincibility by escaping from the grip of his enemies, confidence in his projects soared. The organisation throughout the country was intact and as safe as ever from successful prosecutions. The incarcerated scribes of the *Irish People* were no great loss in military terms. (They began to go on trial before a special commission on 30 November.) The landed and middle classes kept their heads down and their fingers crossed; many of those farmers who still had bank deposits after the series of bad seasons were reportedly noticed withdrawing their money in gold. Little did they know that they had an ally in James Stephens. With neither American expedition nor Anglo-American war in prospect, and having no self-destructive leanings towards symbolic gestures of self-sacrifice, Stephens was determined to temporise. Joseph Denieffe and John Devoy have left two less than satisfactory accounts of Stephens's contacts with his chief subordinates in late November and December 1865, but the picture that comes across clearly is that of the captain in brilliant tactical form endeavouring, in the course of carefully stage-managed meetings and interviews, to make his men feel that they had participated in the decision to postpone action.[85] There was loss of face when the year ended without the promised rising but the arrests provided a pretext for postponement and the fenians in Ireland quickly accepted the notion that the great day had been merely postponed; in any case, expecting the revolution was more important for the fenians than the desire to see it happen. But James Stephens had put himself in the unenviable position of having to maintain the insupportable sense of expectation. Driven by his egotism to keep up the charade, he escaped from Ireland in March 1866 and made his way by Britain and France to New York where he arrived on 10 May 1866 still believing that eventually something would turn up to redeem his promises.[86]

Chapter Five

THE RETURN OF POLITICS, 1866-8

The *Irish People* arrests of September 1865 may have been followed by more disruption of fenianism in America than in Ireland. At the third convention of the Fenian Brotherhood held a few weeks later in Philadelphia, the news from Ireland provided the party of action with grounds for a new strategy — invasion of British North America. Such a policy would be an abandonment of the Irish fenians, a rebuff to O'Mahony's authority, and a tacit admission that American fenianism served the purposes of Irish-America rather than the supposed needs of the motherland. The convention adopted this Canadian policy and along with it some appropriate constitutional changes. Henceforth O'Mahony's title would not be 'head centre' but 'president', and like the president of the U.S.A. his powers would be defined by law and his functions circumscribed by representative assemblies including a 'senate'. One of this body's first transactions was the acquisition, in New York, of impressive and expensive new headquarters for the brotherhood, a fenian White House-cum-Capitol.[1] The new regime was not an Irish government-in-exile but an assertion of Irish-American identity. Far from being affronted by this parody of their own constitution, leading American politicians encouraged it. Swayed largely by electoral considerations, both President Johnson, and Seward, the secretary of state, had led the fenians to believe that the government of the United States would condone an attack on Canada.[2] As part of their overture to the fenians the Washington authorities had agreed in October 1865 to set free John Mitchel (held since the end of the civil war for his support of the confederates) in order that he might act as financial agent for the brotherhood in Paris. He crossed the Atlantic in November and from then until June 1866 he saw to the safe conveyance to Ireland of funds sent to him from America. Securing the support of John Mitchel was a considerable propaganda boost for the American fenians, but that and many other advantages were thrown away by their increasing internal difficulties.

John O'Mahony resisted the Canadian policy adopted in October 1865, as he was bound to do for a variety of reasons. On 2 December the senate deposed him from the presidency, thereby precipitating a split in the Fenian Brotherhood. O'Mahony and his followers held a convention in New York on 3 January 1866; this gathering re-adopted the Chicago constitution of 1863, making O'Mahony once again 'head-centre' rather than 'president'.[3] At the same time the convention declared for war in Ireland and nowhere else, a declaration that was followed up the next month by the issuing of bonds of the Irish Republic, first announced in August 1865. This attempt to raise money on the credit of an independent Irish state had some success: purchasing bonds was at least no less attractive than the making of straightforward subscriptions and these had been flooding generously into fenian coffers since 1864. By the spring of 1866, however, the invasion of Canada appeared considerably more likely than an Irish revolution, and Irish-American interest and money were flowing to the Canadian-bound senate wing of fenianism now under the presidency of William R. Roberts (and issuing its own fenian bonds from April). Succumbing to the temptation to compete for support at any cost, O'Mahony embraced a counter-attraction of similar immediacy. This was a scheme proposed by one of his henchmen, Bernard Doran Killian, for a fenian expedition to occupy for the U.S.A. the small island of Campo Bello, in the Bay of Fundy, of which ownership was disputed with the British crown. Large sums of money were spent on the acquisition of a ship and the fitting out of an expedition. The outcome was farcical failure (in mid-April 1866) and the utter discrediting and bankrupting of the O'Mahony wing.

Arriving in early May, Stephens proceeded to pick up the pieces. The Roberts organisation would have nothing to do with him but he easily took O'Mahony's place as head-centre of the other faction, which he quickly set on the road to recovery. On 15 May large crowds turned out to hear him declare for 'war in Ireland and nowhere else' and that this war would begin — without fail — before the end of 1866. Two weeks later the senate wing's invasion of Canada was under way and by 3 June it had failed. The failure was not ignominious, but it gave

Stephens a large stick with which to beat the proponents of the Canadian strategy. Stephens received further encouragement on 9 June when he obtained an audience with the secretary of state: crucial mid-term elections were in the offing and Seward like many other American politicians was quite prepared to give encouragement to fenianism by word and gesture — if not by deed — with a view to wooing the Irish vote.[4] In any case Stephens never needed anything as substantial as a politician's promise to fuel his optimism. Through the summer and early autumn he toured the U.S.A., promising imminent action in Ireland, and raising almost sixty thousand dollars. The momentum of the campaign led inexorably to a final rally in New York, on 28 October, at which Stephens indicated that his next public appearance would be made in Ireland, at the head of a revolutionary army.[5]

Back in Ireland the fenian organisation had been in great disarray since the spring of 1866. Finding that the arrest and trial of the leaders and the uneventful passing of 1865 — the promised year of action — had not noticeably shaken the strength of the conspiracy, Dublin Castle resolved to abandon the attempt to combat subversion by ordinary legal processes. The securing of a handful of convictions that were supported by masses of incriminating documentation had been tedious work. It would be impossible, simply relying on the courts, to pin anything on the hundreds of brazen fenian activists throughout the country known to the police, or on the scores of returned Irish-Americans standing around the street corners of Dublin in their square-toed shoes awaiting the call to action. The only answer was the suspension of habeas corpus: a bill was rushed through parliament on 17 February 1866 permitting the indefinite detention of any person in Ireland on warrant of the lord lieutenant.[6] The haste was intended to give the Irish police the advantage of surprise. Hours before they could have received confirmation of a formal enactment they had moved against scores of suspects; within a week hundreds were in detention. For every one fenian held an incalculable number fled to America (or Britain, where the immunities of the subject were untouched), went to ground, or simply abandoned the conspiracy. The suspension of habeas corpus wreaked havoc on fenianism in Ireland, shifting the odds in favour of the authorities. Stephens's deputy in Ireland in his absence was Edward Duffy. He was in poor health, and, having been arrested with Stephens in November 1865, he had been released on bail. By the autumn of 1866 he seems to have been in a state of helplessness and despair.[7]

All of this had little enough effect on Irish reception of the news of Stephens's declarations for action by year's end, because just about everyone realised that however good or bad the state of the I.R.B. was a rebellion while Britain was at peace with the great powers was doomed to failure. On the other hand, whatever the condition of the fenian organisation in Ireland, or the state of international relations, James Stephens seemed determined to have a rising. By late November people of substance — of all denominations — were holding breath and worrying about their material assets. 'Business of many kinds is greatly checked', the *Nation* reported on 1 December, and there are numerous other pieces of impressionistic evidence to the same effect for November and December.[8] Among those charged with the government of Ireland there were differences of opinion about how precisely to deal with the threatened rising, but there was an unfaltering assumption that it would be dealt with successfully. Better than any successful suppression of a rising would be the avoidance of one. To ensure the achievement of either one objective or the other, gunboats were deployed off the southern and western coasts and the number of troops in the country was topped up. Between 1 October 1866 and 1 March 1867 the total of officers and men increased from approximately 20,600 to approximately 24,000.[9]

Stephens disappeared from the New York scene after 28 October, thereby giving the impression that he was on his way to Ireland with the secrecy appropriate to his business. In fact he went to Philadelphia and then to Washington, returning to New York in mid-December. He thereupon called a meeting of the officers who had been commissioned to accompany him to Ireland and proposed another postponement of action. His frustrated subordinates poured forth their recriminations on his head. They soon deposed him from leadership, first of the Fenian Brotherhood and then of the Irish organisation, and took charge of affairs themselves.[10] Foremost among them was Thomas J. Kelly, a former captain in the federal army now bearing the title of colonel in the army of the Irish republic. He had been close to Stephens since arriving in Ireland in 1865 as one of O'Mahony's envoys. (He had remained until April 1866.) Kelly and the others were scarcely less realistic than Stephens in their assessment of the prospects, but unlike Stephens they felt that too many promises had been made, too many hopes had been raised, and too many subscriptions had been taken up to permit of any turning back. As they saw things, they had burnt their boats, both as individuals and collectively, and the credibility of fenianism was at stake. The steamship used for the Campobello expedition was sold (at a considerable loss) and the proceeds were utilised by Kelly to finance a resumption of revolutionary effort. By the end of January 1867 a contingent of military leaders (including Kelly himself and two European mercenaries hired earlier by Stephens — Cluseret and Fariola) had reached London which was now the most suitable base from which to organise Irish operations because of the continuing vitality of English feniansm, the suspension of habeas corpus in Ireland, and the close navy and police surveillance of the Atlantic approaches to Ireland.

Kelly and his companions found that preparations for a rising without Stephens were already in hand. The feelings of shame and betrayal felt by men who had believed, and repeated, the solemn promises of action before 1 January 1867 had induced a group of Irish-based centres taking refuge in London to band themselves into a self-constituted directory with the single-minded objective of showing the flag early in the new year. The standing of this directory cannot be determined with great precision but the members felt sufficiently confident to threaten the American military men waiting in Ireland and Britain for many months past with the cutting of their money supplies unless they went along with the idea of an immediate show of force, independently of any further transatlantic aid. The Americans refused to entertain such a reckless idea, with the exception of the newly arrived Captain John McCafferty, an Ohio-born veteran of the confederate army and a desperado. He was admitted as a member of the directory and played a prominent part in the formulation of its desperate and short-sighted plans. News from New York of the deposition of Stephens caused the directory to pause, awaiting the arrival of Kelly. He tried but failed to temper their course of action. They went ahead with preparations for a raid on the military arsenal at Chester to be followed by a filibuster to Dublin via train and mailboat.[11] At least one thousand fenians turned out on 11 February to take part in this venture, an indication that the directory had considerable influence, at least among English-based fenians. The authorities were warned just in time by an informer and Chester castle was so strongly guarded on the day that no action was possible. On the following day, 12 February, one hundred or so fenians assembled under arms in the Iveragh peninsula, beyond Killarney, and seized a coast-guard station, emptying it of arms. Through fear of them a number of constabulary barracks were abandoned and news of their actions created quite a stir in military and official circles. However, they disbanded in a few days and before being seriously challenged.[12] The episode had all the marks of confusion and uncertainty and lack of co-ordination or communication with the movement at large, but the timing was probably determined by some awareness of the directory's plans for the preceding day.

The Chester fiasco, followed as it was by the arrest of McCafferty, spelled the overthrow of the directory. Already a body of greater weight had been pushing it aside. This consisted of one representative from each of the four provinces — Edward O'Byrne (Leinster), Dominic Mahony (Munster), William Harbison (Ulster), and Edward Duffy (Connacht). They seem to have been chosen by some electoral process, the details of which are unknown. Certainly, these delegates considered themselves to have very extensive authority over the I.R.B., for, having met at Kelly's London lodgings on 10 February, they established what purported to be a provisional government. It is not certain that all four of them were members of this government which did include at least one other area representative, probably of some section of the I.R.B. in Britain. A *modus vivendi* was worked out with Kelly. He surrendered all executive power to the delegates and in return one of the first moves of the provisional government was to co-opt him as a member. Recognition was also accorded to his leading military aides (Cluseret was appointed commander-in-chief) but it is doubtful if they too were co-opted, as has been suggested, since the provisional government did not at this stage exceed six in number. The provisional government, on or about 10 February 1867, took the decision which led to the attempted rising of 5 March 1867, though the actual date was set by Cluseret about 25 February.[13]

From their arrival in London Kelly and his associates had been endeavouring to win the support of English republicans, and serious discussions were held with Charles Bradlaugh and others. The affair went sufficiently far for Bradlaugh to be given a large say in the wording of a proclamation adopted by, or on behalf of, the provisional government on 19 February and intended to cover the fenian rising. The proclamation reflected the much more *doctrinaire* rhetoric of English republicanism and the intention of Kelly to persuade Bradlaugh and his associates that the planned rising was not inimical to 'the plain people of England':

> We intend no war against the people of England. Our war is against the aristocratic locusts, whether English or Irish, who have eaten the verdure of our fields; against the aristocratic leeches who drain alike our blood and theirs. Republicans of the entire world, our cause is your cause.[14]

To what extent the fenians might be able to ignore national antipathies was not to be put to the test. No practical co-operation ensued because the course of military action on which the fenians were set made no sense in either Ireland or England under prevailing conditions. But the episode serves as a salutary antidote to the all-too-prevalent notion that fenianism was evidence of the 'otherness' of Ireland, evidence of Irish irreconcilability on the edge of an otherwise complete British mid-Victorian consensus. Bradlaugh and the other leaders of the Reform League were at this very time organising mass demonstrations by discontented Englishmen in favour of the ballot and manhood suffrage. One such demonstration in the previous July had resulted in the Hyde Park riots that had military and populace facing one another menacingly for three days. As for republicanism, it is as certain as such things can be that Bradlaugh had among his followers a far greater number of principled detesters of monarchy and aristocracy than was to be found in Ireland. Influenced by later contingencies, myth and historiography have minimised English disaffection and high-lighted Irish disaffection. Similarly, Irish disaffection has been associated inordinately with physical force. But many of Brad-laugh's followers, like their 'physical force' chartist predecessors would have had no objection to an armed revolution, if it were feasible. The fenians were not 'given to the gun' in any intrinsic way. They were locked into a hopeless policy of armed insurrec-tion largely because of their American dimension and the earlier manœuvrings of James Stephens. But for the American dimension Ireland would not have seemed to be a particularly troublesome part of the United Kingdom in 1867.

Thanks to the deliberate policy of James Stephens, lines of communication within the I.R.B. were personalised and unstructured, and in spring 1867 the emerging representative government of the organisation had not yet had sufficient time to set up a network. Deficiencies of communication and command structure ensured that the rising of 1867, which had so much else working against it in any case, was a particularly sorry fiasco. The plans for the rising of 5 March had about then an air of rather cavalier improvisation. (They were devised by Captain Kelly and General Cluseret, who did not intend being in Ireland on 5 March.) The basic strategy (insofar as there was one) was to raise the flag and keep it flying for long enough to galvanise Irish-Americans into supportive action. Direct confrontation with the forces of the crown was to be avoided except where superiority of numbers absolutely assured victory. So there would be no attack on the by now fully-alerted military barracks or arsenals. Instead there was to be hosting on the hill-sides; and railway lines were to be torn up to impede the movement of troops.[15] The latter point displayed awareness of a factor which over much of Europe had tilted the scales in favour of the state and against insurgency.[16] In any case the arrangements were reported in much detail to the authorities by spies and informers.[17] This flood of information reflected not simply the efficiency of the detective system, but the demoralisation of the I.R.B. The realisation that under prevailing conditions any attempt at armed rebellion was ridiculous left many with the inclination to salve conscience by confiding in authority. General Massey, the senior military officer in the conspiracy to be actually on Irish soil was arrested alighting from the train at Limerick Junction (near Tipperary town) on the evening of 4 March, following information received. Once lodged in Kilmainham jail he told an official from Dublin Castle everything that he knew about the fenians. Meanwhile, the leaderless rising was working itself out. The plans provided for a massing of Dublin fenians outside the city, and on the evening of 5 March men were seen to leave in groups, moving south. The intended rendezvous was on Tallaght hill. Upwards of one thousand fenians went there directly. A somewhat smaller group, intending to approach Tallaght from the south-east, went from Dublin to the vicinity of Bray, picking up reinforcements on the way. This group, or contingents from it, took possession of Stepaside and Glencullen police stations before facing towards Tallaght. But the rebels at Tallaght had scattered in confusion quite early on the night of 5-6 March, indeed before they had assembled properly. An exchange of volleys with a party of a dozen constabulary — in which one fenian was killed — began the rout. There was no more shooting, but along the Dublin mountains throughout the night, amid intermittent snow showers, a flying column of military rounded up fleeing fenians. The great majority in fact escaped and made their way home, but more than two hundred were taken prisoner.[18]

Like their Dublin brethren the Cork fenians left the city in their hundreds on 5 March for an assembly under arms. Their destination was Limerick Junction. They lost heart long before they could reach there but breakaway groups and separate local musterings caused excitement in various places in Cork. In parts of Counties Cork, Limerick and Tipperary bands of fenians were abroad for days or even weeks after 5 March. They avoided any contact with the forces of the crown apart from rare occasions such as the attack on Kilmallock police station (6 March), attempted resistance to a military patrol at Ballyhurst near Tipperary town, and a futile attempt to resist arrest at Kilclooney Wood, on the borders of Waterford and Cork, in which Peter O'Neill Crowley was killed (31 March). There were also minor manifestations of rebellion in Clare, Queen's County and Louth. The frequent transversing of the most disturbed countryside in the south by small mobile flying columns of regular soldiers appears to have been very reassuring to peaceable subjects, and would no doubt have influenced waverers.[19] However, the rising of 1867 was self-defeating; the reasons for this were many but none was more important than the absence of that foreign aid — be it French, American, or Irish-American — the promise of which had at all times been the only basis of the credibility of fenianism as a military movement, even in the eyes of its most naïve supporters. When a single small ship, the 'Erin's Hope' arrived off the Irish coast in May 1867, landing a few dozen Irish-Americans who were quickly arrested by the constabulary, it served to highlight the extent to which the fenians had allowed their hopes to outrun reality.

While journalistic and popular attention were focused on fenianism, more important developments were taking place in the arena of constitutional politics. Lord Palmerston died in October 1865 and was succeeded as prime minister by Lord John Russell. John Blake Dillon who was then barely three months in parliament saw in the change a further move towards the era of reform the prospect of which had brought him back into politics. Displaying a sense of purpose that was quite unusual among them, Dillon lobbied the other Irish M.P.s representing catholic-popular interests, intent on making the most of the coming opportunities. Twenty-one of them joined him for a conference on strategy held in Dublin on 5 and 6 December 1865. They included The O'Donoghue, Maguire, and Gray.[20] At least eleven of them had (like Dillon himself) been elected as independent oppositionists. Dillon's objective was to re-unite the two factions of Irish catholic M.P.s on the basis that satisfactory policies were being advocated by a sufficiently important section of the Liberal party to justify a promise of support for the Liberal government. One of the resolutions adopted referred to the 'advanced' section of that party as largely sharing 'our political views' and being sympathetic with 'our efforts'. The continuation of the meeting into a second day suggests that the proceedings were not perfunctory, and the major subject of debate must have been whether or not independent oppositionists had sufficient grounds to declare themselves in support of the government. They had to bear in mind the feelings of their faction in the country, which for long had been a matter of postures rather than policies: A.M. Sullivan in the *Nation* was making no secret of his opposition to the meeting and its objective. In the event the fourteen resolutions agreed on by the assembled M.P.s did not commit them to support of the existing government; but they reiterated in very forthcoming language readiness to give support if the government

The Tipperary flying column. Small mobile detachments of military, criss-crossing the most potentially troublesome counties were admirably suited to dealing with the Fenian military threat in March 1867. (*Illustrated London News*, 30 March 1867)

adopted acceptable policies on Irish questions.[21] Significantly these were extended beyond the land and church questions of the 1850s to include also education. Dillon might not have achieved all that he hoped for from the meeting, but he had gone a long way towards re-uniting the old independent Irish party and persuading it that its distinctive strategy no longer served a purpose.

Just how far Dillon had moved matters became evident in the spring session of parliament when political life began to revolve about the government's reform bill. This was the clearest possible evidence of the new-found responsiveness of the administration to popular demands, but the extension of the franchise that it proposed was deeply distasteful to much of the whig element in the ruling party. A whig revolt in the lobbies could defeat the bill, and in turn would entail the fall of the government, for reform was patently an issue of confidence. On the strict interpretation of independent opposition principle this was a situation where — irrespective of the desirability of the measure under debate — the government should be opposed, unless it had adopted a satisfactory policy on Irish questions. Faced with the same dilemma just seven years earlier, the independent opposition members had divided almost equally.[22] In 1866 Dillon was determined to ensure that they would as a body support the government.

The *Nation* of 14 April pointedly reminded its readers that the government had 'failed Ireland' on the land, church and education questions; the insinuation was that the independent oppositionists were obliged to vote against the administration in the forthcoming divisions on the reform bill. Dillon replied in a letter addressed to the next weekly meeting of the committee of the National Association, but clearly intended for public consumption. He had decided, he said, to give unconditional support to the bill because the extension of the franchise which it proposed would ensure the continuing rule of the Liberal party, and that, he implied, was essential to the realisation of cherished objectives.[23] The *Freeman's Journal* was strongly in support: the constituencies should put pressure on members who might be thinking of opposing the government; Gladstone had said that henceforth Ireland should be governed in accordance with Irish wishes: was this to be rejected? A highly significant aspect of Dillon's letter was that he spoke in it for The O'Donoghue as well as himself. The *Nation* subsequently protested in dismay that the chieftain of the Glens had left Ireland only a short while before still determined to remain independent of, and in opposition to, the government.[24] The day of decision came on 27 April, with the vote on the second reading of the reform bill. One independent oppositionist (McKenna of Youghal) voted against; two abstained (Corbally of Meath and Greville of Westmeath); all of the others supported the government. It is to 27 April 1866 and not to any date in the late 1850s that we must look for the demise of the independent opposition party in parliament. Charles Gavan Duffy, the prime mover of independent opposition in the 1850s, was back on an extended visit after a decade of making his mark in the antipodes and already assuming the air of an elder statesman. In a public letter to Dillon he declared that he, too, would have voted for the reform bill. He did not seek to prove, his old newspaper pointed out rather sourly, that such a vote would have been in accordance with his old independent opposition principles.[25]

Dillon and his followers had not supported the government purely on promise: already a bill was on its way to the statute book that would modify the parliamentary oath required of catholics; and serious discussions had begun between the Irish catholic bishops and the government to find an accommodation on the university question.[26] But the promise was most alluring: Gladstone was in the ascendant and the proposed extension of the franchise seemed certain to richly enhance his prospects. The vote of the popular Irish members on 27 April 1866 marked the effective inauguration in parliament of that phase of alliance with the Liberals which eventually produced disestablishment. It was also of very immediate consequence, for the government's majority in the voting was a mere five, so that victory would have been impossible without the support marshalled by Dillon. The bill was eventually lost (and the government ousted from office) on 18 June 1866 in a vote on the committee stage. The anti-government majority of eleven included eight Irish members on the Liberal side of the house. Six of those, however, were whigs, who, with their fellow 'Adullamites', revolted against the bill because they were opposed to further democratisation of the franchise. Only two of the eight – McEvoy of County Meath and, again, McKenna of Youghal – were independent oppositionists. Dillon's initiative was holding well and it continued to hold in the period of political flux and uncertainty that was beginning with the inauguration of a minority Conservative government under the Earl of Derby. Dillon did not live to see the fruits of his work; he died suddenly on 15 September 1866 after a highly impressive parliamentary career of just over one year.

While the Conservatives were in office, from June 1866 to December 1868, the predominance of the radicals within the Liberal party became an accomplished fact. And to say that is, indeed, to understate the significance of what transpired. For during those years the party was transformed into the spearhead of a mass movement for reform that made Gladstone, in a very definite sense, the first popular parliamentary leader in British history.[27] The man who did most to whip up and stage manage this movement, John Bright, did not ignore the great potential for participatory politics of the Irish portion of the United Kingdom. His studied reservations about the usefulness of the suspension of *habeas corpus* in Ireland in February 1866 earned him the honour of an engraved portrait in the *Irishman* of 3 March. When he visited Dublin in the late autumn of the same year, it was evident that Bright commanded the support of a far wider spectrum of Irish opinion and interests than any living Irishman. He was hailed by the *Nation*, the *Irishman* and the *Freeman's Journal*, the latter proclaiming that he was the first Englishman to make himself thoroughly popular in Ireland.[28] The O'Donoghue, M.P. and Dean Richard O'Brien were among the speakers at a banquet in his honour; he was received by Paul Cullen (a cardinal since June); he met a delegation from the Cork Farmers' Club; and he addressed a gathering of the Dublin trades convened in the Mechanics' Institute.[29]

This range and level of support could have been expected as a matter of course to issue in mass meetings, and indeed such demonstrations formed a spectacular part of Bright's campaign in Britain. That particular form of political expression was as highly developed in Ireland as anywhere else in the world. Yet it was not brought into play for Bright's visit in 1866, and the reason was that, as we have seen already, the fenian threat was paralysing more conventional political expression. While revolution appeared to threaten, normal political activity was impossible. The events of 5 March 1867 and subsequent days and weeks established conclusively that there was not going to be a serious fenian rebellion, and the gradual re-emergence of normal public political expression is observable over the following months. The easing of tension was greatly assisted by the government's avoidance of any executions in the aftermath of the rising. Hundreds of those arrested were detained for short periods under the terms of the Habeas Corpus Suspension Act and then released. Approximately 170 were put on trial and, like the leaders arrested in September 1865, they were tried by a special commission. This was a 'special court' only in the sense that it was convened outside normal dates to deal with specific business; in every other aspect it was identical with the normal bi-annual county assizes, complete with grand and petty juries. At its first session, in Dublin, at the beginning of May 1867, the special commission sentenced to death Thomas F. Bourke (an

Irish-American soldier who had come over to lead the rising in south Tipperary) and Patrick Doran (who was deeply implicated in the seizure of the police stations at Stepaside and Glencullen). The jury recommended clemency for Doran and this was quickly granted. Meanwhile, Bourke's execution was fixed for 29 May. A campaign for Bourke's reprieve in the middle weeks of May 1866 saw the resumption of conventional style political activity in Dublin city, culminating in a public meeting in the Mansion House. The lord mayor, Peter Paul McSwiney, catholic business tycoon, was in the chair, supported by an array of Dublin city councillors and catholic clergymen; a letter of warm approval from Cardinal Cullen was before the meeting.

These were all staunch opponents of the fenian organisation and they would have approved of the sternest measures against it, if it still posed a threat. As soon as the fenians proved themselves incapable of bringing about a revolution the attitudes of many opponents began to soften. There was a feeling of immense relief that the threat had passed with so little loss of life and without (on either side) any of the outrages or atrocities that might be expected in association with a rebellion. In particular the fenians impressed and surprised almost everyone by the respect for private property displayed by those of them who had been 'in the field' for a few brief hours or days. For this they were subsequently awarded unsolicited testimonials by judges, policemen and English politicians. The dominant interests among their catholic fellow-countrymen were particularly gratified. Irish farmers, priests and shopkeepers obtained in March 1867 a large instalment of what came more gradually to the English middle classes in the 1850s and 1860s — the realisation that the chartist scare was dead, that the propertyless had accepted the moral assumptions of the liberal-capitalist system and that they sought not to destroy the existing order but to obtain a share in it. Specific to Ireland was the reassurance that the famine emigrants would not be returning *en masse* to claim their birthrights. Irish catholics, generally, expected the government to be as relieved as they were themselves and to feel similarly lenient. (This latter presumption was strengthened by the fact that both major parties at Westminster were courting popularity as never before in British history.) As the fenians taken in rebellion at Tallaght were being brought in to Dublin on 6 March the mother of one of them was reportedly heard to shout: 'They will not hang you, thank God, and you'll all be out of prison in a few months'.[30]

Those assembled in the Mansion House on 13 May were, in any case, reasonably confident that the authorities would give Bourke a reprieve. They may be seen as ostentatiously pushing against what they believed to be an open door. Besides, they were all of that section of Irish catholic opinion for long attached to the Liberal party interest and now more so than ever; they took pleasure in this opportunity to campaign against the minority tory government in office since June 1866 which was temporarily delaying the triumph of their emerging champion, Gladstone. They and many others received a rude shock about 24 May when it was realised that all arrangements were going ahead for an execution on the twenty-ninth. A few tense days ensued, in the course of which the government was importuned by President Johnson of the U.S.A., Cardinal Cullen, and a very large number of public figures in Britain and Ireland. News of a reprieve for Bourke came on the twenty-seventh and in due course mercy was extended to the six others condemned to death by the special commission.[31] The exercise of clemency (and especially its dramatisation in Bourke's case) was taken by Irish catholics as confirmation that the wide world shared their feeling that the once-dreaded fenians were really well-intentioned, if misguided, young men who meant no harm to anyone and whose hearts were in the right place. It was not that they received retrospective approval for the rising, but that they were forgiven for it because it was so harmless.

After March 1867 the fenians no longer represented a serious threat of violent revolution by a section of the lower classes. Instead, those of them in prison became invested — partly by default — with the role of symbolising the grievances of the Irish catholic community at large, just at a time when popular grievances were achieving political respectability in Britain. There was indeed an attempt to extend the agitation in its English form to Ireland by founding an Irish Reform League. The *Irishman* of 21 December 1867 reported the abandonment of the experiment, which had never prospered: the catholic ecclesiastical and middle-class people who were the leading Irish allies of Bright and Gladstone, did not wish to have propagated in Ireland the radical and secularist ideas that were the stock in trade of the most active English allies of Bright and Gladstone. After all, the English Reform League stood for many of the godless iniquities that fenianism once (but no longer) was feared to represent. So catholic Ireland joined (belatedly) in the general political mobilisation of the United Kingdom, but under its own distinctive banner — that of the fenian prisoners. Nothing would be more misleading than to suggest a dichotomy in popular attitudes, between feeling for the prisoners on the one hand, and an intense interest in concessions on land, church and education on the other. But as a rallying cry the prisoner question was far more acceptable than the other to the small core of doctrinaire nationalists who were so very well represented among the editors and proprietors of Irish newspapers. Following the suppression of the *Irish People*, the *Irishman* (owned from June 1865 by Richard Pigott) had become the informal press organ of fenianism; it moved easily to the question of the prisoners. The *Nation* had opposed both the parliamentary alliance with the English Liberals, and fenianism. A.M. Sullivan was clearly relieved when conditions from spring 1867 onwards permitted him to drop these negative themes and take up the cause of defeated fenians. For newspapermen the fate of incarcerated fenians possessed the advantage of having very great 'human interest', and the press was just reaching the level of technical and commercial sophistication necessary for the exploitation of 'human interest' stories. The prominence of the prisoner question in 1867 and 1868 owed much to the *Irishman* and the *Nation* (and also to the *Freeman's Journal*). The two weeklies in particular undoubtedly found that fenian prisoners were good for circulation. In the *Nation* office T.D. Sullivan developed a spinoff industry by compiling selections of patriotic Irish speeches from the dock (including the most eminent contributions of the fenian prisoners) and issuing them in pamphlet form. By August 1867 volumes one and two were being reprinted to meet the great demand.[32] All of this was the very stuff of modern popular nationalism, but it was not a campaign on behalf of the separatist nationalism of the fenians. The implicit objective was a future within the United Kingdom in which Ireland would be ruled in accordance with 'Irish ideas', as Gladstone was soon to express it. No proper appreciation of the period is possible without an awareness of this sense of an impending new deal giving 'justice' to Ireland (meaning concessions to the catholics of Ireland). It was an attitude intensely coloured by a sense of relief at the peaceful passing of the fenian business. Together, the commutation of the capital sentences and the promise of 'justice for Ireland' were taken as pledges of a new relationship between English power and the Irish majority. As is the way with such relationships the gratitude of the receiving partner was not explicitly expressed; instead, there was an obvious sense of self-satisfaction which produced much verbal truculence of a kind that the question of the prisoners was admirably suited to highlighting.

John Bright got the measure of the Irish situation very quickly. As early as 3 May 1867 he was presenting to the house of commons a petition concerning the treatment of fenian convicts in English prisons.[33] The prisoners in question were mainly those arrested in September 1865 and sentenced to long terms of penal servitude which they were sent to serve, for security reasons, in the English convict prisons. They included O'Leary, Luby, Kickham and O'Donovan Rossa. On 16 March 1867 the *Irishman* had published a letter of Rossa's smuggled from Portland Jail and alleging that he was being subjected unfairly to bread-and-water diet. Far more startling charges about the treatment of fenian prisoners appeared on 13 April in the same paper: there were allegations about the vindictiveness of prison officers, the fatiguing labours in the quarries at Portland, nauseating chores in the prison laundry, dampness of cells, uncongenial diet and the death of a prisoner owing to inadequate clothing. These allegations were reported in full in the London *Morning Star* and induced a number of English radicals to formulate the petition presented to parliament by Bright. In the commons on 3 May it was supported by at least five Irish members, including Gray and Maguire; the latter quoted the *Irishman* allegations at length. Blake of Waterford city had a question on the subject down for answer by the chief secretary for Ireland.[34] As a direct result of this discussion in parliament the government set up a commission consisting of a magistrate (Knox) and a medical doctor (Pollock) to investigate the treatment of the fenian prisoners. They began work on 13 May 1867, visited the prisoners involved, and reported to the home secretary early in June. The tone of their report was hostile towards the prisoners; all charges of cruel treatment were rejected but it was pointed out that penal servitude was a severe punishment and was intended to be so.[35] This was not calculated to ease concern in Ireland. However, even the *Irishman*, which denounced the Knox-Pollock report as a white-wash, had to admit that the visit of the commissioners to Portland prison had been followed by a relaxation in the regime of the fenian convicts there.[36]

Funerals provided an opportunity for indications of popular attitudes. In March 1866 John McGeough had died in Belfast jail where he was being held under the Habeas Corpus Suspension Act as a suspected fenian; he was buried apparently without any striking demonstration.[37] After the death of William Harbinson in the same prison in September 1867 an estimated 30,000 to 40,000 people took part in the funeral.[38] Harbinson, admittedly, was a more prestigious fenian than McGeough, but the principal explanation of the difference between their funerals is to be found in the dates. Richard J. Stowell of Dublin had been the first fenian prisoner to be interred with spectacular obsequies.[39] He died in May 1867 immediately after release from imprisonment in Naas jail which was believed to have caused his death. In October 1867 a demonstration of massive proportions marked the funeral in Limerick of William

Kelly, recently released after a year of imprisonment without trial.[40]

Colonel Thomas J. Kelly was arrested in Manchester on 11 September 1867 along with another Irish-American officer, Timothy Deasy. A week later they were rescued from a police van returning them from a court appearance to prison. The rescue was carried out by about thirty armed fenians and in the course of the operation an unarmed policeman was shot dead. A few dozen suspects were arrested for the affair and by the second week of November five of them had been sentenced to death for complicity in the murder of the policeman. In the dock four of them made use of defiant gestures and statements, and of the slogan 'God save Ireland'. (This was an obvious adaptation — previously used in a few fenian documents — of the motto 'God save the queen'.) In Ireland their 'manly bearing' and defiance (lovingly reported in the popular press) won admiration on top of the sympathy that was theirs from the start. For there was a fixed belief in Ireland that the death of the policeman was unintended, an unfortunate accident in the course of what was otherwise a splendid exercise in Irish gallantry. The apparent defects of the trial weighed heavily even with those Irish catholics farthest removed from popular prejudice. The fifth condemned man was reprieved because of well-founded doubt about the evidence on which he had been convicted. One of the defiant four, Edward Condon, an American citizen, was also reprieved. There was widespread hope in Ireland that no executions would take place. But the Manchester affair had followed on serious disturbances in Birmingham and other cities (the Murphy riots) and a spate of tradesunion-related armed murders in Sheffield. An opportunity to re-assert authority could not be missed. So, for reasons unconnected with Irish politics, the cabinet decided against reprieve and Allen, Larkin and O'Brien were hanged at Salford jail on Saturday, 23 November 1867.[41]

The reaction in Ireland can only be understood in the context of the mood of preceding months. The executions were seen as the violation by the government of the unspoken understanding that drastic measures had been abandoned and that in future 'Irish ideas' would be taken into account. Touching details of the last moments on the scaffold (in view of a large multitude of hostile sightseers) were circulated in Ireland by the press with an immediacy and a thoroughness that would not have been possible even a decade before. From top to bottom Irish catholic opinion was outraged. William J. O'Neill Daunt, in so many ways the antithesis of fenianism used the phrase 'judicial murder' in his private diary.[42] On the morning of Sunday 24 November many priests referred to the executions at mass and prayed for the souls of the deceased. Over the following weeks hundreds of public requiem masses were celebrated up and down the country, most of them arranged quite spontaneously by the clergy. Spontaneous public gatherings began on the very evening of 23 November; these were soon formalised as *ersatz* funeral processions, which could be represented as religious functions.[43] On Sunday 31 November, tens of thousands walked in such a cortège in Cork city, while smaller demonstrations were taking place in other towns. The natural leaders of protest were soon moving into position: an *ad hoc* committee was formed in Dublin, with John Martin as chairman, to co-ordinate preparations for a procession in the capital.[44] On 8 December 30,000 'mourners' marched through Dublin in cruel weather, following a route that took them past such evocative locations as St Catherine's church, the old parliament building and the site of the O'Connell monument, ending outside Glasnevin cemetery. After an address by John Martin silent respects were paid at the graveside of Terence Bellew MacManus. No banners had been carried, but contingents from the various trades could nevertheless be distinguished among the marchers. The banners had been omitted in an attempt to maintain the fiction that the procession was of a funereal and not a political character, but green ribbons or sashes were worn by most of the marchers.[45] Midway through the following week the government overcame initial indecisiveness and banned the impressive series of 'funerals' planned for the following Sunday throughout the provinces.[46] At the same time Martin and others were charged in connection with the Dublin demonstration, being, however, eventually acquitted. A.M. Sullivan and Richard Pigott were brought to trial for publication of seditious material in their newspapers; each served a term of imprisonment in the spring of 1868. Part of the contribution of the *Nation* to the cult of the 'Manchester martyrs' was a 'Song' (so titled) for singing to an American civil war air ('Tramp, tramp, tramp, the boys are marching') published in the issue of 7 December 1867; this made telling use of the phrase 'God save Ireland', under which name it quickly became the anthem of Irish nationality and so remained for half a century.

On 13 December 1867 an attempt to free Richard O'Sullivan Burke — the organiser of the Manchester rescue of 18 September — from Clerkenwell jail by blowing a hole in the wall caused death and injury to dozens of inhabitants of nearby houses. This disaster took some of the steam out of the 'Manchester' indignation in Ireland. Now it was the turn once again of English opinion to be outraged. Some Irish writers canvassed the rather implausible line that the explosion was part of a police plot to blacken the reputation of the fenians.[47] In due course English indignation produced a counter-reaction and the episode was subsumed in the ongoing wave of Irish self-righteousness.

The affair of the Manchester martyrs produced the fullest possible mustering of the sentiment of Irish catholic identity. The point is nicely illustrated by a comment from a *Freeman's Journal* reporter on the Dublin procession of 8 December. Though himself fully in sympathy with the demonstration, he was taken aback by the participation of children. The marchers included a couple of thousand 'of tender age and innocent of opinions on any subject'. The city had seen many demonstrations during the decade but there had not been anything quite like this in any 'previous displays of popular strength'. Earnestness, he reflected, must have been strong in the minds of parents who directed a son or daughter to walk in saturating rain and painful cold through 'five or six miles of mud and water'.[48] But all the intensity of feeling and all the expenditure of indignation did not have any remarkable political consequences, and were not expected to have. This was because the entire business was simply an intensification of the peculiar Irish form of the wider mobilisation of the time. Gladstone went along with the prevalent English attitude to the executions but in such a way as not to cause serious offence in Ireland. Speaking at Southport on 19 December 1867 he gave a clear signal that the excitements about Manchester and Clerkenwell would not affect his unwritten alliance with Irish interests: he declared that Ireland had real grievances which it was England's duty to remove, implying that 'Irish ideas' should be taken into consideration in dealing with Irish problems.[49] The entire business marginally strengthened Gladstone's position in Ireland by decreasing the ruling conservatives' chances of wooing Irish catholic opinion. This was something they were working at intently, particularly Disraeli, the chancellor of the exchequer. From May 1867 he had been in negotiation with the Irish catholic bishops using Archbishop Manning of Westminster as intermediary.[50] The government in August 1867 had set up the Powis commission to enquire into primary education in Ireland; this opened up the prospect of changes in the national school system along lines desired by the bishops. With Disraeli's succession to the premiership in February 1868 the pace of negotiations increased. On 10 March 1868 the chief secretary for Ireland (the earl of Mayo) informed the commons that the government had decided to concede one of the prime demands of the catholic bishops, a charter for their Catholic University in Dublin. (Whether or not the government's detailed terms would be acceptable to the bishops remained to be seen.) The most that Disraeli could realistically hope to gain from concessions to Irish catholic opinion was an extension of the life of his government. Once a general election came catholic Ireland would rally to Gladstone, not simply because he was able to promise more, but because of the long-established bonds between the Liberals and 'non-independent-opposition' catholic politicians. That applied also to Paul Cullen. However, the cardinal was shrewd enough to see that on the university question the tories could give concessions along denominational lines that would be very difficult for Gladstone by reason of his dependence on the radicals and voluntaryists. If an agreement could be negotiated with the tories, so much the better.[51]

The government's offer of a charter was made in the course of a debate on a motion by J.F. Maguire for a committee to enquire into the state of Ireland, in effect a debate on Irish policy. Maguire's initiative was even further rewarded, for the opposition trumped the ministerial offer. Gladstone poured cold water on the university proposals and sought to upstage them by raising the subject of the church establishment and making the declaration that the Irish church must cease to exist 'as a state church'.[52] He followed up this line on 23 March with a notice of resolutions for the disestablishment of the Irish church. Here was a stone intended to kill a number of birds, one of them being, as E.R. Norman has explained, the government's university proposal. It was effectively disposed of when the commons approved Gladstone's resolutions in the face of government opposition, by majorities of fifty to sixty on 3 April 1868.[53] Cullen clung to hopes of salvaging something of the university offer for a few weeks longer, but the disestablishment resolutions reinforced his loyalty to Gladstone, just as they won the Liberal leader renewed popular devotion in Ireland.

The *Irishman* of 11 April 1868 hailed the commons vote for disestablishment as a victory for fenianism, declaring that what had been impossible in 1865 was now practical politics because of the fenian 'show of force'. It could cite in support of this view no less an authority than Gladstone himself. In the course of the debate on the resolutions he had been challenged by Disraeli to state why he and his party had not brought forward legislation on the subject when they were in office less than two years before. The answer of any accomplished politician to such a question, under such circumstances, would be unlikely to amount to an unveiling of 'the truth, the whole truth, and nothing but the truth'. Gladstone's reply had as its main point the assertion that 'circumstances were not then ripe in so far as we did not know so much then as we do now with respect to the intensity of fenianism'.[54] This calls for some interpretation.

The threat of fenian rebellion was self-evidently smaller in April 1868 than it had been two years before, when things looked bad enough for the Liberals to have suspended habeas corpus. On 31 May 1869 Gladstone, again in the commons, referred to the influence of fenianism in a speech from which sentences can be quoted to support two quite contradictory views of the matter.[55] This ambiguity runs through his statements on the subject when taken as a whole. The fact is that Gladstone exaggerated or minimised the role of fenianism depending on what line of opposing argument he was endeavouring to downface at any particular time. Clarification was rendered even less probable by the ambiguity of the term 'fenianism' itself. Its connotation received an important extension from about mid-1867 onwards especially in the usage of government officials, English politicians and English newspapers. 'Fenian' and 'fenianism' came to be applied to examples of nationalist activity and sentiment that were neither directed by the I.R.B. nor inspired by its principles. These terms were being used indiscriminately to refer to the upsurge of popular 'nationalist' expectation among Irish catholics that had no intrinsic connection with fenianism proper but found a convenient emotional focus in imprisoned leaders of the safely-defeated revolutionary movement. Fenianism in this extended sense had indeed grown in 'intensity' between early 1866 and early 1868. And it was fenianism in this sense that brought parliament to vote for disestablishment in April 1868. But in this sense John Martin was a fenian, as was A.M. Sullivan, and Sir John Gray, and O'Neill Daunt, and, even, some bishops. In other words, Gladstone's policy of 'justice for Ireland' was not a response to the military threats of the I.R.B. but was an overture-cum-response to a 'democratic' demand that was in essence distinct from the fenian conspiracy.

There is one limited respect in which physical-force fenianism exercised influence over Gladstone's policy. The Manchester rescue in September 1867 and the Clerkenwell explosion in December 1867 gave rise to fenian panic in Britain, a fear of ruthless and indiscriminate violence by Irish malcontents. There was political advantage to be gained from offering a solution to this. Partly for that reason Gladstone fought the election of 1868 in *Britain* (as well as in Ireland) on the issue of Irish disestablishment (which, it was implied, would assuage the unruly Hibernians): he was offering an answer to the fenian threat that would be utterly painless to the average Englishman. There were, however, other, and far more cogent, reasons for his championing in Britain of Irish disestablishment; for example, it enabled him to avoid issues such as the ballot which might have divided his support in Britain.[56] In any case, the fact that Irish concessions were being highlighted for English electors must not take from the prior fact that they were originally devised to meet Irish wishes. Gladstone offered 'justice for Ireland' initially and primarily in order to win seats in Ireland; he did so, not because fenians had guns and gunpowder, but because other Irish catholics had votes.

A glance at the public visit of the prince and princess of Wales to Ireland in April 1868 provides a salutary antidote to any notion that the nationalist enthusiasm of the time was an endorsement of militant fenian principles. The royal couple disembarked at Kingstown on 15 April (he sporting a green cravat and a bunch of shamrock, she with bonnet of Irish lace) and left one week later. From start to finish they received an even more enthusiastic popular welcome than the queen had in 1861. Enthusiasm could be more adequately expressed in 1868 because public attention was encouraged by the organisers of the affair to an extent that the queen did not tolerate in respect of herself for another decade or so. It may be no coincidence that the 1868 visit was arranged within weeks of the accession to the premiership of the imaginative Disraeli who was eventually to persuade the queen to turn the monarchy into a popular spectacle. In 1868, however, he was learning rather than giving instruction. That came largely from the Irish chief secretary, the earl of Mayo, who had been the prime mover of the visit.[57] On 16 April prince and princess proceeded from Dublin Castle to the horse races at Punchestown. This event had been originally selected by the chief secretary — himself a County Kildare man — as the centrepiece of the royal visit. It was the bait by which the prince's interest in coming to Ireland had been captured in the first place. There were other advantages. Then as now, almost all public and private business came to a standstill over much of north Kildare for the duration of the festival, such was the enthusiasm for the occasion, transcending all social, political and confessional cleavages; in addition there was a large attendance from farther afield, including Dublin city. So, big crowds in festive mood were assured and they could be expected to show appreciation of the royal visit. On the day, the number of racegoers was swelled beyond all expectations by well-wishers trying to see the royal visitors. Enthusiastic expressions of loyalty and affection were the order of the day. The town of Naas was thronged and fully decked out with flowers, banners, triumphal arches, and large signs with such inscriptions as 'Cead mile failte'.[58] So pleased was the prince that he returned to Punchestown the following day on his own initiative.

The formal reason for the Irish visit was not Punchestown

but the investiture of the prince as a knight of the order of St Patrick. This took place with great ceremony on 18 April in St Patrick's Cathedral. Proceedings begun with a procession from Dublin Castle to the cathedral. On a previous visit (in 1865) the prince had been rushed through Dublin in closed carriages. Now he was shown to cheering crowds thronging the streets of the Liberties. Another major departure from royal reserve was the participation of prince and princess in a grand ball at the Exhibition Palace, Earlsfort Terrace. This was not exactly mixing with the plain people of Dublin — the 4,000 people present had paid thirty shillings each for their tickets — but it was nevertheless a tremendous condescension: many of Dublin's middle class had learned their manners quite late in life. The prince's round of institutional visits took in the charterless and unendowed Catholic University, where he was greeted warmly by Cardinal Cullen.[59]

On the occasion of the prince's wedding in 1863 celebratory flags had been torn down in Dublin, and in Cork illuminated windows had been broken, to the undisguised pleasure of the *Irishman*.[60] But not even the *Irishman* attempted to deny that the prince received an uninterruptedly warm welcome in April 1868.[61] The welcoming multitudes must not, of course, be assumed to represent support for any definite views on constitutional matters. What they do show beyond doubt is the minimal extent of attachment to fenian republican ideas. There were, of course, people in Ireland in 1868 who both believed, and felt passionately, that the country's salvation was to be found in violent rejection of all that the visit (and the visitors) represented. But the utter silence and inactivity of these people in relation to the visit shows how few they were within six months of the Manchester executions, when 'God save Ireland' had just become the national anthem, and 'fenianism' was reputedly rampant among the populace. Here, too, is a salutary warning against assuming that such separatist ideas were on their way to some 'inevitable' eventual success. The clamorous Irish catholic nationalism of 1867-8 was a proclamation of grievance, a loud assertion of identity, and a strident call for a new deal for 'Ireland' — within the United Kingdom. Repeal of the union did raise its head: Dean O'Brien and some other Limerick priests launched a clerical petition in support of the old formula in late December 1867. Nobody regarded it as practical politics. In any case even support for repeal was a far cry from fenianism. Not alone did the prince receive an enthusiastic welcome, but his Irish visit was widely regarded as a boon conferred on the country. As such it was seen as further evidence that 'England' had changed its attitude to 'Ireland' and as a token of esteem for Ireland and Irish opinion.

Irish protestants realised that they would lose something when Irish catholics received the 'new deal' being offered them by English politicians. 'Irish ideas' meant majority Irish ideas. If the country really was about to be ruled in accordance with majority opinion that meant the end of the security that went with the protestant ascendancy. The growing threat to the church establishment provided most emphatic justification for their fears. But they were more affected by indignation than by fear. Not too much imagination was required in order to see the promised catholic triumph as the reward for a general perennial disaffection and in particular for the recent gross disloyalty of fenianism. The orange order was the obvious vehicle for popular protest, but its characteristic modes of action were severely inhibited by the Party Processions act. On 12 July 1867 a large orange parade from Newtownards to Bangor deliberately defied the act. At the head of the march was a minor County Down landlord, William Johnston of Ballykilbeg. He was subsequently charged with a breach of the processions act and as a consequence was sentenced to one month's imprisonment in February 1868. The continuing enforcement of the act against orangemen when catholics appeared to be able to evade its restrictions was a source of deep resentment. In October 1867 Mayo had written to Disraeli in rather despondent mood not so much about the state of the country (which was under control) as about the spirit of the country. Now, the very intense wave of Irish catholic self-assertion that could be felt after March 1867 exhibited an attitude to 'England' that was complex and ambivalent and that in a certain light was indistinguishable from 'hatred'. But the 'hatred' that most depressed the earl of Mayo was not that on its own but in combination with the rising hostility that he felt on the part of Irish protestants, including those of the higher social classes.[62] Mayo was one of that small knot of sophisticates that was endeavouring to extend the appeal of the Conservative party (which they controlled) by transcending the unleavened toryism of the gentry and the church. Few enough Irish protestants were sufficiently well placed to be able to share his breadth of vision. They were coming to realise that even a Conservative administration could not be relied upon to protect their interests or, much less, their sensibilities. When Gladstone's resolutions on the Irish church were being debated in the commons very few M.P.s other than Irish protestant members defended the establishment.

The renewed polarisation of Irish politics dragged presbyterians in opposite directions. The majority sided with the anglican establishment, sensing a threat from rampant catholicism to all the protestant persuasions. Besides, presbyterians shared in the religious establishment to the extent that their clergy were supported by an annual grant from the government, *the regium donum*. At a protestant demonstration on 30 October 1867 in Hillsborough, County Down — evocative scene of a similar gathering over thirty years earlier — the influential former moderator of the general assembly, Dr Henry Cooke, made a thundering declaration of support for the continued establishment of the Anglican church in Ireland.[63] However, the overthrow of establishments also had its practical and emotional appeal for presbyterians. Quite as much as catholics they were nurtured in an ethos of resentment against anglicanism. Their co-religionists in England were in the vanguard of the voluntaryist campaign. Besides, more was at stake than church matters: for example, a tilt of the land law in favour of tenants as against landlords would be in the perceived material interest of very many Ulster presbyterians.

While a broad democratic movement was becoming dubbed as 'fenianism' the secret oathbound conspiracy was being reorganised. Shortly after the attempted rising Colonel Kelly was promoting the reconstruction of the provisional government and the selection of replacements for those who had been arrested (and whom, it was subsequently alleged, he tried to use as scapegoats for the disaster). The revived body had but a short life, its dissolution being brought about by Kelly after the majority had gone against him on an important point of policy.[64] Thereupon Kelly resumed the title 'chief executive of the Irish Republic' (C.E.I.R.) which had been given him in New York in late December 1866 and which was a modification of the title 'chief organiser, Irish Republic' (C.O.I.R.) devised originally by the Fenian Brotherhood to denote, in their high American style, the position of James Stephens in the Irish organisation down to 1866. On a visit to Ireland in the summer of 1867 Kelly showed signs of adopting the dictatorial manner to match Stephens's title, and he attempted to gather into his own hand all the threads of communication within Irish fenianism.[65] Meanwhile a determined attempt to take control of the I.R.B. was being made from another direction.

The failure of March 1867 permitted the Roberts (or senate) wing of the Fenian Brotherhood to argue forcibly that the I.R.B., in siding at Stephens's behest with the O'Mahony wing, had backed the wrong set of Irish-Americans. Seizing the opportunity with remarkable speed, Roberts had despatched two discreet envoys to Ireland before the end of April. The secretary of the Roberts movement, Daniel O'Sullivan, followed on 10 May. They induced a respectable number of I.R.B. activists in Ireland

and Britain to accept that the best prospects for the future lay in co-operation with the Roberts faction, and by early June they had assembled a contingent of them in Paris, there to meet Roberts himself. In return for promises of money, arms, and general fraternal support these I.R.B. men agreed not only to acknowledge Roberts's organisation as the one, true, fenian brotherhood, but also to give him, in effect, ultimate authority over the home organisation. The agreement provided for the setting up of an elected body to direct affairs in Ireland and Britain, and to be called the supreme council.[66]

Success for Roberts's initiative would obviously spell the end of Colonel Kelly's authority in the I.R.B., if only because he was so closely identified with the O'Mahony wing (now also known as the Savage wing in reference to John Savage its new head-centre). Indeed it seems probable that he broke up the provisional government because it was responding positively to Roberts's overtures. In an endeavour to secure his position and offset the Paris agreement, Kelly held an I.R.B. convention in Manchester on 17 August 1867. Like the Paris gathering, the Manchester convention had rather doubtful credentials as a representative body (for one thing it seems to have been dominated by British-based fenians), but it was much larger, with perhaps a few hundred participants. Kelly seems to have had himself ratified as C.E.I.R. without too much difficulty, but disillusionment with his American friends was evident among the assembled fenians; by way of compromise with those who were leaning towards considering Roberts's overture it was resolved to seek out the 'honest' members of both wings of the Fenian Brotherhood and co-operate with them. The arrangements made for the management of I.R.B. affairs indicate that American military men (such as Kelly himself) were still quite numerous and very much involved in his plans.[67]

Fortified by the Paris agreement Daniel O'Sullivan set about the task of arranging seven credible district conventions (four in Ireland, three in Britain) to elect the members of the supreme council. At a congress of his American brethren on 3 September 1867 he was able to report the successful conclusion of two of these. An ambitious Lancashire-based fenian who attended this congress as an observer, John O'Connor Power, was commissioned to assist O'Sullivan in the completion of his task. Completed it was in due course (notwithstanding O'Connor Power's detention without trial from February to July 1868) with the aid of judicious financial expenditure, but with an outcome profoundly disappointing to the source of the money — Roberts. For, once assembled, the delegates at the various conventions, while clearly happy to establish elected and responsible government within the I.R.B., displayed great hostility to the prospect of that body being subject to control from America. Thus, according to one source, when the centres from the north of England convened to elect their supreme council representative, they gave their chosen man firm instructions not to recognise any American faction whatsoever. O'Connor Power went along with this trend, if he did not actually encourage it. The adoption of this 'plague on both houses' attitude reflected a strong movement of feeling in the fenian ranks, but it also contained an element of compromise with those who were fundamentally sympathetic towards the O'Mahony-Savage wing and would never countenance support for Roberts.[68]

When the supreme council met for the first time in Dublin, on 13 or 14 February 1868, O'Sullivan was excluded on the pretext that he did not represent any district of the home organisation. Power, however, was admitted, a probable indication that he had secured election as provincial representative by one or other of the district conventions, probably that for his native Connacht. At the meeting of the supreme council Power was one of those who advocated the adoption of an independent line in dealing with the Americans. Immediately afterwards O'Sullivan upbraided him, and informed him that his services would no longer be required, and that no more money would be forthcoming. The first known public statement of the supreme council, issued in April 1868, probably after a second meeting, this time in Manchester, proscribed any attempt by Irish-Americans to interfere in the running of the I.R.B. Copies of this particular document, with an addendum, were posted up surreptitiously on the night of 27 June 1868 in numerous villages and towns throughout Ireland and Britain, apparently as a demonstration of the extent of the supreme council's authority.[69]

In November and December 1867 Cork city and its environs witnessed a number of daring arms raids by I.R.B. men. Gunshops in the city were raided in broad daylight; a Martello tower was taken over and its complement of arms and ammunition removed; and the gunpowder factory at Ballincollig was robbed of half a ton of powder. This fell far short of a threat of rebellion, but the authorities were nevertheless very worried and moved large contingents of extra police and military to the city and district.[70] Apart altogether from political considerations, this kind of thing was outside the conventional norms of criminal activity in Britain or Ireland in the 1860s, and the criminal classes might get dangerous ideas if the perpetrators were not brought to justice. The ringleader in fact was an Irish-American, William Mackey (alias Lomasney) who had already been expelled from Ireland before returning to participate in the rising of 1867. In the autumn of 1867 Captain Kelly had put him in charge of arms acquisition in the south, but scarcely in the expectation that Mackey would carry out his duties in such a provocative fashion. Mackey was arrested on 7 February 1868 but only after he had put up a resistance in which a policeman was fatally wounded. He was sentenced to twelve years penal servitude for treason felony. Mackey, McCafferty, Kelly and Rickard O'Sullivan Burke (organiser of the Manchester rescue) introduced from across the Atlantic a distinctively American (perhaps frontier) style of violent lawlessness.

All prospects of a rising might have been scotched, but, as Mackey's adventures illustrated, that did not prevent the use of guns for more limited objectives. Colonel Kelly, whatever his capacity or incapacity for conventional warfare, was (by contrast with James Stephens) a natural gunman, a man for whom the revolver (usually in the hands of instinctive subordinates) was a natural extension of the personality. The real fenianism was in any case a better basis for gangland-style gunmanship than for field operations. As early as 1859 there had been plans to assassinate an informer; these were scotched by Luby in Stephens's absence.[71] Thomas J. Kelly had set up a 'shooting circle' or assassination squad, with or without Stephens's approval. Various attempts (successful and otherwise) made on the lives of informers and detectives in late 1865 and early 1866 were probably the work of this gang and may have been directed by Kelly. In the second half of 1867 Kelly revived the system (or more correctly, perhaps, resumed control of it). By early January 1868 the principal members of Kelly's squad had been rounded up by the police. One of them was named Patrick Lennon. Dublin Castle heard from an informer that on the evening of 7 January Lennon had lain in wait near the gate of Dublin Castle for the earl of Mayo, who, however, happened to be away for the first time in more than a week.[72] Was Lennon really intent on assassinating the chief secretary? If so, was this on Kelly's orders? Despite all the tensions of the times, the 1860s (with the 1850s and most of the 1870s) constituted by later standards an epoch of limited political hatreds in Ireland and Britain. At least the hatreds did not reach the level of intensity at which they could corrode the customary deference that invested the lives of dignitaries and public men with a certain immunity. But in foreign parts fenian passion might be less controlled. On 12 March 1868 the Duke of Edinburgh, a younger son of the queen, was shot and wounded (not seriously) in New South Wales by Henry James O'Farrell who was motivated by sympathy with the fenians. Thomas D'Arcy McGee, the Young Irelander, was shot dead in Ottawa on 7 April 1868 following many threats received on account of his outspoken criticisms of Irish and Irish-American republicans.

The fenian assassin is not, however, an adequate symbol for these years. Neither is the fenian martyr, 'high upon the gallows tree'. The best encapsulation of what was most important in this period is the meeting in a parlour in Eccles Street in November 1866 of Paul Cullen, cardinal, and confidant of Pius IX, with John Bright, nonconformist hero and representative of so much in the 'spirit of the age' that both pope and cardinal deplored. The forgetting of this symbolic event, and of the remainder of Bright's visit matters little: much more serious is the overlooking, in so many accounts of the period, of what was symbolised — the alignment of Irish catholics with the wider contemporary reform movement under the aegis of Bright and Gladstone.

Chapter Six

Ireland between Gladstone and Butt, 1868-72

Parliament remained in session for nearly three months after the debate on Gladstone's disestablishment motions, but its days and those of the minority Conservative government were clearly numbered. For tactical reasons Gladstone wished to delay a dissolution. Meanwhile, electoral reform measures were enacted for Scotland and Ireland. The Irish act was but a shadow of the English reform act of 1867. There was no redistribution of seats. In the counties the rated occupier franchise remained at the level of £12. This was reduced in the boroughs from £8 to 'over £4', and a lodger franchise was introduced. These changes created almost 15,000 more voters — an increase of 47% in the borough franchise.[1] Nobody displayed much enthusiasm for the Irish measure but neither was there any significant opposition to it. Even members in the Irish 'popular' interest did not show overwhelming concern for extending the franchise. They were much more eager for the secret ballot, and John Gray unsuccessfully moved an amendment to prescribe it for elections in Ireland. Following a long recess during which the election campaign began in many constituencies, parliament was dissolved early in November.

The general election of 1868 mobilised and polarised the Irish electorate more thoroughly than any other since 1852. Nevertheless, the crude antagonism of the earlier contest were largely avoided, thanks to a greater appreciation of relative weaknesses and strengths of parties. When all the returns were made, the Liberal leader had the following of 66 of the 105 Irish members; this provided a handsome proportion of his overall majority in the United Kingdom as a whole. Of the increase in Liberal seats in Ireland by comparison with the 1865 general election, the greater proportion came not by way of gains from the Conservatives but through the annexation of the independent opposition interest which had already been accomplished in parliament before 1868. The most salient fact about the 1868 campaign was that anyone seriously seeking catholic votes was obliged to promise support for Gladstone. This the former independent oppositionists did and so they are quite properly labelled as Liberals. But behind the labelling the old factional conflict continued. Certainly, the catholic whigs had not forgotten the vendetta, and they pressed home their tactical advantage against candidates identified with the other clique, and defeated two of them, Bowyer in Dundalk and McKenna in Youghal. This internal party contest was by no means one-sided. With the support of Archbishop MacHale, G.H. Moore, out of parliament since 1857, was returned for County Mayo, ousting a sitting whig (Lord Browne) in the pre-nomination manoeuvrings. In County Cork McCarthy Downing, a typical local leader of the independent-opposition faction vied successfully with a young aristocrat (Hon. Robert Boyle) for the honour of sitting on the Liberal benches. Unlike G.H. Moore, Downing had to wait for the poll to secure his victory. The seat in contention between Boyle and Downing had been held by a Conservative (M.P. Leader) since 1861. In 1868 the Conservatives did not even contest the seat. Four Liberal gains at Conservative expense were made in this way, that is by the failure of the tories to enter a contest in counties where they had one of the two members in the outgoing parliament; with Cork the other three counties were King's, Queen's and Wexford. Similarly, in the borough of New Ross, the tories did not defend the seat they had held since 1856. These were all constituencies in which the weight of property and personality could secure seats for Conservatives at times of normal levels of partisanship, but where they saw no hope in 1868. County Sligo had been represented since 1832 exclusively by conservatives with the exception of one independent who served from 1852 to 1857; in 1868 the Liberals challenged successfully for one of the two seats. However, in most other counties where the Conservatives had a hold the status quo was not challenged at the polls. Thus the representation continued to be shared between the parties in Cavan, Clare, Leitrim, and Wicklow, and two tories were returned without Liberal opposition in counties Carlow, Antrim, Down, Londonderry, Armagh, Tyrone, Fermanagh and Donegal. The Liberals did challenge the Conservative dominance in Counties Monaghan and Dublin, unsuccessfully in both cases.

Altogether only a handful of counties were contested between the parties, and the most important contests occurred in some of the larger boroughs. In Dublin city an extremely close contest left the parties still with one seat each (although the successful Conservative, Sir Arthur Edward Guinness, was subsequently unseated on petition). The most interesting contests were in three northern boroughs where the major parties fought one another for the urban presbyterian vote. What Gladstone promised was attractive to a sufficient proportion of presbyterians to win both Derry city and Newry from the Conservatives. In the two-seat constituency of Belfast the Liberals returned a member for the first time since 1847. The other Belfast seat was won by William Johnston of Ballykilbeg standing as a Conservative, but unofficially and on the policy which had led to his imprisonment for defying the Party Processions Act on 12 July 1867. His victory was an expression of the anger and frustration of popular protestant opinion and its distrust of the Conservative party, whose candidates were soundly defeated. The same sentiments prevailed in the single-seat borough of Carrickfergus where the sitting Conservative gained less than forty per cent of the votes cast in a straight contest with an unofficial Conservative.

Gladstone's victory meant that the disestablishment of the Irish state church was a foregone conclusion. What was by no means so clearcut was the disposal of church property. How much of it would the church retain? And on what basis? Would the surplus be allocated to other churches or used for secular purposes? The outcome was an elaborate compromise between the various interests, especially as represented in parliament. Gladstone's Irish Church Bill introduced in the commons on 1 March 1869 and passed finally by the lords on 22 July 1869 provided for a Church Temporalities Commission which would take possession of all the property of the state church. Under the terms of the legislation about half the property (approximately £8,000,000) was returned to the church to make provision for the income of existing occupants of livings and for other purposes. On the principle that henceforth (from 1 January 1871 to be precise) the state would have no involvement with any church in Ireland, the presbyterians lost their long-standing civil subsidy, the *regium donum*, and Maynooth college lost its annual grant; the sum of £1,000,000 went as compensation for these. The remaining £7,000,000 was set aside for eventual expenditure on charitable purposes.[2]

While the Church of Ireland was disestablished on terms that were generous in the financial sphere, the entire experience was deeply distressing for Irish protestants. They could not argue with much conviction that any injustice had been done to them, but the manner in which it had all come to pass did not enhance the prospects of religious equality being accompanied by a flowering of inter-confessional goodwill. 'The poor protestants are all very irritated. They never did imagine that England would have abandoned their cause'; so wrote Cardinal Cullen, privately, on 31 July 1869, barely suppressing the note of triumph.[3] When he held a triduum of thanksgiving in his archdiocese in September, even O'Neill Daunt was repelled by this 'crowing for three consecutive days over a fallen foe.'[4] Disestablishment was a victory for the Irish catholic body but it proved to be a negative one. 'In the future, the protestants will find themselves as the catholics, without any privileges', Cullen wrote again in the first flush of success.[5] Technically he was correct, but time was to show that Irish protestants possessed advantages of wealth, education and connection that would not be offset by mere legal equality.

The most important result of disestablishment was possibly the assumption by Irish catholics that the determinant of Irish questions was henceforth to be majority Irish opinion. This was their interpretation of the whole Gladstonian overture with its invocation of 'Irish ideas', and disestablishment was seen as simply the first of many concessions. By early 1870 Gladstone was firmly insisting that he had never bound himself to concede to 'Irish opinion' *simpliciter* in the formation of Irish policy and he proceeded to act accordingly. However, much had been conceded: on a fundamental constitutional issue — one legislated for by the Act of Union — exceptional arrangements had been made for Ireland in line with majority Irish sentiment, and indeed with much invocation of the religious statistics of the 1861 census. Despite Gladstone's subsequent stickiness on other issues, the impression remained firmly embedded in the consciousness of Irish catholics that their right to determine the nature of Irish institutions had been conceded. Disestablishment can be seen as a stepping stone to the eventual dismantling of the union, but only at the risk of subjecting the past to the tyranny of the present. One can with at least equal justification see in disestablishment the making of a new and more workable basis for the union. Distinctive local arrangements, especially in ecclesiastical matters, had proved to be the foundation of success in the union with Scotland. Irish disestablishment was no more a subversion of the union than was the boost given by Gladstone to Welsh distinctiveness when he addressed the Eisteddfod of 1873.

Disestablishment was but one of many boons and concessions expected from Gladstone. Another was the freeing of the fenian prisoners. The last of those detained without trial under the Habeas Corpus Suspension Act had been released in late July 1868, but there were about 100 fenian convicts (including twenty-four soldiers sentenced by military tribunals) in jails in Britain and in Western Australia. Various individuals had already called in the popular press for an amnesty. In August 1868 Cork city council adopted a motion demanding that the prisoners be set free, and over subsequent months many other town councils followed suit. On 5 November 1868 a small meeting in Dublin organised by John McCorry — an inveterate espouser of radical causes, but not a fenian — initiated a formal organisation to work for the release of the prisoners.[6] In heavy-handed ironic allusion to a rather different English body it was initially called the Irish Liberation Society, but soon became known as the Amnesty Committee. With the general election at hand, it set about having as many Liberal candidates as possible challenged to publicly adopt the policy of amnesty; up to twenty seem to have done so.[7] Virtually all Irish Liberals in fact expected that Gladstone when in government would set the prisoners free. However, they avoided making any loud references to it, for fear of causing their leader any embarrassment with British voters. With the elections virtually over a special meeting of Dublin city council was held on 21 November 1868 to discuss petitioning parliament on behalf of the prisoners. The Liberal lord mayor, Sir William Carroll, who had declined earlier in the month (that is, before the elections) to be associated publicly with the amnesty movement, now bubbled with enthusiasm and was eager to be the bearer of a petition to parliament in favour of the prisoners. Such a petition was soon in circulation. Carroll clearly expected with confidence that a fenian amnesty was imminent. So too did many others, such as J.F. Maguire M.P. who made a bold public speech on the subject in early December.[8] A meeting organised by the Amnesty Committee and held in the Rotundo on 26 January 1869 received letters of support not just from nine or ten M.P.s but also from half-a-dozen bishops, including Leahy of Cashel. By early February a total of 100,000 signatures was being claimed for the petition, including those collected by hundreds of parochial clergy. Meanwhile, the new lord lieutenant, Lord Spencer, was giving the issue painstaking attention. On 2 February he placed his conclusions before the cabinet, which considered them and then decided against a general amnesty but in favour of releasing those not guilty of violent acts and not involved in the running of the conspiracy; also excluded were the military prisoners. On 22 February the chief secretary, Chichester Fortescue, announced in the commons the names of 49 fenian

convicts (15 in English gaols, the rest in Australia) who were to
be released. They included only one of the well-known convicts, Charles J. Kickham, whose health was particularly precarious.[9]

Kickham was quickly back in the thick of conspiracy, but
two of the younger men released with him proved to be far
more effective. These were James O'Connor from Wicklow and
James F.X. O'Brien from Cork. Largely, it would appear, at the
initiative of this pair the supreme council of 1868 was superseded
in the summer of 1869 by another supreme council, which on
18 August 1869 adopted the first known I.R.B. constitutional
document.[10] An 'address of the supreme council of the Irish
Republic to the people of Ireland' was issued in January 1870
on the occasion of 'the re-assembling of the supreme council
for this its second session', a clear indication that the session
of 18 August had been its first.[11] The same document dwells
on the confusion that reigned in the I.R.B. before the 'recon-
stitution' of the supreme council and contrasts this with successes achieved during 'the past six months'. The supreme
council referred to here, and whose system of election is described, consisted of eleven members, whereas the supreme
council of February 1868 had consisted of only seven.[12] The
constituencies had not changed but the four Irish provincial
representatives on the new body had elected in committee four
honorary members who then had equal standing with the
seven provincial representatives.

The intensification of fenian effort and organisation from
March 1869 onwards was facilitated not only by the release of
some convicted activists but by the lapsing in the same month
of the legislation suspending habeas corpus. Life was once
again relatively safe for conspirators in Ireland. O'Brien and
O'Connor were joined in their work of reorganisation by a
band of young men rather similar to themselves in many respects, except that they had not served prison sentences (though
some had been detained by virtue of the Habeas Corpus Suspension Act). They included John O'Connor Power, James J.
O'Kelly, John O'Connor (younger brother of James) Mark
Ryan, Joseph P. McDonnell, Charles G. Doran, John 'Amnesty'
Nolan, John Daly and Patrick Egan. An exactly comparable
contemporary group among the Lancashire fenians included
Arthur Forrester, Michael Davitt and John Barry; indeed
O'Connor Power and Mark Ryan had been part of this Lancashire set a few years earlier. One of the unreleased fenian convicts fitted the same bill; he was John Devoy, sentenced to fifteen years penal servitude in 1866. At twenty-seven years of
age in 1869, Devoy was older than many of the group. Like

Devoy most of the others are known to have been sworn fenians before 1867, but few of them had had the opportunity for whole-hearted participation that Devoy enjoyed as organiser of fenianism in the British army in Ireland from October 1865 to February 1866. In general, Stephens's system (or non-system) had failed to provide ambitious and energetic young men like these with the promotional outlets that they needed. Thanks largely to the national schools they had all had a good elementary education. They were thus fitted for employment — as clerks and such — of a type that would never give them the opportunities for leadership and direction which they craved. Some of them procured professional education in later life by dint of exceptional effort, but none of them was from a socio-economic background that could secure automatic access to higher education or the professions. That serves to highlight how different they were from the neo-Young-Ireland elite that provided the leadership cadre of early fenianism. Most of the older group came from well-to-do families, and many of them would have been in the professions but for accident or their own waywardness. O'Leary, Kickham, Luby and O'Mahony were all, in the technical sense, gentlemen, and Stephens could do a better-than-passable imitation of one. The 'new fenian' élite possessed neither such substance nor such airs. The older set were mainly men who had passed up material opportunities for the sake of political visions; the younger men were using politics to create opportunities that would not otherwise come their way: they lacked the dreamy quality and were endowed instead with strong pragmatic instincts. In Revolutionary France half of them would have become generals. James Stephens's attitude to themselves and their ambitions they had found to be patronising. They were determined to be done with him and they made him the scapegoat for the disgrace of March 1867. J.F.X. O'Brien brought powerful support to this policy by announcing that from his prison conversations with John O'Leary and T.C. Luby he knew beyond doubt that these two worthies were opposed to the revival of Stephens's regime. Within a short while Kickham, the most celebrated of the released fenians, had been prevailed upon to espouse the same line.[13]

In 1869, as for decades before and many decades afterwards, journalism was the most congenial occupation for the politically hyper-conscious. The office of the *Irishman* quickly became the effective headquarters of the new fenianism, and James O'Connor was soon on the editorial staff. The proprietor, Richard Pigott, threw himself uninhibitedly into fenian affairs and was soon indispensable. He profited handsomely from the role he was playing both through the assured readership it brought him and also through his handling of the monies that were sent to the *Irishman* in aid of various fenian-related collections. To conclude that he was, therefore, insincere in his professions of republican faith would be to trivialise human motivation. In many ways he was one of the band; he too had worked his way up in life, his father having been a lowly-placed employee in the office of the *Nation*.[14]

The 'Constitution of the Irish Republic' adopted on 18 August 1869 vested all authority, ultimately, in the eleven-strong supreme council. That council would freely elect its own president, secretary and treasurer, who together would constitute the executive: the entrusting of executive power to any single individual was explicitly proscribed. As a further precaution against the emergence of one domineering leader, it was provided that in the execution of their collective functions any two of the officers could over-rule the third. Almost all the proper functions of the president and the executive were subject to the approval of the supreme council. Each of the seven members representing an electoral division had certain executive powers within his own division, which powers he shared with two other elected officials. As an essay in democracy the system had serious limitations. All of those elected to country or provincial authority and all members of the supreme council were deemed to be elected 'finally' or 'permanently', and could be removed from below only by an initiative on the part of two-thirds of the relevant electors. A member of the supreme council could also be deposed by a two-thirds majority of his fellows. The election of a member of the supreme council, on the rare occasions that it would be called for, would be made by an *ad hoc* committee of five elected from among, and by, the county or district centres of the province or electoral district. As these in turn would have been elected for life by the ordinary centres of their respective areas, the supreme council existed at three removes, if not more, from the votes of the plain member. Indeed the constitution was silent on the credentials of the ordinary centre and gave the rank and file no guaranteed say in his appointment. The Stephens dictatorship had been replaced not with democracy but with safely entrenched oligarchy.[15]

The desire to undo one of the more damaging (even if misleading) impressions created in the Stephens era explains the article in the 1869 constitution which declares that 'no member of the supreme council or officer in the employment thereof shall be in receipt of salary from the funds of the Irish republic'. (Obviously that did not preclude the payment of expenses in connection with offical work.) Again as part of the endeavour to put past calamities behind them, the members of the brotherhood in the late 1860s repudiated the term 'fenians' in favour of 'I.R.B.', ostensibly on the grounds that the former was imposed by outsiders. However, even 'I.R.B.' was still for informal use only. It was employed in a revised constitution of 1873, but not in the 1869 instrument, in which the supreme council was represented as the ruling authority of the 'Irish republic' and its subjects as the 'army' or 'citizens' of the 'Irish republic'. Outsiders (followed by later commentators) understandably continued to talk of 'fenians'. Another noteworthy terminological development of the late 1860s is the regular use of the word 'nationalist' to indicate advocates of separatism, especially physical-force republicans. The term 'advanced men' was used with similar connotations.

The seriousness of the 'new fenianism' shines through much of its activities, especially in the early years that concern us here. The 1869 constitution required each member to make regular financial contributions, and it appears that full status in the organisation may have been reserved for those who had acquired possession of their own firearms. Guns were purchased in England and shipped to Ireland, in a business-like fashion previously unknown in the I.R.B. Arms committees were active in the Irish port towns. In January 1870 the Dublin Castle authorities were informed from several sources that the fenians were better armed than ever before. During that same year a total of seventeen cases of arms (some containing up to a dozen rifles) were interrupted on their way to destinations in Ireland, and the police were left to speculate on how many others were getting through.[16] By early 1870 fenianism in Ireland was probably as formidable in military terms as it had been in the mid-1860s (which is saying something but not a great deal). Prospects of a great international war had not diminished; many people believed, correctly as it was to prove, that a European war was imminent; less accurately an Anglo-American war could still be envisaged, as the diplomatic dispute continued about indirect British aid to the confederates in the civil war. The better-armed fenianism of 1869-70 probably counted among its adherents thousands more with firm convictions on the subjects of physical force and republicanism than had ever followed James Stephens: the rhetoric of any cult, however lightly it may flow from the pens of leader-writers is apt to be taken to heart by a small proportion of youth, and the cult of the fenian prisoner-martyrs was no exception. But the impact of fenianism on Irish public perception was now far less marked than in the mid-1860s. March 1867 had broken the spell. In particular the notion of a great Irish-American filibuster was seriously discredited. The fenianism of the mid-decade had mesmerised popular politics; by 1869 there was so much political activity that even a fully active member of the I.R.B. might feel tempted to think the world was passing him by unless he was also participating in politics.

The homecomings of many of the convicts released from English prisons in March 1869 provided occasions for popular demonstrations of welcome (though most of those concerned avoided inflammatory speech-making). These quickly merged with the inevitable wave of complaint about the failure to release all the prisoners. The Amnesty Committee conducted a church door collection — styled a 'national tribute' — on 17 March 1869, that was designed to capitalise on the prevailing mood. By the end of April this had produced over £2,000. There was no public clarification about who was to share this money and in what proportions. Some certainly went to a Ladies Committee which for a few years had been allocating subscribed funds to the wives and families of prisoners. And a portion went to the coffers of the Amnesty Committee itself which promptly split asunder in a disagreement about how to spend the money. As a consequence, by May 1869 there were two competing bodies in being, the Amnesty Committee and the Amnesty Association.[17] As a publicity gesture the Amnesty Association launched itself formally at a public meeting in the Rotundo on 28 June 1869. The Association was intended by its founders (many of whom had been among the founders of the Irish Liberation Society and of the Amnesty Committee) to recover control of the amnesty movement from the hands of the pro-Gladstonian clique that moved on to the Committee after the general election and controlled it by the spring of 1869. Very much to the forefront was John Nolan, an employee of McSwiney's drapery house in Sackville Street and an I.R.B. activist. There is no way of telling how much official fenian support he had for his entry into amnesty campaigning but two things are certain: that he became involved because of a natural talent for the work; and that he used his position in a way that pleased a great many fenians. The Amnesty Association was not simply a fenian affair, official or unofficial; its controlling body included John Martin and A.M. Sullivan. Presiding over them all was Isaac Butt, who since losing his parliamentary seat for Youghal in 1865 had been seeking a role for himself in Irish political life and at the head of something entending beyond his 'native' constituency — ascendancy protestantism. Through his work as counsel for the fenian prisoners from December 1865 onwards he had re-established himself as an esteemed figure with the popular catholic side. He saw in the campaign on behalf of his incarcerated clients something that could be turned to his own political advantage. (This is not to deny that he also felt genuine sympathy for their plight.) Although he posed as an honest broker between the two amnesty factions in early summer 1869 he used his influence all along to undermine the Committee to the advantage of the Association.[18] On 28 June he was declared president of that body and over the following months himself and Nolan (as secretary) directed it in a sometimes uneasy partnership. The Amnesty Committee survived drawing away portion of the available subscriptions and advocating a conciliatory attitude towards the government.

The antagonistic approach favoured by the Amnesty Association drew sustenance from a renewed press campaign about the alleged ill-treatment of fenian prisoners. The core of this was a series of articles in the *Irishman* beginning on 6 March 1869 and running right through the spring and summer; by May a collection of them had appeared in pamphlet form. In that same month Richard Pigott obtained permission to visit Chatham prison (as part of his preparations for a court hearing in a renewed bout of litigation between the *Irishman* and the *Nation*). He met a number of the fenian prisoners including O'Donovan Rossa and emerged with the story that was to dominate the debate in subsequent months: that Rossa had been handcuffed continuously for thirty-five days.[19] In subsequent weeks other sources added details, such as the claim that because he was handcuffed behind during this period Rossa had had to lap his food like a dog. The whole matter was taken up in parliament, eagerly by G.H. Moore, cautiously by Sir John Gray and others who did not wish to embarrass the government. All of these events were alleged to have occurred before the accession of Gladstone's government but it now had the task of providing explanations which inevitably identified it in the public mind with the infliction of continued suffering on the prisoners. In fact the fenian convicts' prison regime had been relaxed in various informal ways on Gladstone's accession. The government's embarrassment was heightened when grave doubts were cast on a statement by the home secretary in the commons (4 June 1869) that special punishment of Rossa had extended over 28 days only, rather than 35. The truth appears to be that until he eventually knuckled under, late in 1868, Rossa was an extremely obstreperous prisoner who constantly provoked the prison officers. (This was a reflection of personal psychology, not of any indomitable fenian principle: John O'Leary subsequently made a virtue of having, as he liked to recall, stoically borne all his sufferings without complaint.) Rossa's insubordination reached a climax on 17 June 1868 when he emptied the contents of his chamber-pot over the governor of Chatham prison. For almost five weeks after that he was manacled behind; however, the handcuffs were removed at night and were put at the front for mealtimes. This punishment undoubtedly exceeded prison regulations and so was illegal.[20] On the other hand a convict with no political connections would almost certainly have been flogged — quite legally — for the same offence; he might also have been punished illegally in all kinds of ways and never have had his case taken up by a newspaper.

The fenian convicts in English prisons undoubtedly suffered in the early years by antagonism on the part of some prison officers. Prejudice apart, as members of a serious conspiracy they were seen as potential jailbreakers (something underlined by the Clerkenwell affair) and so for some time had to undergo regular searches of their clothing. Most of their sufferings were the common lot of all convicts in a system that had been rationalised (by legislation of 1853, 1857 and 1864) without having been greatly humanised. Increased bureaucracy undoubtedly provided increased safeguards for prisoners in general, but sometimes redtape could be a real menace. John Lynch was transferred with others from Dublin's Mountjoy to Pentonville prison, London, in January 1866 wearing (underneath the regular convict garb) flannels ordered for him on medical advice. In accordance with regulations all his clothing including the underwear was returned to Mountjoy while he and his companions dressed from the Pentonville wardrobe. That did not include flannels. To have them supplied Lynch had to go through the tedious procedure of consultation with the prison medical officer. Meanwhile he spent many mid-winter days without adequate clothing. The cold that resulted cannot have helped his already weak constitution and it was inevitably blamed for his death, which occurred a few months later.[21]

Calls for the fenians to be treated as political prisoners had been made from early in their imprisonment. However, British law, unlike that of some other European countries, had no provision for such a distinction. When special treatment was given to Daniel O'Connell in 1844 and to the Young Irelanders in 1848 that was done on an informal basis. Because they belonged to an organisation that posed a serious threat of revolution, the fenians initially received no such sympathetic consideration; besides, the making of informal concessions was much more difficult in the more bureaucratised prison system of the 1860s. By 1869 certain concessions were being made to the fenian convicts, depending on the circumstances of the particular prisons. In particular, attempts were being made to allow the fenians to remain separate from other prisoners, insofar as practicable.[22] There is evidence, too, that with the passage of time the hard labour requirement was treated as purely perfunctory in the case of fenian convicts. Little of this impinged on popular perceptions. Instead, the public read stories of the sufferings of prisoners that mixed undeniably harsh facts, with distortions and fabrications. These were used as arguments not for amelioration of the convicts' lot, but for their liberation.

The Amnesty Association sponsored an important series of public demonstrations in the summer and autumn of 1869 that exploited and further whipped up popular feeling for the prisoners, and demanded their release. The demonstrations were not quite spontaneous. The first efforts, at the end of June, produced nothing larger than a gathering of four thousand in Cork city. The organisational genius of John Nolan, and the enthusiastic efforts of local fenian activists were required to build up an impressive countrywide campaign. In any case, demonstrating for amnesty was in effect protesting against the government, and catholic opinion could not readily be mobilised to embarrass Gladstone while he was putting through disestablishment. By the early autumn larger crowds were turning out and the high point of the series, a meeting at Cabra on 10 October, had an attendance estimated by the police at 200,000 people, of whom three quarters had travelled from the provinces. The campaign was a painful business for the popular M.P.s on Gladstone's side. The continued detention of the fenians was an embarrassment to them; they dearly wished for an amnesty so that there should be no blot on the popular reputation of the prime minister and no shadow over their own positions. The Amnesty Committee, representing their point of view, deplored the stridency of the demonstrations and advocated respectful petitioning. Individual M.P.s privately beseeched Gladstone to look to his reputation in Ireland (and theirs).[23] The hundreds of thousands who eventually turned out in support of the demonstrations were not, of course, rejecting Gladstone: they were, rather, letting him know how much they expected of him. But the sight of the masses marching in protest before the ink on the disestablishment act was dry was a severe shock to Irish Gladstonian Liberals. However, following the basic principle of democratic leadership, they were impelled to follow their supporters and almost a dozen Liberal M.P.s eventually graced amnesty platforms.[24] Sir John Gray is a striking case in point. His newspaper, the *Freeman's Journal*, was very lukewarm about the meetings until one was arranged for Kilkenny city (Gray's constituency) for 12 September. The *Freeman's Journal* of 11 September waxed enthusiastic about the 'universal demand for amnesty', while adding a caveat about exaggerated and extreme language. Next day Gray was on the platform in Kilkenny: when constituents are rallying a politician finds it difficult not to show his face. In the same way many of the catholic clergy came to the fore at amnesty meetings, jumping on a bandwagon which they feared to ignore, and then by their weight increasing its momentum. Maurice Johnson, in the most thorough study made of the amnesty campaign, has accounted for a total of fifty-four meetings in 1869.[25] Priests were prominent platform figures at over forty of these and seventeen were actually chaired by priests (some of them long-standing independent oppositionists, others not). The Queenstown meeting of 17 October was held on church ground, with Rev Dr Rice, Administrator, in the chair.

The only M.P. who supported the amnesty demonstrations without any apparent concern about embarrassing Gladstone was G.H. Moore. He was with Isaac Butt on the platform at Cabra, the only one of the meetings actually addressed by the president of the Amnesty Association. Both must have realised fully that the campaign, far from advancing its ostensible purpose, in fact made the release of the prisoners impossible for the time being. On 20 October Gladstone spelled out the realities in characteristic style: some of the meetings 'seemed to be demanding as a right what could only be granted as an act of clemency'; and 'were public mischief to arise in consequence of an ill-judged act of indulgence, wishes expressed even by large numbers of the people would not avail to excuse the advisers of the crown'.[26] Gladstone personally favoured early releases but nothing could be done while the strident campaign continued. Butt, indeed, was attempting before mid-October to have the series of demonstrations ended, despite which Nolan and his collaborators went ahead to organise more than a dozen further meetings.[27] Butt's call reflected his genuine concern for the prisoners, but he was at this time engaged in such a complicated game of balances that little can be taken for granted about his motivation on particular issues. One point especially worth noting is that the task Butt had set himself — the creation of an alternative to the Liberal alliance — required much more sophisticated efforts than simply nurturing disappointment with Gladstone, though that, of course, was essential, and was fostered by the amnesty campaign.

From all that has been indicated above about the vitality of the land question in those decades it might be expected to loom large in the era of 'justice for Ireland', and so it did. Gladstone could possibly have worked up a substantial Irish following without fingering the church establishment; but without the promise of concessions to the tenants he would never have raised much of a stir in the country. That promise was made implicitly and explicitly in 1866 and 1867; those voting for Gladstone in 1868 expected land legislation from him as surely as they expected disestablishment.[28] The precise content of that legislation was not specified, and in the absence of detail people tended to think in general terms of the emasculation of landlordism. So, the general feeling of national euphoria that was abroad in Ireland by 1868 included a conviction that the duties and burdens of the tenant farmers were about to be relieved. In anticipation of legislation, there developed an attitude of truculence on the part of many tenants that led to demands for lower rents and to a considerable rise in the number of agrarian outrages. The most spectacular of these occurred at Ballycohey near Tipperary town on 14 August 1868. The landlord concerned, William Scully, was one of the impatient, business-like kind. When the tenants of Ballycohey refused to accept leases with new and unfavourable terms, Scully moved to evict them. As he endeavoured to deliver ejectment notices on the fateful day, he and his party were ambushed; a bailiff and a policeman were killed and others, including the landlord, were injured.[29] The incident, sensationalised by newspapers throughout the United Kingdom, added to the strength of the belief that something was rotten in Irish land law. That in turn increased the expectations of the tenants and their inclination to resist the exercise of landlord rights, as the Ballycohey tenants had done. Tenant expectations received a fresh boost on 30 April 1869 when John Bright, now a cabinet minister, made a passionate plea in the commons for the Irish population in large numbers to be put 'in possession of the soil of their own country'.[30]

Isaac Butt, when he set about making a national leader of himself after the 1865 election, lost little time about making a play for tenant support. In 1866 he published in Dublin a pamphlet, *Land tenure in Ireland: a plea for the Celtic race*, which advocated legislation for security of tenure and independent arbitration of rents. Another publication along the same lines followed in 1867.[31] Farmers' clubs that emerged in various counties as means of influencing and exploiting the coming change in the land law turned to Butt as to a mentor and guide. Unquestionably Butt did wish to have the farmers made secure in their holdings; however, he was in no hurry about it, whatever his pamphlets and speeches may have suggested. If Gladstone should succeed in delivering a sufficiently attractive measure the tenant-right lobby might very well weaken and with it one of the most powerful forces that Butt hoped to harness. Butt's ambition made it obligatory for him to be seen as the tribune of the tenants: the same ambition required him to appear as the new pathfinder of Irish toryism, and so as a friend of the landlords. To maintain his ambivalent posture he had to discourage clamorous public agitation on the tenant-right question if at all possible.

Such a campaign was set in motion early in 1869 by Sir John Gray and the *Freeman's Journal*. The passing of disestablishment in the summer was an obvious cue for the land agitation to be stepped up. At that very point, Butt gave his blessing to the Amnesty Association's programme of public demonstrations: here was a means not only of causing confusion to the Gladstonites, but of stifling an inconvenient agrarian agitation. It is significant that the *Nation* displayed very little enthusiasm for the amnesty meetings. In this, A.M. Sullivan, unlike Sir John Gray, was not motivated by any desire to avoid embarrassment to Gladstone's followers: he was a founder member of the Amnesty Association. But he did care about the land question (as most certainly many of his readers did) and in the late summer and autumn of 1869, as the amnesty meetings captured the headlines, he repeatedly expressed regret that a golden opportunity was being lost of pushing to the limits the concessions long sought for the tenants and now acknowledged by the prime minister of the day to be to some extent deserved. During these months the *Nation* repeatedly urged efforts to organise the tenants and vocalise their demands.[32]

Butt persisted in his balancing act. He went along with the farmers' clubs when they resolved upon the formation of a national organisation. He attended and dominated the meeting in Tipperary town on 28 September 1869 at which the representatives of the clubs inaugurated the Irish Tenant League. It is noteworthy that the league thus placed under Butt's direction did next to nothing. Meanwhile, largely through Gray's endeavours, the land question began once again to get an airing at public gatherings. Tenant-right was advocated at an amnesty meeting in Kilfinane, County Limerick on the 5 September 1869 and the same happened at up to seven subsequent amnesty meetings. Since the great majority of the participants would just as readily have participated in a campaign for tenant-right or on any other emotive issue, speeches on tenant-right were enthusiastically received. By late October tenant-right meetings, under Gray's auspices, were being held with the same impressive processions and displays that marked the amnesty meetings. Public response was at least as good and almost certainly better. For instance, the police estimated that the attendance at a tenant-right meeting in Kilkenny on 18 October was four times as large as that at the amnesty meeting there five weeks earlier.[33] In late November the *Freeman's Journal* claimed a total attendance of two and a half million at tenant-right meetings since the beginning of the year. Butt claimed no more than one million for the series of amnesty meetings,[34] and yet there is a widely-received assumption in the historiography that sympathy for the prisoners swept aside all other political emotions in the Ireland of 1869.

A fenian element within the amnesty movement took serious exception to the success of tenant-right on the public platform. At some of the amnesty meetings where the subject was introduced, hissing and disturbance ensued. The antagonism was continued to the point of interference by fenians in purely tenant-right meetings. The most celebrated instance of this intervention occurred in Limerick city on 1 November 1869 when a local group dismantled the platform at the beginning of a tenant-right meeting and thereby prevented a number of lay and clercial dignitaries from making their speeches. This and similar episodes were defended on the grounds that the tenant campaign violated a pledge made by 'the country' not to seek or accept any favours in advance of amnesty for the prisoners.[35] Butt, from his more sophisticated point of view, was also unhappy with the emergence of a tenant-right platform campaign, but he dared not discountenance it in any way for fear of alienating the most important of all constituences. Almost equally disastrous for his schemes would be an open conflict between amnesty activists and tenant-righters. Even more delicate balancing was now necessary. A meeting of the committee of the Amnesty Association held on 12 November 1869 had before it a letter from the conveniently absent president which was subsequently sent to the newspapers and in which amnesty enthusiasts were admonished against undervaluing the truly national content of the tenants' campaign.[36] A public tenant-right meeting held in the Rotundo on the evening of 14 December 1869 was essentially a move by Butt to defuse a threatening crisis. The main thrust of his address was to persuade amnesty enthusiasts that no appeal to nationalism could be used to justify hostile action against tenant farmers. And the main achievement of the evening was not any declaration for tenant-right, but the fact that the anti-tenant activists present in large numbers were prevailed upon, by Butt's eloquence and authority, not to cause disruption. That was the meaning behind the *Nation*'s subsequent anxious assertion that 'the proceedings were orderly and characterised by great unanimity'.[37] Persuading all of Butt's horses to pull as a team would call for quite exceptional leadership. In 1869 and 1870 Butt seemed capable of just that.

The apparent clash between amnesty and tenant-right forms

the essential background to the celebrated Tipperary by-elections of November 1869 and February 1870. Butt was pressed to stand from many quarters. He rejected the suggestion on the pretext (highly dubious in view of his previous and later records) that he had reservations about the usefulness of serving in 'an alien parliament'.[38] It seems reasonable to conjecture that the major consideration deterring him was the difficulty that he would have experienced in the autumn of 1869 in conducting an election campaign, or even drafting an address, without exposing the ambiguity that enabled him to retain the allegiance of the farmers and of the disruptive fenian wing of the amnesty movement, while at the same time not alienating the Irish Conservatives. With Butt out of the running the tenant and clerical interests in the county turned to Denis Caulfield Heron, a catholic lawyer, a supporter of Gladstone, an eminent champion of tenant-right and a declared advocate of fenian amnesty. When Heron's return seemed a foregone conclusion, a group of amnesty activists, led by Peter Gill of the *Nenagh Guardian* and J.F.X. O'Brien, put forward the name of Jeremiah O'Donovan Rossa, by now the most widely-known of the prisoners. They undoubtedly arrived at the idea from reading of developments in France where Victor Hugo and other exiled or imprisoned opponents of the second empire were being nominated for parliamentary seats. The original intention in the case of O'Donovan Rossa was merely to propose him at the nomination meeting but the affair quickly assumed a momentum of its own and the challenge was pursued beyond nomination to polling, on 25 November. If Rossa were seen by the electorate as the standard-bearer of an amnesty movement inimical to tenant-right interests (which is how his nominators viewed him), he would have suffered overwhelming defeat at the polls. But fenianism was no longer a bogey for the farmers and the prisoners had come to symbolise all popular grievances including those of the tenants. The choice between Rossa and Heron was a confusing and meaningless one for many voters. The most significant result of the poll was the number that did not vote at all — almost seventy per cent of the electorate.[39] The election is described by David Thornley as 'an unmistakable struggle for predominance between the fenian-amnesty and Liberal-land-reform parties'.[40] However, it was seen as such only by a few activists on either side and by outsiders; for most people in Tipperary, and throughout the country, there simply was no conflict between amnesty and tenant-right. Under the circumstances the fact that Rossa obtained a small majority (103) of the 2,171 votes cast was, in itself, of no great significance. Or at least it did not signify the upsurge of support for fenian revolutionism that English politicians and leader-writers discerned at the time. The complexity of the situation escaped the comprehension of many contemporaries and indeed of many subsequent commentators.[41] Ironically, although Butt had not encouraged Rossa's candidature, the election did much to advance his objectives by hardening English opinion against a far-reaching land bill. Rossa was declared incapable, as an unpardoned felon, of membership of parliament, and so another by-election was necessary.[42] On this occasion Heron was opposed by C.J. Kickham who was nominated without his own consent. In a somewhat larger poll Heron was victorious by four votes on 28 February 1870.

While Butt dragged his feet — with a purpose — on tenant-right agitation, Gray, as we have seen, was pressing ahead with a lively campaign. Its climax was the land conference held in Dublin on 2 and 3 February 1870. Virtually every prominent personage in the country who had evinced any interest in land reform was invited to attend. About fifteen M.P.s were present, including The O'Donoghue and J.F. Maguire.[43] G.H. Moore absented himself on the pretext that the conference was in some way offensive to his patriotic sensibilities; however, he could have been confidently expected to find an excuse of some kind to avoid supporting an initiative by Gray. Butt, all things to all men, could not afford to be touchy and accordingly he attended. Because of the esteem and authority which he enjoyed he had to be accorded a prominent place in the deliberations. His contribution reflected the difference between his political motivation and Gray's. He pushed the conference into formulating the largest possible demand so as to open up the widest possible gap between that and the eventual government offer.[44] Any imaginable measure would have been an anti-climax; the bill actually produced on 15 February 1870 was a source of serious disappointment. Butt played on this disappointment in order to nurture disenchantment with the Liberal alliance. He might have boosted this disenchantment enormously by means of a great public agitation, for which the materials most certainly existed. That, however, would have mortally offended the tory landed interest. Instead Butt proposed to the farmers that they place their hopes of further amelioration in a new political formula. At the end of March 1870 the County Tipperary branch of the Irish Tenant League dissolved itself, with the declaration that 'nothing was left for the people but to agitate for repeal of the union'.[45] Not all of the farmers' clubs went as far as self-dissolution, but they largely accepted Butt's strategy.

The Landlord and Tenant (Ireland) Act became law on 1 August 1870.[46] By its terms the 'Ulster custom' was given the force of law wherever it existed, and an attempt was made to initiate and support analogous practices elsewhere. Tenants would henceforth be entitled to compensation for disturbance, within specified limits, in the event of eviction for causes other than non-payment of rent. An outgoing tenant not otherwise compensated might claim for improvements made at his own expense. There was nothing in this complex bill that could be dressed up colourfully as a great boom for the farmers. The legal guarantee of the Ulster custom was welcome, but that only underpinned something already taken more or less for granted. The principal effect of the other measures was simply to make capricious ejectments – such as William Scully had attempted at Ballycohey – expensive and practically impossible.[47] Though real, that threat was so rarely inflicted that deliverance from it was unlikely to evoke much euphoria. Little though it may have amounted to in practice, the 1870 act involved what appeared (and still appear) to people concerned with such things to be very great matters of principle. Here was parliament invading the rights of property as sanctified by the orthodoxy of the age, and violating the closely related doctrine of freedom of contract. This has sometimes been seen as striking a blow for collective rights as against the inflated claims of individual proprietorship. By the late 1860s, in European thought generally, notions of historic communal property rights were providing a counterpoint to the prevailing individualist doctrines of the age on land property. Gladstone was one of those listening, and he saw himself, in the 1870 act, making some small recompense to the 'dispossessed' 'Celtic race'. Such whimsies had little bearing on what was actually happening – except perhaps to make it more palatable. The heave for control of Irish landed property, insofar as it involved collectivites at all, was a tussle between two sets of capitalists. Like disestablishment, the land act of 1870 was the recognition of a distinctive feature of Irish life; in this case it was the peculiarly heavy weight (by British standards) of the country's tenant-farmer interest as against that of the landlords; it was not the weight of any attachment to communal notions about property in land, though such notions might be invoked for purposes of propaganda or apology.

The part of the 1870 act that evoked most popular appreciation in Ireland was a section inserted at the behest of John Bright which provided for support for farmers buying out the landlord's interest in their holdings and so becoming owner-occupiers. Here in an otherwise disappointing act was an emotionally satisfying symbol of greater things, even though on inspection the actual terms of the 'Bright clauses' were not such as were likely to produce much change. The government would make loans available (up to three-quarters of the price) to purchasing tenants. However, the financial terms were not very attractive to the prospective purchasers, and in any case there was no compulsion on any landlord to sell. There was a small trickle of purchases in the following decade, but in general the 'Bright clauses' were more important for what they symbolised than for anything they made possible.

Gladstone had hoped that his land legislation would pacify the widespread unrest that the authorities had been perceiving in Ireland especially since the summer of 1869. This unrest was to a considerable extent the result of the great expectations that the prime minister himself had personified (and to a considerable extent still did). A concomitant factor was a sense of liberation from constraint, which was represented by the restoration of habeas corpus (and the accompanying feeling that any further interference with it was rendered impossible by the spirit of the age). Intimations of deep-seated agrarian unsettlement were added to the evidence of fenian reorganisation, and to uncertainty about the import of the amnesty campaign and such episodes as the election of O'Donovan Rossa. In late 1869 extra regiments were moved into Ireland and in the early months of 1870 the army — on government instructions — reconstituted the flying columns that had been used to quell insurrection in 1867.[48]

Another indication of the apprehension felt by authority at this time was provided by the explicit papal condemnation of fenianism, on 12 January 1870. The British government had been seeking this for many months and its representations undoubtedly carried much weight. However, the decisive initiative came from the Irish bishops — in Rome for the Vatican Council — when in late December 1869 they decided to request the Vatican for a condemnation. MacHale and one other bishop remained aloof from this move which was spearheaded by Cullen.[49] During the year the cardinal had resumed his verbal attacks on fenianism and had displayed considerable hostility to the activities of the Amnesty Association. He tended to reduce the confused political exuberance of the time in Ireland to the simplicity of a godless fenian conspiracy. The *Irishman* was now his *bête noire* as once the *Irish People* had been. Indeed at this time Pigott's paper was in many ways more outspoken (and more dismissive of ecclesiastical authority) than ever the *Irish People* had been. It provided, throughout the spring of 1870, a stream of arguments and sophistical posturings intended to show that the Vatican condemnation carried no weight. Cullen replied with a series of pastoral letters.[50] The solemn papal declaration that fenians were subject to excommunication caused a handful of I.R.B. members to pause, but its overall impact was predictably slight.

Conditions in the period from mid-1867, but especially from mid-1869, were conducive to an increase in activity of the kind that the police and others dubbed as ribbonism. This gave rise, especially in south Ulster, to a rash of factional conflicts, in which the attitude to fenianism (and especially to the amnesty meetings) became one of the many *casus belli*. Attempts by authority to rationalise what was happening produced references to 'ribbon-fenians' and descriptions of clashes between pro- and anti-fenian ribbonmen and between ribbonmen and fenians.[51] By late 1871 significant detachments of the 'ribbonmen' had given their allegiance to the I.R.B. on the same ideologically indifferent basis as in the mid-1860s. The principal difference was that the attachment was now on a much larger scale. Decades later John O'Leary remarked that it was easier to make a rebel, or a fenian, of an orangeman than of a ribbonman.[52] This may reflect O'Leary's knowledge of affairs before his arrest in 1865. It certainly does reflect his preoccupation in the 1890s with attacking the Ancient Order of Hibernians, which he and others (for reasons that pertained to the 1890s) were then seeking to brand with the mark of some kind of doctrinal leprosy. What O'Leary's remarks do not reflect is what had actually happened in the late 1860s and early 1870s.

The general sense of unrest ensured the renewal of the Peace Preservation Act which was due to expire at the end of the 'then next session of parliament' after 1 July 1870. The Peace Preservation (Ireland) Bill was introduced at Westminster on 17 March 1870 and enacted on 4 April 1870.[53] For the most part, the new measure repeated the features of the previous legislation, with the important addition of provisions for the suppression of treasonable newspapers. The latter were widely blamed for fomenting unrest. The prime target of the new law was the *Irishman* which had been particularly provocative, secure in the belief that Gladstone's government would never bring itself to infringe the freedom of the press. Following the passing of the act the tone of the *Irishman* became noticeably more cautious. Yet another modification of the ordinary law to meet Irish circumstances came in June 1871 with the Protection of Life and Property in Certain Parts of Ireland Act.[54] This permitted the contravention of habeas corpus principles in districts proclaimed in connection with agrarian crime. The area particularly in mind was County Westmeath with adjacent portions of County Meath and King's County where the countrywide unrest had both issued in a large number of outrages, and had been particularly persistent. The powers conferred by the act were, characteristically, used rarely and with reluctance. There were pockets of continuing ferment such as parts of Westmeath and Cork city,[55] but by and large the country was settling down again by the middle of 1871. Meanwhile, the Franco-Prussian war had thrown some interesting light on the Irish political scene.

News of the declaration of war between the two great continental powers produced an almost immediate mass demonstration of pro-French sympathy in Dublin on the evening of 19 July 1870.[56] Throughout the weeks and months that followed, innumerable gatherings up and down the country re-echoed the sentiment. The mark of the Amnesty Association may be discerned in a few of these, but only a few; most were called more or less spontaneously by ad hoc local groups, with no fenian affinities. Indeed what is most striking is how widespread the public demonstrations were, despite the absence of co-ordination. Like the many other displays of mass enthusiasm we have considered, these manifestations of francophilia must not have assigned to them any specific ideological or political content. But it is clear that the sympathy expressed for France went much deeper and extended over a much wider spectrum of Irish society than, say, sympathetic feelings for the fenian prisoners did. To put the matter plainly, the Irish catholic community identified wholeheartedly with France in the war of 1870-71 as it had done with the beleaguered papacy in 1860, with disestablishment in 1868, and (very briefly) in late 1867 with the Manchester martyrs. By comparison the MacManus funeral, the Catholic University, and fenian amnesty, while appealing to the same community had evoked only a limited enthusiasm. The role of ancient Franco-Irish links in this should not be overstated, although of course they were repeatedly cited. France was sympathised with in 1870 because in 1870 she appeared as the catholic champion facing the protestant Bismarck; and in Rome the pope was relying on French arms for his independence and safety. Cardinal Cullen displayed his sympathy for the French cause (and was subsequently rewarded with the Legion of Honour). By the late autumn, when the French garrison had been withdrawn, leaving Rome at the mercy of the Italian state, pro-French meetings merged with meetings in sympathy with the pope.

The extent and depth of the pro-French sentiment was proved by the criterion of financial subscriptions. As early as 26 July 1870 the *Freeman's Journal* carried a call for material donations and within a few weeks funds were being raised on a large scale as an expression of public sympathy with France. Substantial sums were sent to the Empress Eugénie before the collapse of the empire. On 15 September the committee in charge of the funds decided to channel its burgeoning resources into the fitting out of an ambulance corps, which eventually set sail for Le Havre on 7 October 1870 consisting of over two hundred volunteers supplied with wagons, uniforms and equipment.[57] A few days earlier the *Irishman* had admitted, ruefully, that 'Ireland had contributed more for the relief of French soldiers in one month,' than 'all Ireland and Irishmen all over the world' had subscribed in five years for the fenian prisoners' funds.[58] This is indeed eloquent testimony.

Just as Irish catholics identified with France, many Irish protestants rallied to the other side, physically challenging pro-French meetings in some places and holding their own series of demonstrations to affirm solidarity with the king of Prussia. Irish interest in the continental war, at first sight improbable and even exotic-seeming, turns out on further inspection to be simply a manifestation of familiar preoccupations. Irish catholics and protestants endeavoured to score against each other vicariously in the continental war rather as some of their successors would later do with Glasgow football teams. It would be a mistake however to think that the polarisation was as complete for protestants as for catholics. Many Irish protestants held aloof from the pro-German mood and indeed there were ardent francophiles among those enabled by education or circumstances to rise above insular perspectives.

The Franco-Prussian war had helped to switch interest from one of the two perennial Irish issues (land) to the other (religion, or more exactly, confessional rivalry). The latter was by far the more manageable, in the view of authority, and by October 1870 there was talk of the return of tranquillity. Gladstone took the opportunity to press on his cabinet colleagues and on Dublin Castle the advisability of an early release of fenian prisoners. The fact that nothing had been heard from the Amnesty Association for some months was of crucial importance: a release while the association's truculent campaign was in full spate would have been impossible. Now the government could concede something without appearing to give way to threats. The cabinet eventually agreed on 11 November to an amnesty, leaving the announcement and timing to the prime minister and the Irish government. Irish Liberals with intimations of what was afoot — including Sir John Gray — took up the prisoner question eagerly in November and December (and of course with a conciliatory manner). However, the gloss was taken off the releases by the condition attached to almost all of them (contrary to Gladstone's instincts) of exile from the United Kingdom for the term of the original sentences. Finding a watertight legal formula to provide for this took time, as did the business of persuading all the prisoners concerned to accept the condition of exile.[59] By mid-January 1871 the necessary arrangements had been made and over thirty fenian convicts had been liberated. They included John O'Leary, T.C. Luby, Jeremiah O'Donovan Rossa, John Devoy and Denis Dowling Mulcahy. After the release the government issued the report of a commission set up in the previous spring under the chairmanship of the earl of Devon to investigate the treatment of fenian prisoners. Its balanced composition ensured the credibility of the information it presented which is excellent source material for the historian. Its judgements were couched in such qualified and measured terms as to leave nobody feeling very aggrieved.[60] However the best service that the Devon commission gave had been to put the amnesty debate on ice throughout most of 1870.

The fenians emerged from jail with some feelings of gratitude towards the internationalist movement, which had given strong support to the amnesty campaign. Seeing in fenianism more possibilities than it actually possessed, Karl Marx had made a young fenian and former N.B.S.P. activist, Joseph P. McDonnell, a member of the general council of the International Workingman's Association as representative of Ireland.[61] John Devoy actually joined the International sometime after January 1871.[62] O'Donovan Rossa offered the organisation some words and gestures of thanks, but went no further. In the *Irishman* of 1869 and early 1870 there is occasional evidence of some appreciation of socialist ideas. For instance, the issue of 27 November 1869 had an editorial denouncing John Bright as 'a capitalist imbued with all the prejudices of his class' and a warning from its correspondent in Paris to beware of 'mere class revolutions' as that of 1789 in France 'which liberated only the bourgeoisie'. Some of the new breed of fenian leaders might very well have gone along with socialism if that had happened to suit their circumstances. However, reaction to the beginnings of the Paris commune showed that even the *Irishman* had very little stomach for socialism. The journal which had complained so vociferously about the way in which fenian convicts were treated in jail now urged the government of France to shoot out of hand a few of the fomentors of 'red republicanism' in that country, *pour encourager les autres*.[63]

James Stephens had joined the International, probably in 1866.[64] There was scarcely anything about it that he would have found intrinsically objectionable, and he might have devoted his great talents to it, if he could have been himself its leader. By the same token there was no possibility that he would ever accept the new I.R.B. of the supreme council. He still had admirers and followers in Ireland. Unfortunately for him, they were preponderantly of the lower ranks. The bright young men with pretensions had mostly turned against him. Yet even there he still had a friend or two: one of them actually produced a newspaper in Dublin for some months in 1869 in opposition to the *Irishman*.[65] Stephens was never for long without contacts in Dublin and he was ready to exploit any opportunity to present himself once again as a credible leader. In early September 1870, on the collapse of the French empire, he immediately cast himself as the man who could obtain the support of an incoming French republican government for the setting up of an Irish republic.[66] In the autumn of 1870 the police in Dublin saw much undeniable evidence of a revival of Stephens's party. Large meetings were held in public houses at which letters from the captain himself were passed from hand to hand. Money was subscribed in some quantity. A concert held in the Rotundo on 7 November 1870 to raise funds for Stephens realised £80. However, the situation in France soon lost all appearance of promise, even for the most devoted Irish nationalist, a serious dispute developed within the Stephens group in Dublin, and before the end of the year metropolitan police intelligence indicated that the supreme council had regained the initiative. That was not to say the Stephens group had disappeared. From some of Stephens's surviving correspondence it emerges that his followers were making very ambitious plans in 1871. And the captain himself was showing that failure had not caused him to modify his methods. In the effort to organise and recruit, his adherents found themselves quite spontaneously resorting to a committee system. Not having money to send a peripatetic agent who could counteract this development, Stephens acquiesced in it; he even issued a formal certificate to validate the work of a 'committee of reorganisation'. But, reading between the lines, his distaste for all this was manifest. In an example of his blackest tactical style he rounded off the certificate by solemnly forbidding the committee to collect money until specifically authorised by himself to do so, and in order to obviate any argument on this point he went to the extreme of saying that he was in no need of money. Stephens would have autocratic power or nothing. In one small respect he had altered his formula: he now referred to his followers as the I.R.B., and he instructed them to cherish that title.[67] Stephens retained a following in Ireland throughout the 1870s but he was limited in his use of it by lack of money: he sparkled only when he was in clover, financially, and for most of the decade he lived in Paris in conditions of near-starvation.

Declaring for Stephens seems to have been frequently a rationalisation of defection from the authority of the supreme council for one cause or another. Fr Charles ('Kit') Mullen, a very untypical Meath diocesan priest, had controlled groups of young men in the midlands since the early 1860s, in the same way as other, non-clerical, busybodies, who were referred to as 'Ribbon leaders'. For a few years in the early 1860s he had enrolled them under the banner of the National Brotherhood of St Patrick.[68] At some later date he established links with fenianism; he attended the Paris conference of June 1867 as the representative of Leinster and became a member of the first supreme council. Perhaps because his talents were not sufficiently well appreciated, he had withdrawn his allegiance from the supreme council by 1869 and was maintaining an independent organisation that may have extended as far as County Armagh. In April 1870 he was in contact through an envoy with American fenians. The following month he made peace with the supreme council, but two years later he was alleged to be still paddling his own canoe and it is not clear when a final reconciliation was achieved.[69]

The disenchantment arising from the land bill of February 1870 was an obvious cue for Isaac Butt to unveil his alternative to the alliance with Gladstone. There were others who had the same general idea. The enthusiasts and ideologues who had deliberated ineffectively on 'national organisation' a decade earlier were deliberating once again. Denis Holland was in America, Smith O'Brien was dead and The O'Donoghue remained loyal to Gladstone, but otherwise the personnel was virtually the same: G.H. Moore, J.A. Blake, O'Neill Daunt, John Martin (again writing long letters to the papers), A.M. Sullivan, Dean Richard O'Brien (launching another clerical petition every so often) and P.J. Smyth. Butt was more than a match for them but he did have to expend a certain amount of time and effort in order to get them lined up behind him. This task was considerably facilitated by the death of G.H. Moore on 19 April 1870.

Butt set out his formula for the country's constitutional future in the pamphlet *Home government for Ireland; Irish federalism: its meaning, its objects and its hopes*, published in Dublin in 1870. Its kernel was that 'England, Scotland and Ireland, united . . . under one sovereign, should have a common executive and a common national council for all purposes necessary to constitute them, to other nations, as one state, while each of them should have its own domestic parliament for its internal affairs'. Under this scheme Ireland would have its own executive, answerable to the Irish parliament. In that parliament a reconstituted house of lords would have the same powers of veto as the upper house had at Westminster. Butt's plan — which from an early stage was called 'home rule' — obviously owed much to debates about federalism that he had witnessed in the 1840s, but equally obviously he brought it forward now because his observations and reflections over the intervening years had convinced him of its wisdom, and because he believed it would attract support. On the first score he was almost certainly right. Something along the lines he was suggesting was needed to create the possibility of a satisfactory development of relations between the two islands and between the different parties in Ireland, something more sophisticated than either the union as it stood or separation. Butt's was, however, the kind of project that could be forwarded successfully only by those with executive power. As a formula for winning support — not to speak of power — it could only succeed by being misunderstood, distorted or simplified.

Both David Thornley and Laurence J. McCaffrey have quite rightly warned against exaggerating the level of protestant-conservative support enjoyed by Butt's Home Government Association at its inception in the summer of 1870.[70] Be that as it may, his overtures to the conservatives did at least disarm their opposition on an impressive scale and this in itself was a notable achievement. At the outset he also secured himself against attack by the fenians. He had a conference with two members of the supreme council in advance of the private meeting on 19 May 1870 at which the Home Government Association was founded. The I.R.B. men promised him the 'benevolent neutrality' of their organisation, and on that basis Butt promised his followers that his 'experiment' would not be 'thwarted' by the fenians.[71] The fenians were not simply repaying a debt of gratitude to Butt, defender of their prisoners and champion of amnesty. Many of the new fenian élite felt no qualms about mixing armed conspiracy with conventional political activity and they responded eagerly to the prospect of *action* on any front. G.H. Moore had been in the closest contact with members of the supreme council for more than a year before his death, endeavouring to create an alliance.[72]

As early as 1868 some fenian activists had obtained a taste of electioneering. Mark Ryan (and, no doubt, other Connacht fenians) worked for the return of G.H. Moore in the general election of that year.[73] Dublin-based fenians intervened in two constituencies. At Dungarvan they supported an anti-Gladstonian candidate in a bitter factional contest; in the two-seat Limerick city constituency Richard Pigott stood (unsuccessfully) as a candidate in a pact with a Conservative contender. The most significant aspect of the County Tipperary by-election of

November 1869 (in which Rossa was elected) was the appearance on the popular side of a local cadre independent of the clergy and capable of organising a successful campaign. They obtained useful support from outside the county but relied mainly on their own resources. The most prominent personage among them, Peter Gill of Nenagh, was not a fenian at all. At least he was not a fenian in 1865 when he stood unsuccessfully as a nationalist candidate for the county in the general election in opposition to clerically-approved and clerically-supported Liberal candidates. Without the support of either clergy or fenians Gill succeeded in obtaining over nine hundred votes. Gill was a good example of the kind of reasonably prosperous individual not receiving the recognition he felt he deserved under the existing scheme of things who was to become an important factor in the politics of the 1870s. People like him are to be found participating in, and leading, cadres of activists many of whom were fenians or ex-fenians, who entered politics not because they wanted to spread any gospel but because they needed to have something to do in public life. The supreme council in its address of January 1870 advocated that 'persistent efforts should be made to obtain control of all local bodies such as corporations, town commissioners etc.', but at the same time it instructed I.R.B. members 'to refrain from taking part in parliamentary elections'.[74] As the second Tipperary by-election approached a few weeks later, the I.R.B. leadership issued firm instructions against participation. In defiance of that, the local activists put Charles J. Kickham in nomination and campaigned to within inches of victory.[75] Meanwhile, in December 1869, supporters of the Amnesty Association, enthused by Rossa's election, had run John Martin as a candidate in a by-election in Longford, a county in which the local whig aristocracy in alliance with the priests had not been seriously challenged for over twenty years. The Martin camp drew a team of activists from all over the north midlands for what turned into one of the more bitter election campaigns of the era. The catholic clergy deployed their influence and power as tellingly as they had done in constituencies over much of the country, whenever circumstances demanded, for nearly half a century. The difference was that, as in Tipperary in 1869 and 1870, they were in conflict not with the old antagonist — landlord influence — but with a new activist élite from within their own community. In the event just over twenty per cent of the votes went to Martin in what was a high poll.

The I.R.B. members who were so much part of these new electioneering cadres can of course be seen as deviationist fenians. As against that, it should be recalled that most of these people had participated in the national petition campaign of 1860-61 or in the National Brotherhood of St Patrick in the early 1860s, before being drawn into the I.R.B. as the newest attraction of the hour. They moved on as naturally to amnesty and to home rule politics when the time was right.

The first candidate to offer himself for election on the platform of home rule was Major Laurence Knox, proprietor and editor of the *Irish Times*, and a founding member of the Home Government Association. Standing as a conservative at a by-election in Mallow on 3 February 1870 he had been defeated by eight votes. The successful candidate was unseated on petition and in the subsequent by-election on 10 May 1870 Knox presented himself as an advocate of home government; he again lost by eight votes. Six days later a home rule candidate stood in County Longford (the Liberal who defeated John Martin having been unseated on the grounds of undue clerical influence). He was a landowner of tory stock, E.R. King Harman, another founder member of the home rule movement. Despite considerable support from home rule headquarters in Dublin, he obtained no more than forty three per cent of the vote. On 18 August Harman carried the home rule flag once again, this time in a Dublin city by-election. Against the Liberal, Sir Dominic Corrigan, he again scored just forty three per cent. Not alone had he failed to win over Liberal supporters, he had not even held the Conservative vote in Dublin.

The turn in the electoral fortunes of home rule came in 1871, beginning on 17 January with a by-election in County Meath. This was caused by the death of M.E. Corbally who had been returned in tandem with Edward McEvoy in four successive general elections without any serious opposition, first in support of independent opposition in 1857, finally in support of Gladstone in 1868. The first instinct of the clergy was to find a Gladstonian to replace him and they quickly adopted one who presented himself, the Honourable George J. Plunkett, scion of an old catholic landed family. In a constituency where the electoral influence of landlords (of any complexion) had been minimal for decades past, where the tenant-right interest was especially strong, and where consequently Gladstone's land act was a source of great disappointment, the nomination of Plunkett did not evoke much enthusiasm. He might nevertheless have been returned automatically but for the intervention of John Martin who had attached himself to the Home Government Association a few months earlier.[76] In sharp contrast to what had happened when he was a candidate in Longford thirteen months earlier, the Meath clergy did not campaign against Martin; that was partially a reflection of

John Seery, Co. Westmeath, farmer. Arrested in 1871 under the West-meath Act as a so-called 'ribbon man'. (Fenian photographs, State Paper Office, Dublin Castle)

Statue of Sir John Gray erected in Sackville Street (O'Connell Street) shortly after his death in 1875. The high building on the right partially obscured by the plinth is the retail store owned by another Liberal-nationalist political magnate, Peter Paul McSwiney. In the far background on the left is the Rotundo, location of numerous political gatherings. (From a stereoscopic negative in the National Library of Ireland)

contrasts between the two counties, but it was principally owing to the changed level of the tenant-farmers' confidence in Gladstone. They showed their disenchantment principally by not voting at all in the election (the turnout was less than 44 per cent), and to a lesser extent by voting for Martin, who won by 1140 to 684. This home rule victory was not spectacular, being based on the support of less than 28 per cent of the electorate of Meath, but it was interpreted by a large section of Gladstone's Irish supporters as a cue to take to the lifeboats. In the subsequent crush on the home rule decks the newcomers pushed many of the original hands overboard.

In fact Martin's victory coincided with the increased identification — both deliberate and spontaneous — of home rule with catholic and tenant interests. Thus identified, home rule quickly became a powerful votepuller.[77] When a by-election arose in County Galway just a few weeks after Martin's victory all three candidates on offer proclaimed themselves advocates of home rule; two withdrew before the end leaving the seat to the third, Mitchell Henry. When Patrick J. Smyth was put forward as a home rule candidate for a County Westmeath vacancy in June 1871 the clergy sprang to his support so enthusiastically that the Gladstonian Liberal hopeful, J.A. Dease, withdrew in despair.[78] The introduction of home rule into a by-election campaign in the Conservative-dominated constituency of County Monaghan in July 1871 gave rise to so much confusion that Butt himself was induced at a late stage to carry the flag. He was defeated by the Conservative. Recompense came in September when he stood for a vacancy in Limerick city. A team of campaigners of the same kind as those who had supported Rossa and Kickham in Tipperary, and Martin in Longford, immediately took up the running on his behalf. The bishop and some of the priests wished to have a pro-government candidate, but the ground was taken from under them when Butt declared for a catholic university and denominational education more fulsomely than any Gladstonian could have done. He was returned unopposed. By now home rule had the support of Sir John Gray M.P. and the *Freeman's Journal*, and of John F. Maguire M.P., and the *Cork Examiner*. In October it lost the support of the *Irish Times*.

Two by-elections in February 1872 — one in Galway, the other in Kerry — confirmed the appeal of the home rule label. In Galway county it was carried by a catholic landowner, Captain J.P. Nolan. He had made amends for evicting fourteen tenants some years before by accepting the adjudication of A.M. Sullivan, John Gray and Fr Lavelle in the matter. Indignantly, almost all his fellow landlords of every complexion supported his rival, the Conservative, Captain William le Poer Trench. A small number of them succeeded in delivering their tenants' votes, but most of the voters chose to face landlord wrath rather than the rival intimidation. The priests were exceptionally active. Their determination and unanimity is not to be explained as a product of convictions about the constitutional question. They saw in the contest (indeed, they made of it) a straightforward conflict between catholic and protestant, and that perspective was sharpened by the association of Trench's family with protestant evangelising activists in the west, and by the awareness that he would, if elected, be the first tory returned for the county in a quarter century. In the event Nolan had an easy victory. While the clergy were the dominant element in his supporting group it also included a local version of the fenian-related cadres who had been in evidence in other recent by-elections. Mark Ryan later recalled marshalling car-loads of supporters of Nolan armed with cudgels.[79]

In Kerry clerical identification of home rule with catholic self-assertion was less complete. This was largely because the local bishop, Moriarty, was strongly attached to the Liberal alliance, which was represented in the contest by J.A. Dease. Moriarty, like Cardinal Cullen, hoped for worthwhile concessions from Gladstone on the university education system, with which the prime minister had still to deal. Neither prelate cared much for the likely shape — under the existing circumstances — of a Dublin-based legislature. More to the point, they felt unhappy about two kinds of people who were likely to gain political prominence even in agitating for home rule. These were, firstly, Butt's small band of upper-class protestant followers, and secondly, the fenian and ex-fenian activists. Moriarty warned the voters against the latter:

> Farmers of Kerry, beware: it is not the place of parliament that these agitators so much desire to change. It is the representation of the county that does not please them. If you give them their way you will have household suffrage and then manhood suffrage; and then your labourers and servant boys, and the journeymen of your towns, will choose your representatives and become your masters, and then . . . .[80]

The bishop's advice was undermined by a considerable number of his priests taking the opposite side. The parish priest of Ardfert, Fr O'Donoghue, was the formal proposer of the home rule candidate, R.P. Blennerhassett (a protestant landowner) at the nomination. The 'fenian' cadres were busy at work for home rule. The cause was helped by the 'benevolent neutrality' of some tory landlords. On the other side were ranged many of the clergy and most of the landowners, including The O'Donoghue, M.P. for Tralee. Money was expended freely on both sides. But the decisive factor was the attraction of home rule as the popular slogan of the hour, something that was strongly confirmed by news of the Galway by-election. In both constituencies the pro-home-rule sentiments of the unenfranchised were successfully harnessed to pressurise voters. When polling day came in Kerry, Moriarty himself deemed it wiser to abstain. In Kerry the opposing forces were more closely balanced than in Galway and while Blennerhassett had a clearcut victory, Dease was not overwhelmed.

In Galway, the defeated candidate, Trench, lodged an appeal against Nolan's return. His petition was tried by Judge William Keogh whose judgement was delivered on 27 May 1872. Nolan's victory was quashed on grounds of undue clerical interference. Much more startling than this verdict was the accompanying verbal attack on the Galway priests and on the catholic clergy in general. This was so outspoken that even many of those who agreed with it were taken aback by its tactlessness.[81] Catholic newspapers of every shade of opinion united in denunciation of Keogh. The judge was burned, drowned and hanged in effigy up and down the country, and public bodies called for his removal from the bench. Against his own inclinations Butt was forced to participate in a parliamentary attack on Keogh.[82] All of this produced a predictable counter-reaction, and when Keogh went on assizes in the summer he received expressions of support from the grand juries of various counties. The catholic earl of Granard was obliged to tender his resignation from the lord lieutenancy of Co Leitrim for criticising Keogh. The entire business was an example of spontaneous polarisation, and a reminder of where one of the really important lines of cleavage in Irish politics lay. It undoubtedly strengthened home rule as the most obvious rallying point on the catholic side, and further eroded its already greatly diminished attraction for protestants.

The home rule formula had won little support in its own right; it prospered at the hustings when it acquired connotations of the standing grievances of the catholic majority. But it is equally important to note that the formula of itself did not alienate 'nationalist' support to any extent. That is to say, the proposition that Ireland should remain subject to the crown and to the imperial parliament did not evoke the slightest popular opposition. Only a handful of ideologues expressed reservations. In the early 1870s, as for long before and long after, popular Irish nationalism was a matter of the self-assertiveness of the catholic community and of a search for material benefits, rather than a question of yearning for constitutional forms.

Chapter Seven

The Uses of Home Rule, 1873-8

After Gladstone's ecclesiastical and land legislation, and the defusing of the amnesty question in January 1871, the one major subject for Irish initiative left to the prime minister was education. In itself the education question did not arouse the deepest political feeling in the country. The catholic masses were enjoying ever-increasing access to formal schooling and churchmen had not so far succeeded in making a popular political issue of the inter-related questions of denominational education and ecclesiastical control. To say that the laity were uninterested is to say that in general the local clergy also were unperturbed. It was primarily the bishops (led by Cullen) who were agitated about the issue, which they saw as affording the occasion for their particular, and mandatory, contribution to the world-wide vindication of the prerogatives of the catholic church in the era of *Kulturkampf*. The increasingly-evident international aspect of the question rendered even more remote any chance that Gladstone might gain the consent of the radical wing of his party for concessions to denominationalism in Ireland. The definition of papal infallibility by the first Vatican council in 1870 and Pius IX's conflict with the Italian state in Rome itself, beginning in the same year, had heightened anti-catholic sensibilities in Britain as elsewhere. In Ireland the spectre of rampant ultramontanism had been raised by the case of Fr Robert O'Keeffe, parish priest of Callan, which raged through the early 1870s.[1] In essence this was an elaborate faction fight sparked off by personal animosities, but it did air substantial questions such as that of the force of catholic canon law in the country, a question which, once raised in a contentious context,

195

was bound to arouse intense emotions.

Against this background Gladstone prepared his promised legislation on Irish university education. The plan finally revealed on 13 February 1873 envisaged the abolition of Queen's College, Galway and then the setting up of an Irish National University incorporating every university institution in the country including Trinity College Dublin and the Catholic University, so that students at the latter would for the first time be enabled to earn degrees. It would, however, receive no direct endowment. Cullen tried, somewhat unrealistically, to get Gladstone to change his mind about endowment, having first obtained the backing of the hierarchy as a body for his rejection of the Irish university education bill as it stood.[2] Only two bishops dissented, one of them being Moriarty. Cardinal Manning of Westminster recommended acceptance of the proposed measure, as being the best available. The serious difficulty about the bill from Cullen's viewpoint was not simply that it failed to offer financial assistance for his favourite institution, but that if passed without amendment it would make matters much worse: Trinity College, retaining its old endowments and now part of an 'approved' national system, would be more attractive than ever before to catholics, and the hierarchy's prospects of controlling the university education of catholics might thus disappear for good. Nevertheless, it was with obvious regret that Cullen looked to the fall of Gladstone that would be the likely consequence of a vote by Irish Liberal M.P.s against the bill. By contrast, those bishops such as MacHale, and Keane of Cloyne, who were enamoured of the home rule movement were eager to precipitate the collapse of the Liberal alliance, and their encouragement helped persuade nearly forty of Gladstone's erstwhile Irish supporters to oppose, and defeat, the second reading on 12 March.[3] There might be little popular concern with the university question as such, but members in the popular catholic interest were unwilling to risk episcopal disapproval while home rulers were waiting to take advantage of any opening. The collapse of the Liberal alliance is quite rightly seen as having given a boost to the home rule movement, but it is equally true that the abandonment of Gladstone by most of his Irish supporters in the commons over the university bill was conditioned by the growing success of home rule. The Liberal M.P.s of 1860 could ignore episcopal pressure about education with impunity. By 1873 home rule (not as a policy but as the rallying cry of an alternative 'party') had induced a new sensitivity.

The defeat of 12 March 1873 destroyed the authority of Gladstone's government, and although it was re-confirmed in office within a week the likelihood of an early general election loomed large. In preparation droves of Irish ex-Gladstonians were manoeuvring with varying degrees of dignity to dress up as home rulers. With a view to absorbing and controlling this influx Butt agreed to hold a public conference on the future of the movement.[4] This met and deliberated in the Rotundo from 18 to 21 November 1873 and set up the Home Rule League in place of the Home Government Association. Butt presided over the new organisation as he had over the old; however, recent refugees from the Gladstonian alliance could feel that much more at home in the new body for having participated in its formation and influenced its orientation. It was intended that the league would create a coherent countrywide party organisation, but before any serious progress could be made with this a general election was called. This pressure of time facilitated the informal entry of a fresh band of supporters. In the general election of February 1874 a home rule candidate was anyone who described himself as such: there was no time to enforce formal requirements about adherence to the league or to the decisions of the conference.[5]

Home rule was the popular catch-cry of the 1874 general election in Ireland and it captured 60 seats, leaving 33 to the Conservatives and a mere 10 to the Liberals. (The total number of Irish seats had been reduced since 1868 from 105 to 103 with the disenfranchisement of the boroughs of Cashel and Sligo.) 'Home rule' was popular because it represented for most an assertion of Irish catholic identity (in the same way that Gladstone and disestablishment had in 1868) that was all the more attractive for its lack of definition. But behind the facade of home rule unity were various conflicts, latent and open. One of them was the factional division going back to the 1850s between Liberals and those who used to be independent oppositionists. The latter had been at a major disadvantage in 1868, but at both candidate and constituency-activist level they had been early recruits to home rule. For that reason, and because home rule was an assertion of 'independence' as opposed to co-operation with the British Liberal party, they were at an advantage in 1874. Their electioneering successes included the return of Bowyer in County Wexford, McKenna in Youghal, Conyngham in County Clare, Morris in Galway city, and, indeed, A.M. Sullivan in County Louth. But there was no question of overwhelming the other faction which was by far the larger of the two with many more candidates and would-be candidates, and much more widespread support among the clergy. To this attachment belonged almost all of the 26 outgoing Liberal M.P.s who sought re-election as home rulers. Eighteen of them were successful, and perhaps a dozen or so of the first-time M.P.s returned under the home rule banner had this same basic allegiance. Only twelve Liberals sought re-election without changing colours and only three of these were successful.

The general election of 1874 was the first in Britain and Ireland to be conducted by secret ballot. There had been some by-elections since the passing of the Ballot Act in July 1872 and the course of these provided evidence that home rule would have done well in 1874 under the old system or the new. This is not to say the ballot had no effect in Ireland, but that effect was not dramatic.[6] Especially in the countryside, the individual's loyalty remained generally a matter of public knowledge. Thus, the County Limerick contest in 1874 was notable for a ferocious clash between rival home rule factions in which mob warfare resulted in one death.[7] In any case, voting — even secret voting — is not simply the product of individual choice but also of organisation and social pressure. However, the disappearance of the moment of highest tension — at the point of voting — undoubtedly had a calming influence on the day itself. Besides, the Ballot Act provided for a large increase in the number of polling stations, something which helped to disperse the opposing forces of intimidation. By and large Irish voters, at least since 1852, had been voting in accordance with their inclinations (insofar as they had any); in future they could do so more freely and more frequently.

The Ballot Act was followed by a reduction in the number of uncontested elections. At the 1868 election 69 seats in 40 constituencies had gone uncontested compared with a mere 17 seats in 10 constituencies in 1874. The change contributed something to the success of home rule in 1874. For example, in both Wicklow and Kildare where there had been no contest for 17 and 22 years respectively, a home ruler was returned at the expense of the occupant of a 'family' seat. In Ulster the increased interest in contesting seats was most evident. At the 1868 election the seven counties of Ulster other than Cavan and Monaghan had each returned without a contest two Conservative members. In 1874 all seven were contested, Tyrone by an extra Conservative, the other six by Liberals. In Fermanagh this was the first contest since 1830, in Donegal the second contest since 1832, and in Armagh the first serious contest since 1826. The Liberals obtained very creditable results, winning the two seats in Londonderry and one in Down while coming within a few score votes of victory in Antrim and Donegal. Such Liberal achievements were made possible by an alliance of catholics and presbyterians at the polls[8] (aided of course by the fact that defiance of landlord wishes was not now as traumatic a step as before the ballot). This serves as a reminder that in taking up home rule the catholic majority in the rest of the country sacrificed the possibility of a political accommodation with the presbyterians. Butt had been imaginative – if only marginally successful – in endeavouring to win protestant interest and support, but he appears to have been thinking only of the landed tory interest, and to have been as unheeding as any southern catholic politician of the presbyterian farming and industrial elements in the north. The fact that the home rule movement was seen even if only in its early stages to be courting landlord support, made it in the eyes of presbyterians an even more dubious proposition than it would otherwise have seemed. A home rule candidate (Joseph Biggar of Belfast) had done extremely badly in a Derry city by-election in November 1872 (the first ballot election in Ireland) because the catholic voters of the city were in alliance with a section of the presbyterians under the only possible common banner, Liberalism. In the 1874 general election there was no home rule candidate in Ulster outside of Cavan and Monaghan.

David Thornley has demonstrated statistically the predominance of people from outside the landowning class among the newly-elected Irish M.P.s of 1874.[9] Of the 24 first-time members in the home rule group he classified only seven as landowners or sons of landowners. Of the seven new Liberal members all belonged to the middle class; the three Liberal M.P.s surviving from the previous parliament were all landlords, reflecting the fact that down to and including the parliament elected in 1868 a preponderance of members of all parties came from among the landed gentry. The second Irish by-election with secret voting, in Cork city in December 1872, had been won for home rule by Joseph Ronayne. He was a highly successful engineer who made a fortune in California and returned to Ireland to become a railway proprietor, and so he was a prosperous individual. There was nothing startling about such a man – rather than a landowning magnet – taking a city seat: he was replacing a newspaper proprietor, the lately deceased J.F. Maguire. What was important was that people of non-landed backgrounds began to win county seats. The most celebrated example of this in the 1874 general election was the return of W.H. O'Sullivan as a home ruler for County Limerick. O'Sullivan, an inn-keeper and farmer, was in effect replacing William Monsell, one of the landed 'quality', who had just been elevated to a peerage by Gladstone. Both Ronayne and O'Sullivan enjoyed the support of fenian-related activist groups (though, of course, they had other interests behind them also). As far as influences on voter behaviour were concerned, secret voting undoubtedly altered the balance in favour of organisation and energy as against mere deference-commanding social position, be it that of cleric or landlord. That is to say that the ballot enhanced the importance of the previously-existing cadres of eager fenian and near-fenian election campaigners. One of Butt's achievements had been to make home rule acceptable to such people. Within the home rule ranks they were most enthusiastic about candidates who, like themselves, were 'coming in from the cold'. The bond between candidate and activists could be clinched by the fenian oath. J.G. Biggar, a Belfast provision merchant, was returned as home rule M.P. for Cavan county in 1874 and had himself initiated into the I.R.B. after the election, thus acknowledging the utility of the connection. Within a short time he was elected to the supreme council and was transacting his business with that body on house of commons notepaper. Biggar's case suggests that attachment to republican ideology was not of the essence. This point is even more clearly illustrated by fenian support for the home rule candidate, Frank Hugh O'Donnell, in a by-election for Galway city that immediately followed the general election of 1874. He had quite recently given public expression to enthusiasm for Ireland's place in the empire. He was being put forward by the bishop and some priests because of his outspoken denunciations of undenominational education. His public pronouncements would not have won him fenian support; nor would the simple fact that at some point he had taken the I.R.B. oath; his real attraction for them lay in the fact that he was in socio-political terms one of their own. The son of a soldier who had risen from the ranks, O'Donnell had by some means been enabled to study at Queen's College Galway, where he had a distinguished scholastic career and excelled as an orator. Apart from this university education, he was the identical type of the young neo-fenian. He was 26 years old in 1874 and had been eking from journalism an income that in no way matched up to his self-esteem and ambition.[10] The sight of this young, penniless, upstart parading the city streets as their potential representative in parliament cannot have pleased the aristocratic catholics of Galway. His clerical mentors became aware in due course of the unwelcome characteristics of an alternativist mentality, most spectacularly when O'Donnell and some members of his clique of young supporters were discovered having meat for dinner in a city hotel on a Friday. O'Donnell won the election with 579 votes as against 358 for his only opponent, a Liberal, Pierce Joyce, but he was subsequently unseated on petition.

Perhaps the most celebrated instance of fenian involvement in elections in 1874 occurred in Mayo, in support of John O'Connor Power, who had been from 1868 one of the leading figures in the new fenian elite. In a move that illustrates well the typical mentality of that group he had taken himself in 1871, at the age of 25, to St Jarlath's College Tuam to study. Archbishop MacHale tolerated here in his diocesan college the cult — among a section of students and staff — of a rhetorical nationalism which was cover for a certain amount of fenian activity.[11] In February 1874 the ambitious O'Connor Power, fortified by three years of advanced education, sallied forth from St Jarlath's to seek a seat in parliament for Mayo as a home ruler. He may have thought initially that he would have support of the archbishop, whose diocese encompassed much of the county. In the event he found bishops and priests lined up against him. They were supporting two landed gentlemen both of whom, predictably, were also home rulers. Power withdrew, leaving in the clerical candidates, Browne and Tighe, without a contest. But the fenian machine had already been at work among the populace and the forcing out of O'Connor Power provoked some sporadic anti-clerical demonstrations in Castlebar and elsewhere. When the election was invalidated on a technicality and a new writ issued, Power and his supporters had sufficient confidence to throw themselves into the contest against Browne and Tighe. The key personalities in O'Connor Power's supporting organisation included locally-based fenians such as Thomas Brennan and P.W. Nally, and individuals from other counties, such as Matt Harris of Ballinasloe and Mark Ryan. Fenians in the north of England supplied vital financial support.[12] The contest with the clerical and landed interests was bitter and tough. At the end a mere 51 votes separated the first and last of the three candidates — Browne and Tighe. O'Connor Power, placed between them, secured the second seat and went to Westminster as the first man of no property to represent the county of Mayo.

On 3 March 1874 home rule M.P.s convened in Dublin to concert parliamentary policy. They resolved that they 'ought to form a separate and distinct party in the house of commons'. But the resolutions adopted also included some very weak-sounding phrases such as 'making all reasonable concessions to the opinions of each other'.[13] As in 1852, the attempt to create an independent Irish party in Parliament faced serious difficulties, the most insidious of them being the innate feeling of most of those concerned that the two-party system was part of the natural order. The inchoate Irish party of 1874 did not hold the balance of power (as its predecessor had done in 1852), the tories having secured an overall majority in the general election. That militated against the possibility of major parliamentary victories, but at least in the short term it should have made for prospects of more coherence than was exhibited by the 1852 party. Then M.P.s who saw themselves as essentially Liberals had deserted to help provide a new government. The large numbers of Liberals in uncomfortable home rule clothes in 1874 had no such pretext for returning to type. Nor were their principal men subject to the blandishments of office in the way that Sadlier and Keogh and company had been in the 1850s: a tory government shared the spoils with a different set of Irishmen. Butt was obviously the leader, in a way that nobody among the independent oppositionists had been in 1852. Yet, he had an essentially modest view of his function. He had neither the ambition nor the means to impose strict parliamentary discipline on followers whose only common bond was the slogan which so many of them had adopted only belatedly and opportunistically.[14]

When parliament assembled Butt moved a very moderate amendment to the queen's speech: far from demanding home rule it simply asked for an examination of Irish political dissatisfaction. As expected the amendment was overwhelmingly defeated, but the real disappointment for home rule enthusiasts was that a dozen or so of their M.P.s failed to put in an appearance to vote for the amendment.[15] Later in the session Butt obtained parliamentary time for a full debate on the home rule issue, on the nights of 30 June-1 July and 1 July-2 July. Again his approach was tactful: his motion called for the house to go into committee 'to consider the present parliamentary relations between England and Ireland'. Butt spoke most impressively, but the supporting contributions were largely disappointing, especially because they exposed blatant disagreements about the meaning of home rule. This scarcely influenced the outcome of the vote. Only ten British members went into the voting lobby in support of the motion. More dismayingly, six of the home rule M.P.s were not there: four of them had paired, while two others simply did not participate in any way.[16] Another home rule motion, two years later, produced similar results — evidence of divided opinion among home rulers, minimal support from English members even for the idea of considering change, and just over fifty Irish votes in support.[17]

From the beginning it had been clear that the parliament elected in 1874 would make no concessions to the notion of self-government for Ireland. However, the aspirations behind the home rule campaign could be satisfied almost as well by less far-reaching moral and material triumphs at Westminster on behalf of the Irish majority. Accordingly, Butt and his colleagues brought forward proposals for legislation on a wide range of issues including tenant-right, universities, local government and the franchise. The results were disappointing, as was the lack of impact of the home rulers on the government's own Irish measures, such as the Peace Preservation Act of 1875. It was lack of success on more ordinary issues rather than failure to achieve its obviously inaccessible formal object, that marked the home rule 'party' with failure and frustration. The Conservative government of 1874-80 did make very important concessions to Irish catholic demands on the education front, by intermediate school legislation in 1878, and university legislation in 1879, but these came far too late for the home rule party to draw credit or benefit.[18]

The fortunes of the home rule party in parliament greatly affected the affairs of the I.R.B. From the very beginning of the decade it appeared that the energy of the neo-fenian cadres might be as readily expended on parliamentary politics as on preparations for armed rebellion. In an endeavour to arrest a decline in morale and organisation that had already set in by 1871, a fenian convention consisting of 50 or so provincial and county officials was held in Dublin in March 1873. The supreme council surrendered its authority to the convention only to have it restored again next day, and in the evident expectation that the council would make changes in the constitution of the I.R.B.[19] The subsequent revision retained the structures and paraphernalia of a secret oath-bound society and reaffirmed the ideology of armed struggle for an Irish republic. But there was also a new element that might have been designed to turn the I.R.B. into a subordinate branch of the home rule movement. This was section three, laying down that:

> The I.R.B. shall await the decision of the Irish nation, as expressed by a majority of the Irish people, as to the fit hour of inaugurating a war against England, and shall, pending such an emergency, lend its support to every movement calculated to advance the cause of Irish independence consistently with the preservation of its own integrity.[20]

The 1873 revision also set a term of two years to all office-holding in the I.R.B., though without any ban on recurrent election. This was a major change from the 'final election' provided for in the 1869 constitution.

Section three of the 1873 constitution provided justification for I.R.B. participation in the launching of the Home Rule League later in the year. Such participation would undoubtedly still have occurred in the absence of justification on paper, but the formal provision obviously helped to smooth the way. The great home rule conference of 18-21 November 1873 was preceded by negotiations in which an understanding was arrived at concerning fenian behaviour towards the movement. The conference could scarcely have gone ahead without this: the experience of The O'Donoghue and company in the early 1860s was sufficient warning of the capacity of a small band of diehards to disrupt public movements. The eve-of-conference bargaining was largely an internal fenian matter with those favourably towards co-operation buying off the less well-disposed. One of the counters used was an alleged undertaking from Butt that if his formula did not produce results — three years was probably mentioned as the time limit — he would admit defeat and give a free hand to people with more 'advanced' ideas on vindicating Irish nationality.[21] One of the more important motions at the conference was proposed by C.G. Doran and seconded by John O'Connor Power. Such sponsorship was evidence of the much-desired fenian goodwill, but the resolution in question appeared also to carry a price-tag, proposing as it did the return at the next elections of M.P.s who 'in any emergency that may arise will be ready to take counsel with a great national conference to be called in such a manner as to represent the opinions and feelings of the Irish nation'.[22] If that were to come about the fenians, as a clique of determined activists, would be in a position to dictate the response of 'the Irish nation' to the 'emergency'. The motion was passed without its substance receiving any serious consideration because attention was distracted by a proposed amendment on a quite different topic — the level of party discipline to be expected of home rule members in the commons.[23]

It is a mistake to represent the fenian participants in home rule politics as deviationists from some established twenty-four carat I.R.B. standard. As we have seen already, Stephens in the 1860s opposed open political movements not because they offended his ideology but because he could not control them. The concept of a pure fenianism incapable of compromise with a corrupt political world is largely an invention of the 1870s. It had as a corollary a cult of physical force and that alone, which for many was, unconsciously, a cult of inaction. The most influential of the intransigents were John O'Leary and C.J. Kickham. O'Leary, like the other fenian convicts released in January 1871, was obliged to live abroad till the expiration of the period of his sentence — in O'Leary's case 1885 — but his views were eagerly sought and used in internal fenian wars of propaganda. Kickham alone of the leading fenians from the 1860s was resident in Ireland in the 1870s and by 1874 (or perhaps earlier) he was president of the supreme council.[24] Being totally deaf and almost totally blind, he was physically disposed

to intransigence rather than to action, and he was similarly inclined by temperament. Personal temperament had much to do
with the division of the leading lights of the I.R.B. into intransigents and activists. As with most political divergences,
personal inclinations were overlain by interpersonal antipathies
and further complicated by the formation of factions. Instead
of seeing the supreme council in the mid-1870s as divided
between those who were pragmatists and those who were principled in striving for the same objective, we can look upon the
I.R.B. leadership as divided between those who obtained ful-
filment from the fenian posture in itself, and those who felt
the need for action as well. Most of the latter group were prepared to countenance action over a broad band of the spectrum
running from home rule politics to terrorism. But when all has
been allowed for, the division was not ideological but factional,
and an 'intransigent' like John Daly of Limerick was ready for
anything from storming platforms to dynamiting. In 1876-77
the intransigents purged the I.R.B. leadership of home rule
supporters, the lead being taken by C.G. Doran (who had changed
his attitude shortly after the home rule conference of November
1873) with the whole-hearted support of C.J. Kickham. The
crucial date was 10 August 1876 when, after some months of
preparatory manoeuvring, the supreme council resolved, by a
majority of one vote, that all I.R.B. members having any connection with the home rule movement should 'withdraw from it
their active cooperation' within six months. In the following
year four members of the supreme council who refused to com-
ply resigned or were expelled; they were O'Connor Power M.P.,
Joseph Biggar M.P.; John Barry and Patrick Egan.[25]

The supreme council's move against the home rulers was
made with encouragement from America. From its inception
the supreme council of the I.R.B. had been cautious in its dealings with American fenianism and it refused to align itself with
either of the organisations into which the Fenian Brotherhood
had been split since 1865. Since 1867 there existed also Clan na
Gael (otherwise the United Brotherhood) founded with the
objective of creating common ground between the two wings
of fenianism, and in 1870 it established some form of rapport
with the supreme council. Scandalised by the competition for
their support the fenian convicts released in 1871 resolved to
join none of the existing organisations but to make a fresh start
themselves in the form of the Irish Confederation. In 1873
this body had collapsed and its founders had gone in different
directions. The most able and determined of them, John Devoy,
joined Clan na Gael and by the middle of the decade it was
largely directed by himself and Dr William Carroll, a Donegal-

born presbyterian resident in Philadelphia. It appears that even before Devoy came to prominence in its affairs Clan na Gael had been making serious overtures to the supreme council.[26] These bore fruit in a 'compact of agreement' between the two bodies originally proposed by the American body and ratified by the supreme council in June 1875. The basis of the agreement was financial: the supreme council needed money and Clan na Gael could provide it. But the Clan drove a hard bargain and under the terms of the compact it was entitled to get an account of how its money was spent.[27] From this bridgehead Devoy pressed ahead to bring the I.R.B. more fully under his control. That objective was forwarded immeasurably by the expulsion of the home rulers from the supreme council. They were the ones least amenable to manipulation, and O'Connor Power in particular was too able and too obviously ambitious to become a subordinate. When he visited America in the winter of 1875-76 so much antagonism developed between himself and Devoy that a vicious public row ensued.[28] In the spring of 1876 Devoy sent by way of Denis Dowling Mulcahy (who was returning from a visit to the U.S.A.) a message to Kickham in Ireland and to O'Leary in Paris. Mulcahy at this time was breathing fire at mention of O'Connor Power and the home rulers, and his mission from Devoy was undoubtedly to encourage the intransigents to push to a speedy conclusion their intensifying conflict with the home rule fenians. The purge was set in train almost at once.[29] Devoy, Carroll and Mulcahy rationalised their interest as being a matter of concern for revolutionary purity while in fact they were motivated largely by ambition and personal animosity.

Devoy's influence among Irish revolutionaries on both sides of the Atlantic was greatly enhanced when in the spring and summer of 1876 a Clan na Gael mission rescued six fenian convicts from prison in Western Australia and brought them to America on board the 'Catalpa'. Just as news of this spectacular success was riding high in the press headlines, Devoy wrote to Kickham — on 11 June — proposing a project advocated by Dr Carroll some months previously, namely the establishment of a 'revolutionary directory' with authority over both Clan na Gael and the I.R.B.; left unspoken was the obvious fact that Devoy would be all set to dominate the directory. Kickham's response was dismissive, but in little over a year he and the supreme council accepted the force of Devoy's logic.[30] The death of John O'Mahony in dire poverty on 6 February 1877 served as a reminder of the decrepitude of the Fenian Brotherhood of which he had been head centre until a week before, and of its supersession by Devoy's organisation. The bringing of O'Mahony's remains to Ireland for burial in Glasnevin provided cover for a Clan na Gael mission which steeled the nerves of the intransigents for the final stages of the purge, and no doubt promoted the directory project.

Meanwhile the authority of the Clan was being demonstrated in the U.S.A. In September 1875 O'Donovan Rossa had conceived, and in March 1876 he had launched in the pages of the New York *Irish World* (and with the enthusiastic encouragement of that paper's proprietor, Patrick Ford), a fund for the financing of terrorist attacks on English cities — the Skirmishing Fund. Recent technological developments, including the perfection of dynamite, gave plausibility to Rossa's (and Ford's) declarations about the ease of arranging such operations by comparison with the full-scale rebellion that was the more usual objective of Irish revolutionaries. A simplistic and emotive newspaper campaign brought a flood of dollars. Money and power being practically inseparable in such instances, control of the fund became an imperative for Clan na Gael. Application of the appropriate pressures brought results and by March 1877 Rossa had been forced to accept, as fellow-trustees of his fund, Devoy, Carroll, three further Clan na Gael members, and T.C. Luby (who was a member of both Clan na Gael and the Fenian Brotherhood). Over the next few years the title was changed to the 'National Fund' and Rossa was ousted from the secretaryship of the enterprise.[31]

The subordination of the I.R.B. to Clan na Gael was comprehensively illustrated when Carroll arrived on a tour of inspection in early 1878. Having spent some weeks on the continent engaged in Clan na Gael business, Carroll reached Ireland in January. Over the following four or five months he visited at least thirty Irish counties and travelled extensively in Britain examining and reorganising the I.R.B. everywhere he went. By his own account he found a sorry situation and left a much happier one behind him. The forced departures of the home rulers from the I.R.B. leadership had caused confusion in the ranks, in addition to marking a serious loss of organisational talent. Carroll claimed to have won back the allegiance of large segments that had defected in Leinster and in the north of England. Vacancies at every level of the I.R.B. officer corps were filled and existing officers were put on their toes. C.G. Doran who had spearheaded the purge was induced to resign the secretaryship of the supreme council: Carroll was not satisfied with his level of effectiveness as an organiser. He was probably to some extent taking the rap for his friend Kickham who remained on as president, despite his rather obvious physical handicaps. Carroll spent considerable time with Kickham and seems to have obtained his acquiescence in all that was

Suspected fenians arrested per 10,000 of the Catholic population, under the Habeas Corpus Suspension Act, 1866-68. (Sources: H.C.S.A. papers, State Papers Office, Dublin Castle; *Census of Ireland, 1861*)

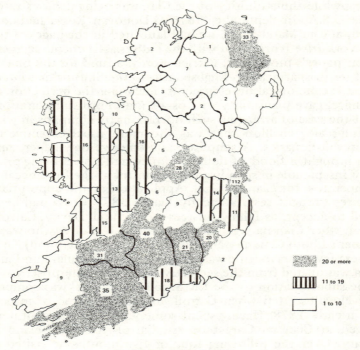

MAPS (pages 208 & 222)

These maps are presented subject to some caveats. In general H.C.S.A. prisoners were suspected fenian activists, but the thoroughness and accuracy of police information would have varied from place to place. A number of those arrested may have been trouble-makers under some other heading, and this is particularly likely in the case of County Westmeath. Nevertheless, the H.C.S.A. list constitutes a very useful country-wide sample. For the purposes of this map those prisoners who are indicated to have come from Britain or America are excluded, except where it appears that they were arrested in their native places having returned after a short exile. That leaves a total sample of just over one thousand.

The map for 1879 is based on John Devoy's report of the strength of the I.R.B. as he was leaving Ireland in the summer of that year. Although he had every reason to claim as large a membership as possible, there appear to be good grounds on which those figures can be challenged. His amazingly low absolute figure for County Kilkenny (17) undoubtedly reflects the existence of a James Stephens organisation there but it does lend credence to the document as a whole. Besides, the distribution of members as given here correspondends remarkably well with contemporary impressions. This is not to credit Devoy with unfailing accuracy: the numbers that he 'recalls' at various points in his published recollections are frequently unreliable.

done, but it is difficult not to conclude that Kickham retained his own position because he combined with his high personal standing an apparent incapacity to successfully oppose suggestions coming from Clan na Gael. Doran's successor as secretary was John O'Connor, younger brother of James. The new arrangements were wrapped up and formally approved by a meeting of the supreme council attended by Carroll in Dublin in the third week of May 1878. One of Carroll's objectives was not achieved, namely the setting up of a newspaper that would serve the I.R.B. (and the Clan) and eliminate dependence on Richard Pigott's *Irishman* and *Flag of Ireland.* However, he did return to the U.S.A. with clear ideas about the management and contributors to be envisaged for the new journal.[32]

Throughout the 1870s amnesty for the remaining fenian prisoners remained on the agenda of Irish political activists, though it never assumed the importance it had attained briefly in the late 1860s. The releases of January 1871 had greatly reduced the capacity of the movement to engage public interest. The agitation continued, however, not only because there were still fenians in prison, but because they were people outside geared towards such agitation as a pastime or way of life. For St Patrick's Day 1872 the Amnesty Association arranged processions and soirées in a number of cities and towns but the popular response was somewhat disappointing. In September 1872 the *Irishman* published a letter smuggled from Dartmoor prison by Michael Davitt, who was serving a sentence of 15 years' penal servitude for treason felony imposed in July 1870 and arising out of his smuggling of arms from England to the fenians in Ireland. Davitt complained bitterly about his treatment. He was indeed suffering the full rigours of penal servitude: the Home Office had taken a deliberate decision not to extend to him that separation from other prisoners that had been informally granted to many of the earlier fenian prisoners and that had been recommended by the Devon commission; this decision was reaffirmed by the cabinet in the wake of the publicity given to Davitt's letter.[33] Before the end of the year sympathisers with fenian convicts had switched their attention to Daniel Reddin, an Irishman just released from five years of penal servitude earned for his part in the Manchester rescue of 1867. He had a story to tell of ill-treatment and torture. A subsequent legal action of his against the prison authorities was dismissed with costs.[34]

John 'Amnesty' Nolan and his associates did not confine their collective attention strictly to the affairs of prisoners. Early in 1872 they engineered a takeover of the controlling body of the Dublin Mechanics Institute. Nolan and others spent a lengthy

period of 1873 in the north of England — by invitation — helping to organise the Irish vote there with a view to the next election. By the autumn of 1873 Nolan was back in Ireland organising a season of public demonstrations (7 September to 23
November) for Amnesty on the same lines as four years earlier.
This was as successful as his formidable expertise and the energy
of the young activist fenian cadres throughout the country
could make it. The *Irishman* claimed a combined attendance of
800,000 but the true figure may have been as low as 200,000.
To the chagrin of the Amnesty Association motions on home
rule were intruded at a number of the meetings. The truth of
the matter was that concern for the remaining prisoners was not
very deeply felt by the public in general. Although Butt and a
handful of M.P.s besides addressed meetings, the home rule
leader was obviously unenthusiastic. He had strong support from
the ranks of fenians and ex-fenians, partly because he was seen
as the prisoners' friend; reminding the country at large of that
fact was not likely to bring him much additional support and
would almost certainly alienate some whose support he was
still hoping to win.[35]

During 1874 the Amnesty Association went into irreversible
decline and its last public appearance was made in August 1875.
A month before, John Nolan had left to make a fresh start in
the U.S.A.[36] Subsequently the amnesty issue was monopolised
by a group of home rule M.P.s, with O'Connor Power to the
fore. The question was not setting the country alight, but it
provided a party starved of achievement with the prospect of a
possible success. Disraeli's government was importuned by
M.P.s' petitions and challenged by motions in the commons,
but conceded nothing until December 1877, when Michael
Davitt was released on ticket of leave. Early in January 1878
three fenian military prisoners were set free in the same fashion.
One of them, Colour-Sergeant C.H. McCarthy, sensationally
collapsed and died in the company of a group of prominent
home rule politicians and newspaper editors who were lionising
the ex-prisoners in an innocent piece of exploitation. The newspapermen ensured that McCarthy's dramatic death caught the
public imagination and was successfully linked in the public
mind with the hardships he had endured in more than a decade
of imprisonment, so that his funeral — held over till Sunday,
20 January — attracted very large crowds. McCarthy's case
almost certainly hastened the release of the remaining fenian
prisoners. They were let go in small groups and by the end of
February 1878 there was no longer anyone in prison for fenian
activities.[37]

Sergeant McCarthy's funeral on 20 January 1878 was at least

as large as Terence Bellew MacManus's, and was the subject of the same kind of enthusiastic comment in the nationalist newspapers of the time. Through historiographical accident one has been invested by later generations with a significance that neither merits. The funerals of 'rebels' might provide occasions for display, but there was no very widespread interest either in rebellion or in the ostensible objects of rebellion. There were in the middle 1870s individuals in Ireland with strong convictions about the desirability of a sovereign Irish state, and they may possibly have been more numerous than they had been a decade earlier, but they still constituted an insignificant proportion of the population in numerical terms. Most (but by no means all) of them were fenians. Conversely, most fenians had an intellectual and emotional attachment to the notion of Irish independence. However, to view the fenians simply as a communion of the separatist 'faith' would be to miss most of what is really important about them. One of the least interesting or illuminating things about most political movements is the ostensible object for which they are conscious of being banded together. Perhaps the most enlightening way to look at fenianism in the 1860s, 1870s and 1880s is to see it as a refuge and base of operations for individuals and interests within the Irish catholic community who for one reason or another felt excluded from their proper place in, or by, that community's establishment. It goes without saying that these people (in common with most of the catholic population) felt excluded from the Irish state establishment. The characteristics of the bright young men of the neo-fenian elite who dominated the I.R.B. leadership in the late 1860s and middle 1870s we have already looked at. Also entering the leadership group at national level and prominent in the cadres at local level in the 1870s were some successful businessmen, such as Joseph Ronayne, Patrick Egan (executive of a Dublin-based milling company with numerous branches and agencies throughout the north midlands and Connacht) and Matt Harris (a Ballinasloe building contractor). Whenever the history of municipal government in mid-nineteenth century Ireland is written it will reveal a small scattering of self-made men of fenian proclivities jostling with Liberals and Conservatives on town councils and commissions. (The supreme council directed in January 1870 that 'persistent efforts should be made to obtain control of all local bodies such as corporations, town commissioners etc, as a means of increasing the power and influence of the Irish republic'.[38] C.G. Doran, employed as clerk of works at Queenstown cathedral in the 1870s became a town commissioner there.) Some of these people undoubtedly found that fenianism was good for their particular businesses: as early as 1870 the resident magistrate at Castlebar observed that the profession of extreme politics was part of the stock-in-trade of Egan's company, giving an added dimension to the commercial bond between employees, agents, suppliers and customers;[39] the clerk of the Castlebar office through much of the 1870s was Thomas Brennan, one of the ablest of O'Connor Power's election workers in 1874. In general the businessmen resorted to fenianism much less for economic than for socio-political reasons: the movement offered them a leadership role that was not yet assured in conventional politics for mere talent or recently earned wealth. Even more provocative than economic deprivation is the denial of socio-political status commensurate with economic success.

Insofar as the businessmen-fenians were motivated socially rather than economically they resembled the group who had constituted the bulk of the fenian rank-and-file in the 1860s, the rebellious young men of the towns. These people were less evident in the I.R.B. in the 1870s. The reduction in their numbers was partly compensated for by the accession of a significant number of marginal rural people. The latter's motivation as we shall see, was primarily economic. Fenianism attracted all of these different kinds of people not by reason of its particular ideology, but because it happened to exist. From the 1860s being a fenian was a mode of life in Ireland in the same way as being an anti-clerical or republican was in provincial France. As we saw in the last chapter many became attached to fenianism not as individuals but as members of other groupings that often were not so much absorbed into the I.R.B. as merely affiliated to it: such group conversions are not likely to have been marked by high rates of individual intellectual commitment. Yet another element in the fenian mixture that diminishes the concept of a society with doctrine as its *raison d'être* was the mutual-aid factor. The March 1873 address of the supreme council announced that the I.R.B. convention of that month had advised (in view of the sad fact of the emigration of members) that branches be established in American cities and added that 'of course, members of the organisation would have a peculiar claim on the friendly aid of such branches.'[40] This casual presumption undoubtedly reflects some level of practice at home, though it cannot be extensively documented. However it is well worth noting that the address of the supreme council to its supporters in January 1870 advised that: 'Common sense would also point out to us the advisability of giving the preference to our friends in all our dealings; we should thus make it the interest of many at present half-hearted or indifferent to openly join the national ranks'.[41]

A return of I.R.B. membership by county that indicates the position in late 1878 and early 1879 gives a picture of very uneven distribution.[42] (See map on page 208). A total of almost 25,000 members were allocated between the provinces as follows:

Leinster	2037	(8.43%)
Munster	4798	(19.85%)
Connacht	7066	(29.24%)
Ulster	10,266	(42.48%)

The figure for Leinster undoubtedly reflected the recent temporary loss of some members to the Stephens organisation, but even at that they are startling. The geographical bias of fenian strength had altered dramatically since the mid-1860s with the focus moving from the areas of (by Irish standards) relatively advanced urbanisation to the region of north Connacht and south Ulster — more or less the old 'ribbon' territory. This reflects the persistence of the attachments set up in the late 1860s and early 1870s when so many 'ribbon' societies were affiliated to the I.R.B., but more than that was involved: for instance the I.R.B. was now very strong in Mayo where ribbonism had not been widespread. The ethos of this agrarian fenianism had crystallised in the period 1868-70 when perennial hopes of a new order on the land received a fresh boost from Gladstone's promise of an Ireland governed in accordance with 'Irish ideas'. The 'idea' dominant among the smallholders of the west was secure tenure of more land with lower rents. In the air of unrest that pervaded the country in the spring of 1870 the resident magistrate at Castlebar dismissed an alarmist report that County Mayo was on the brink of rebellion; on the contrary, he insisted, there was no sign of anyone being about to strike for an Irish republic but every indication of an agrarian movement, unorganised but exceedingly widespread. Its programme was 'fixity of tenure, valuation of rents and the breaking up of the consolidated territorial farms'; farmers with live stock and more than fifty acres of land felt threatened, though such people generally dissimulated their fears.[43] No doubt smallholders throughout the country dreamed the same dreams as those in Mayo, but only in Connacht and South Ulster did such people outweigh in social terms both the substantial farmers and the landless labourers. With cattle prices rising faster than corn prices the inexorable agricultural trends of the age were increasing the comparative disadvantage of small farms. Every year tens of thousands of western smallholders and their sons migrated to Britain for seasonal work with the proceeds of which they supplemented the grossly inadequate incomes from their farms.

In the late 1860s and early 1870s O'Connor Power, Mark Ryan, Matt Harris, Patrick Egan and other activists, building on the work of Edward Duffy in the mid-1860s, had considerable success in presenting fenianism to the marginal farmers of North Connacht, south Ulster and north Leinster as the means of achieving agrarian ambitions. Kickham and O'Leary might cherish platonic ideals about sovereignty and independence but the segment of their following that was expanding most successfully was motivated by land hunger and cared little if anything about broader political questions. Here once again we can see the I.R.B. attracting followers not because of its ostensible nationalist/republican objectives but because it happened to be available to provide a rallying point for people with other preoccupations altogether. The I.R.B. organisation everywhere suffered a decline in the mid-1870s, especially in connection with the banishment of home rulers from the supreme council. William Carroll on his tour in 1878 was particularly successful in restoring the organisation in Connacht, south Ulster and north Leinster. Indeed, so successful was he that the government began to receive reports in April 1878 of a supposedly new 'fenian-ribbon society' in the west. Carroll had reorganised western fenianism but he had not altered its character: he himself adverted to the fact that the great majority of fenians in Connacht and Ulster were 'farmers' or sons of 'farmers'.[44] These people were just as likely to participate in a public agitation as in an oath-bound conspiracy, given the appropriate leadership. Matt Harris had provided this in his own area when (with others) he launched the Ballinasloe Tenants' Defence Association in 1876. At Sunday meetings in neighbouring parishes platform speakers denounced landlords and graziers. Because of the predominance there of smallholders any popular movement on the land question in Connacht was bound to threaten not only the rights of landowners but also the actual distribution of land between the tenants. Those who stood to lose in a redistribution — large and small landlords, graziers, and substantial farmers — carried little numerical weight. But this category included a considerable number of catholics, many of them closely linked to the clergy. Not surprisingly, therefore, the priests were reluctant to initiate a land agitation movement; but one having once started, they had no choice but to give it their support, as indeed happened with the Ballinasloe agitation in 1876 and 1877.[45] The reluctance of the clergy explains the poor response to the repeated calls of James Daly of Castlebar in the leader pages of his *Connaught Telegraph* for a public agitation of the land question. This clerical refusal to vocalise popular feelings on the land provided Connacht fenian leaders with a ready opening. It was not so much fenian principles of secrecy that prevented them from initiating public agitations, as the difficulty of doing so without clerical co-operation. When they could do so they did, as in the case of Harris at Ballinasloe, and of O'Connor Power's regular speaking tours of his constituency after his election to Westminster in 1874.

The balance of agrarian interests was significantly different in the north-east and over most of Leinster and Munster. As in Connacht, the dominant ethos was that of farmers, but of farmers with something to lose, with much larger average holdings and living among a much larger proportionate number of landless labourers than was to be found in Connacht. They had an unchanging interest in the reduction of landlord rights but only in a manner that posed no general threat to property. The purely economic incentive for a tenant-right campaign was at its lowest in the early and middle 1870s as Irish agriculture went through a period of very general prosperity. Nevertheless, farmers' clubs were active in many counties to an extent not seen a decade earlier. The 1870 land act had confirmed the possibility of special agrarian legislation for Ireland, and there was no logical reason why there should not be further concessions to dominant Irish interests. Besides, the 1870 act proved to be an irritant in some respects. The Ulster custom as legalised did not always operate as beneficially as expected. Tenants with leases for periods in excess of thirty one years were excluded from many of the benefits of the act, which prompted many landlords to force leases on their tenants, thereby compelling the latter to contract out of rights to compensation for disturbance and improvement. Within weeks of the general election of 1874 Isaac Butt introduced in the commons a bill to mend the deficiencies — from the tenants' viewpoint — of the 1870 legislation. It came to nothing.[46] A conference of representatives of dozens of local tenants' associations was held in Dublin in February 1875 with the purpose of preparing a land bill for the next session of parliament. Butt was one of sixteen home rule M.P.s who attended the conference; however, the bill was formulated without adequate consultation and was not introduced. In March 1876 Butt produced another land bill of his own which was defeated heavily on its second reading in the commons on 29 June.

Tenant pressures on landlord resources were manifestations of fundamental structural factors in nineteenth-century Irish affairs, but there was nothing happening in the mid-1870s that made a landlord tenant crisis inevitable. Similarly there was nothing in the political life of the period that can be convincingly interpreted as presaging (much less requiring) the mobilisation of the Irish catholic populace into the most impressive explicitly nationalist movement the country had witnessed since the 1840s. However, those addicted to the historiography of ineluctable nationalist progress can satisfy themselves with various supposed intimations of things to come, such as the election of John Mitchel as M.P. for Tipperary in 1875, the determined use of so-called 'obstruction' tactics in the commons by a section of the home rule party, the repudiation by some home rulers of Disraeli's imperial policies or the expression of 'advanced' nationalist views at the O'Connell centenary celebrations in August 1875.

John Mitchell was returned unopposed in a by-election in February 1875 having been nominated by fenian activists. He was shortly afterwards declared incapable of entering parliament, as an undischarged felon. In the subsequent by-election he was again a candidate and was opposed by a Conservative. In the polling, on 11 March, Mitchel had a comfortable majority. Nine days later he died. Mitchel's election is the kind of event that fits all too easily into a myth of manifest national destiny and ever-burning popular zeal for the patriotic. In fact the turnout was low and only thirty per cent of the registered voters actually came out and voted for Mitchel. On the same day in a by-election at Stoke-on-Trent the successful candidate was E.V. Kenealy who had been 'disbenched, disbarred and removed from the list of Queen's Counsel' for his scandalous conduct in the notorious Tichbourne case. He was of such ill repute in decent society that – unprecedentedly – not even one member of the commons was to condescend to perform the immemorial formality of introducing him to the speaker.[47] Yet he received six thousand votes in Stoke-on-Trent. By comparison the voters of Tipperary had been amusing themselves in a quite harmless fashion in returning the ageing and by then totally innocuous rebel, John Mitchel. Kenealy's election cannot be represented now as evidence of the inevitable rise to power of populist charlatanism in England. The course of events over subsequent generations do make it possible to see Mitchel's election as part of a larger pattern. But giving a teleological interpretation to Mitchel's election in this way is as great a distortion of historical understanding as if Kenealy's election were to be given similar weight and significance.

The culmination of the O'Connell celebrations was a great public meeting in Dublin's Sackville Street on 6 August 1875. The attendance which filled the street and surrounding thoroughfares amounted to the scores of thousands that all great popular

occasions regularly attracted. Patriotic oratory was taken for
granted on such an occasion but the precise shades of platform
opinion were of no interest to the massed audience. It so happened that the organisation of the centenary celebrations had
been in the hands of the lord mayor, Peter Paul McSwiney,
a Liberal who, like Cardinal Cullen and some other prominent
catholics, had never gone along with home rule. A contingent
of fenian amnesty activists heckled McSwiney during his
address and jostled him as he left the platform. Subsequent
speakers, including Butt, A.M. Sullivan and John O'Connor
Power, attacked McSwiney, with varying degrees of directness,
for allegedly emphasising O'Connell's work as emancipator at
the expense of his endeavours to undo the union. The conflict
was a matter of faction, not of ideology: McSwiney's principal
ally was P.J. Smyth M.P. who had seceded from the home rule
grouping in parliament shortly after the general election and
had begun to denounce Butt's movement for the incomplete-
ness of its nationalist objectives, in that it aimed at something
less than repeal of the union. After the O'Connell celebrations
McSwiney, with Smyth's support, endeavoured to launch a new
political movement. The home rule leadership crushed his
efforts without too much difficulty.[48]

The home rule 'establishment' was well able to prevent the
emergence of a rival; 'home rule' continued to be, as at the
1874 general election, the key to success at by-elections in
predominantly catholic constituencies. Yet the depth of the
movement's popularity was limited. It did not stir the masses
profoundly and it had no success in setting up any mechanism
that might have had that effect, despite an attempted plan
vigorously promoted by Butt in 1874 for a national roll of up
to 100,000 supporters paying one shilling subscription each.
The intention of emulating the repeal movement was obvious,
but the project was a total failure; three decades after O'Connell's
death there was nothing in being comparable with the Repeal
Association.[49] The contrast with the O'Connell era was further illustrated in 1875 when some of Butt's associates set on
foot a testimonial fund for the benefit of their leader. It was
not a success, largely because chapel gate collections were not
allowed by the catholic bishops; this no doubt reflected some
enduring episcopal antagonisms towards the home rule leader,
but the important point is that the collections could not have
been denied if there had been a great groundswell of popular
interest. Enthusiasm for home rule was more apparent and
better organised among the Irish in Britain where the Home
Rule Confederation was a vibrant social movement continuing
the earlier public role of the I.R.B., which organisation it had

largely incorporated.

The parliamentary leadership of home rule split in two in 1877 on the issue of tactics in the commons. A small group of M.P.s, ignoring the wishes of Butt, pushed beyond the hitherto accepted limits a policy of 'obstruction' of parliamentary business.[50] They included O'Connor Power, Biggar and Frank Hugh O'Donnell (returned for Dungarvan in a by-election in January 1877), but the most striking of them was Charles Stewart Parnell, elected for Meath in April 1875 on the death of John Martin. Obstruction was seen inside and outside the house as retaliation against the government for its blanket dismissal of the Irish party's motions and legislative proposals, and as such it was calculated to win support in Ireland. It was also a highly effective means of gaining coverage in the newspapers. The interest and support generated by their tactics did not prove sufficient to win for the obstructionists that control of the home rule party which they clearly sought. Butt refused to give way or even to compromise, and he easily retained the support of the majority of home rule M.P.s, not because they had any reason to be happy about his performance but because they found the obstructionist policy distasteful. A home rule conference held in Dublin on 14 and 15 January 1878 failed completely to heal or resolve the conflict.[51] By the parliamentary session of 1878 the ex-Liberal (or crypto-Liberal) element among the home rule M.P.s appears to have been largely disillusioned with the whole business of an independent party, if one is to judge by their voting performance. It was now clear that the party of 1874 would be divided against itself at the next general election. The reversion of the ex-Liberals to their former colours would have been a logical development. Yet, the home rule slogan had acquired a measure of popular acceptance that made it difficult to discard without having something to put in its place.

From some date in 1877 Gladstone had been envisaging the prospect of a revival of Irish Liberal fortunes. John Vincent has shown how the former prime minister resumed interest in Ireland in that year as part of the process of re-establishing himself 'as a Liberal leader'.[52] In October-November 1877 he paid his first ever visit to the country. His speeches in (and on) Ireland at this period amounted to tacit overtures to home rule politicians to rejoin the Liberal fold, with intimations of local government reforms to satisfy the demand for 'home rule'; in private correspondence he was quite explicit about seeking a *modus vivendi* with the home rulers.[53] A stay of nearly four weeks gave him time for lengthy visits to the houses of the whig nobility: he spent six days with the duke of Leinster. There was extensive and hectic sightseeing in the Dublin area. And then there was the touching of the strings of popular feeling. In this respect he had notable success. He felt warmly welcomed by all those he encountered including the catholic clergy he met on visiting Maynooth College and other institutions. Cardinal Cullen received him, in spite of the ex-prime-minister's diatribes against the papacy (issued in 1874 at a time when he thought he would never again be counting on the support of ultramontanists). There was contact with organised farmers. However, the tokens of popular support were noticeably fewer and more limited than those bestowed on Bright (acting as Gladstone's *alter ego*) eleven years earlier. In November 1877 Gladstone had opened up the possibility of recapturing Irish catholic support, but all still remained to be played for. One of his more predictable ploys would be some kind of undertaking on the educational front that the bishops could not pass up. When the tories legislated in 1878 on Irish intermediate education and in 1879 on Irish university education along lines that were acceptable to the catholic hierarchy they were bringing to fruition some years of solid work by their Irish ministers; but they were also pulling the rug from under Gladstone's feet in very neat fashion.

Imperial and foreign policy questions throw at least a little light on Irish political attitudes — in parliament and elsewhere — in the years 1876-8. What emerges cannot be justifiably invested with a simplistic significance. That danger scarcely arises in the matter of Disraeli's proclamation of Queen Victoria as empress of India in 1876. While Parnell, Biggar and Butt abstained, two dozen or so of those home rule M.P.s usually regarded as possessing dubious nationalistic credentials actually opposed this manifestation of the imperial spirit. They were not so much taking a principled stand as voting with their Liberal friends. There was a widespread belief that the proclamation would be followed by a release of prisoners including the remaining fenian convicts; Parnell and Biggar would be seeking credit for the fenian releases and so did not wish to be seen voting against the associated measure.[54] Anti-imperialism was a card to be played at convenience: the South Africa bill of 1877 was made the occasion of the most celebrated episode of the 'obstruction' campaign.[55]

The international tension generated from 1875 onwards by Russian advance in the Balkans reached crisis-point in 1878 when Disraeli seemed fully set for war in defence of British interests and the status quo. An issue like this was capable of exposing one of the fundamental ambiguities in the home rule movement: was it the expression of a local patriotism subordinate to support of the United Kingdom and the empire, or of a full-blooded nationalism? Butt and Frank Hugh O'Donnell strongly supported the government in a commons debate on eastern policy in July 1878. David Thornley believed that this pro-imperial line so offended instinctive popular feeling in Ireland that it automatically damaged both men politically. It was certainly used against them, and especially against Butt, for the purposes of internal party rivalry.[56] However, insofar as there was widespread popular feeling on the matter in Ireland that owed less to nationalist instincts than to Gladstone's calculated and highly orchestrated exposure of infidel Turkish atrocities against Balkan Christians. That is to say that Irish popular opinion on the subject was moved in much the same way as British popular opinion. There is no clear-cut evidence for the existence in Ireland on a large scale of an anti-imperial attitude that was stronger than or qualitatively different from the anti-imperial posture of British Liberal parliamentarians in 1878. Only nine home rulers actually voted against Disraeli and 'jingoism' while sixteen supported the government and the majority abstained.

In the years 1876-79, as twenty years earlier, the possibility of war with a major power hung in the air. Considerable tensions ensued, but they were not on a level with those that produced the volunteering movement of 1859: Russia simply did not pose the same kind of immediate threat that Napoleonic France could. In Ireland very few people either hoped or feared that the threatening war would provide 'Ireland's opportunity'. However, the leadership of Clan na Gael made a determined effort (through the Russian embassy in Washington) to interest Russia in the possibilities of Irish disaffection.[57] This overture appears to have received little encouragement and the same was true of an approach to the Spanish government with a view to a joint Spanish and fenian assault on Gibraltar.[58] But William Carroll was still thinking in such strategic terms when he visited Ireland in early 1878. He had been to Madrid en route. There is good reason to believe that his success in reorganising the I.R.B. at this time owed much to his evocation for the small farmers of the west of the expectation of imminent international war.[59] That was the illusion on the strength of which the I.R.B. had been originally launched. The vision of an Irish-American filibuster had lost credibility in 1867, though Carroll still had one in mind. No matter how much trouble the Russians might make for Britain in the east, scarcely anybody could expect them to land in Ireland, as the French had been confidently expected to do at various times in the past. The 'opportunity' that could most plausibly be expected to arise from an Anglo-Russian war was the reduction of British army strength in Ireland as forces were drawn off to the theatre of conflict. This the Connacht fenians envisaged as giving rise to consequences that would be in the first instance economic and localised (reduced rents and division of grazing lands) rather than political and national.[60]

Throughout the 1870s and most of the 1880s James Stephens continued to uphold his claim to be the rightful autocrat of the Irish revolutionary movement, and he maintained his contacts in Ireland, England and America. In the early 1870s he made his only serious attempt at setting up in a regular business. This brought him to New York in September 1871 as partner in, and agent for, a French-based wine firm. The venture was foundering within a year in debt and confusion. Stephens eventually extricated himself by June 1874 when he returned to France, exchanging penury in New York for equal but more tolerable penury in Paris.[61] He had made no impact on Irish-American politics and he left behind no more than a handful of supporters. There was an unexpected accretion of American support within less than two years when the Fenian Brotherhood began to make friendly overtures, in effect recognising Stephens as the head of the 'home' movement. This was done in the hope of counteracting the 'compact of agreement' whereby Clan na Gael had secured an alliance with the supreme council in Ireland. After having disregarded Stephens for years, the Fenian Brotherhood now turned to him as the only one who could prevent its archrival, Clan na Gael, from totally annexing fenianism in Ireland. The support of the Fenian Brotherhood did enable the Stephens party briefly to improve its fortunes in Ireland, and especially in Leinster, where up to several hundred may have defected from the supreme council by early 1877. Clan na Gael took the threat seriously enough to open their own negotiations with Stephens. William Carroll called on him in Paris in December 1877 (on his way to Ireland) to discuss co-operation. The essence of Stephens's response was consistent with all he had done and said for twenty years and can scarcely have surprised anyone: he would support no movement unless he was himself its supreme head. This blunt refusal served Carroll's purpose better than any cooperative talk would, for it enabled him to argue in Ireland that Stephens had spurned a reasonable offer and was interested only in self-aggrandisement. Along with Clan na Gael money, that argument helped Carroll to bring at least a good proportion of the recent defectors back into the fold of the supreme council.[62] With its affairs in ever-deepening decline, the Fenian Brotherhood eventually, in an obviously desperate gamble, brought Stephens to America to assume the leadership of their organisation. He arrived early in 1879 and remained for less than a year.

He was out of his time and out of his depth. Even with Stephens at the helm the Fenian Brotherhood was by now only a pathetic sideshow to the centre-stage activities of Clan na Gael. And meanwhile in Ireland political life was moving into a new phase, yet a further stage on from the brief interlude in which Stephens had seemed to hold sway.

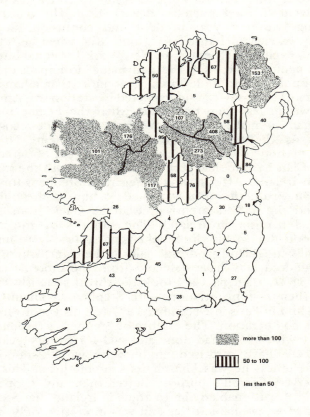

Adherents of the Supreme Council I.R.B. per 10,000 of the Catholic population, Summer 1879. (Sources: Devoy papers (N.L.I., MS 18036); *Census of Ireland, 1881*) See note on p.208 above.

Chapter Eight

A Different Revolution, 1878-82

Making all due allowance for differences of scale and scope, the land war of 1879-1882 is to Irish history rather as the revolution of 1789 is to French history. The resemblance has been highlighted in the past decade or so by a spate of stimulating publication and debate on the background, origins and socio-economic implications of the land war. Another, and far less fortunate, point of comparison is that both episodes have been invested in popular perception and in generations of historiography with a quasi-mystical aura which distorts understanding. Thus, even the clinical and dispassionate writings of recent years on the land war are liable to be suffused in the minds of many readers with the warm glow of old assumptions about this being a highlight of the ever-onward march of human liberty and progress in their Irish manifestations.

Alfred Cobban as part of his contribution to the demythologisation of the French revolution described it as coming like a fall of snow on blossoming trees. Floral metaphors may be inappropriate for Ireland in the 1870s, but the same general point is applicable: examined objectively the land war looks less like salvation and more like disaster. Landlords and tenants had been coping for decades with a secular change in their collective relationship — one that favoured the tenants. As W.E. Vaughan has shown, overall rent increases since the early 1850s had fallen far behind the increase in the value of agricultural production, thus leaving the greater share of the extra agricultural income of the period with the tenants.[1] However limited its practical benefits, the 1870 land act had shown that parliament could

223

be persuaded to change Irish land law in the perceived interest of tenants. Despite the incompatibility of the farmers' way of life with active participation in politics, their social and economic weight was not without its impact on political life, as was shown by the willingness of landlord parliamentarians at least to affect interest in their particular concerns. The general election of 1874 saw the return of two members who could be classified as tenant farmers (although they did have petty commercial interests also).[2] It was apathy tinged with deference rather than deference itself that kept the farmers from wresting control of the boards of poor law guardians from the landowners.[3] Looking at the country overall, and making allowances for regional and local variations, it can be said that while the landlord-tenant relationship in the mid-1870s left much to be desired, it was not self-evidently doomed to disaster. The auguries were for the continuation of conflict, but within the boundaries of convention and politics. The onset at the end of the decade of a severe agricultural recession, drastically reducing the income pool from which both classes drew a livelihood, was certain to increase tension. Unlike the comparable crisis of the early 1860s this one could be expected to have political repercussions, if only because of the implications of the Gladstonian concessions of 1868-70. As it happened, the crisis of the late 1870s gave rise to a form of civil war that incorporated, but went far beyond, conventional politics and poisoned both social and economic relationships. This was no inevitable progress, but rather the result of initiatives by élites and individuals endeavouring to use the crisis for their own purposes. Here various fenian agents and agencies were prominent, and especially Michael Davitt.

From his release in December 1877 Davitt displayed an insatiable appetite for public affairs.[4] He was quickly admitted to the supreme council of the I.R.B. as representative for the north of England. Here was evidence of the esteem in which he was held by many fenians and also of his own unchanged attachments. Within a short time he was displaying symptoms of that leaning towards parliamentary politics for which leading men had so recently been expelled from the supreme council. He had been in contact immediately after his release with a number of M.P.s, including O'Connor Power, F.H. O'Donnell and Parnell. On a whirlwind visit to Ireland in January 1878 he had met Matthew Harris of Ballinasloe — O'Connor Power's replacement on the supreme council, and as enthusiastic as his predecessor for cooperation with parliamentarians. Perhaps more decisive than individual contacts was his experience of fenianism in Britain in the spring and early summer of 1878 as he travelled up and down the country to attend and address functions in support of amnesty for those fenians still in prison. Fenianism in England and Scotland was inextricably identified with the Home Rule Confederation of Great Britain, which had elected Parnell as its president in August 1877 in a gesture of support for his obstructive tactics in parliament. In this environment Davitt grasped that the ideological purity preached by the supreme council was not a marketable commodity. He displayed his acceptance of that fact by calling in his public speeches for harmony and understanding between 'honest home rulers' and 'nationalists'. This brought him a public rebuke in June 1878 from Richard Pigott (in the columns of his *Flag of Ireland*), acting as expounder of the official supreme council line.[5]

By this time the supreme council purists had reason to be on the defensive. The Clan na Gael people who had virtually forced Kickham and company into making a principle of intransigence, were now themselves taking an interest in the parliamentarians, especially in Parnell. The *volte face* was gradual. It had begun in August 1877 when Parnell and Biggar were interviewed by J.J. O'Kelly, a member of the neo-fenian elite of the late 1860s and, since the early 1870s a New York journalist and Clan na Gael activist.[6] O'Kelly strongly advised Devoy to take a positive view of Parnell and his line of parliamentary policy. The result was that when William Carroll crossed the Atlantic at the end of 1877 as Clan na Gael envoy he had instructions to make contact with Parnell. They met in Dublin in January 1878, and again in London in March, with a wider circle of interested parties present on the latter occasion.[7] In all of this Parnell's purpose was to tap the energy of potentially useful activists, successfully conveying the impression that he shared their dreams without actually committing himself in any way. When Biggar wished to fasten his fenian support in 1874, he had joined the I.R.B. and so had become enmeshed in its internal conflicts.[8] By contrast, Parnell in the years 1877-79 won the admiration of key fenian personalities without compromising himself. And he may have sensed that they were far more desperately in need of lifelines than he was.

Parnell's reward for his adroit conduct of this game of nods and winks was Devoy's offer of fenian support, in the celebrated 'new departure' telegram of October 1878. The details of this exceedingly complicated episode have been clarified by T.W. Moody in a masterpiece of historical reconstruction.[9] From this it appears that the offer was unsolicited. It was, of course, a conditional offer, but it was made publicly and without any attempt to extract from Parnell prior agreement to the conditions. Devoy was not so much bargaining with Parnell as throwing himself on the parliamentarian's good will. It is also possible to detect an element of over-eagerness in the supposed occasioning of the offer: Devoy rushed off his telegram on hearing that the Home Rule Confederation of Great Britain, meeting in Dublin on 21-22 October, had re-elected Parnell as its president. That event turned out to have no new significance. Why was Devoy so eager?

William Carroll had returned from Europe in the summer of 1878 leaving the I.R.B. in the kind of condition it had not known for many years, and apparently under secure Clan na Gael control. Maintaining that machinery intact must have been Devoy's principal concern in subsequent months, and that could only be achieved by activity or the early hope thereof. The prospect of Anglo-Russian war had helped Carroll's work considerably, but Devoy knew it was not going to galvanise the organisation indefinitely. Twenty years' experience had demonstrated that fenian organisation would rapidly disintegrate or metamorphose unless guided by pillars of cloud and fire. In 1878 spontaneous disintegration would be exacerbated by the inroads of a clique of ousted leaders keen on cooperation with home rule — O'Connor Power, Barry, Egan and Biggar; the situation would be even more perilous in Britain than in Ireland. Realistically, the only thing for Devoy to do was to lead his united forces into the field of conventional politics before others took them there in batches. Though ostensibly made on behalf of American fenians, the offer to Parnell was equally intended to include the I.R.B. For someone in Devoy's situation the two theatres of action were closely interdependent. If he were seen to be managing I.R.B. involvement in a worthwhile venture in Ireland his influence with Irish-Americans would be further enhanced.

Parnell's new style of parliamentarianism gave Devoy a pretext for abandoning the 'intransigent' policy of which he had been making so much a bare two years before, but he still needed a supply of appropriate rhetoric with which to justify the change. He was ably assisted in developing this by Michael Davitt, who arrived in America on 4 August 1878 primarily in order to visit his family.[10] He, too, was looking for a formula for deliverance from the strait-jacket of intransigence, though his concern was more immediately personal than Devoy's. He was barely eight months out of prison and was in search of a lifestyle. Since his release he had become a public personality and he loved the experience. He could hope to earn a living on the platform, whereas intransigence would condemn him to dig or beg and for such he was physically and temperamentally unfitted. In a fascinating dialogue-by-speechwriting spread over a period of weeks in the autumn of 1878, Davitt and Devoy resolved their common problem.[11] Their principal formulations were reflected in the conditions of Devoy's telegram offer to Parnell, which may be summarised thus: federalism to be discarded in favour of a simple demand for self-government; vigorous agitation for peasant proprietorship; avoidance of purely catholic issues; and disciplined and energetic action by M.P.s at Westminster.[12] The emphasis on the land question was Devoy's doing and it was almost certainly designed to minister to perennial Irish-American sensibilities (and was not the consequence of any awareness of impending economic crisis in Irish agriculture). Nothing else about Ireland set the hearts of Irish-Americans thumping as the agrarian question did, and there was no issue that they simplified more grossly. By spelling it out, Devoy was simply disarming potential critics on his side of the Atlantic with the reassurance that in the new strategy the hated Irish landlord would still be fair game, in the way taken for granted whenever Irish-Americans thought of Irish self-government. There were other themes, too, in the rhetoric of new departure that were not touched on in the formal communication but were spelled out in speeches and letters to the press. One was the insistence that physical force was not being abandoned. ('Alike in the spirit and in the letter, the message of Davitt's speeches in America was that both open agitation and secret preparation, both constitutional action and physical force, would be necessary to free Ireland.')[13] Another regular theme was the need for a tolerant attitude to those 'honest Irishmen' who, while not being separatists, were not 'West Britons' either.[14] And another of these rhetorical glosses (all of which, no doubt, were as important for Devoy's and Davitt's personal peace of mind as for defence against the criticisms of their opponents) concerned the withdrawal from Westminster to Ireland, at some critical juncture, of the fenian-supported parliamentarians.[15]

Devoy took for granted that the I.R.B. was in his pocket and that he could act over the heads of that body's official leaders. He soon discovered that some members of the supreme council were not prepared to go along with unpalatable policies, no matter how the cards might be stacked in Devoy's favour.[16] And resentment against the Clan na Gael leader's highhandedness compounded serious reservations about the content of his proposals. The executive of the I.R.B. joined with the Fenian Brotherhood and James Stephens in denunciation of Devoy, using the very rhetoric of the untouchability of parliamentarianism to which Devoy himself had given so much credence in his vendetta against O'Connor Power. At an important meeting

of the supreme council held in Paris, 19-26 January 1879, Davitt
and Devoy tried, and failed, to have the 'new departure' accepted.
Fenian support for a parliamentary party was ruled out, as was
participation by fenians as such in parliamentary politics.[17]
Nevertheless, the supreme council could not deny their organisation's practical subservience to Clan na Gael, and, accordingly,
Devoy, as envoy of the Clan, was readily granted permission to
do a thorough tour of inspection through the I.R.B. In the late
spring and summer of 1879 he travelled widely in Britain and
Ireland, consolidating Carroll's work of the year before. If the
matter were to be put to the test there would scarcely be any
doubt but that the I.R.B. organisation would prove to be more
amenable to Devoy's influence than to that of the supreme
council. But neither the supreme council nor Devoy could prevent the bulk of fenians from being drawn into a congenial
public movement, especially an agrarian one, the numerical
strength of the I.R.B. being, as Carroll had reported, concentrated among the landhungry smallholders of the west.
Devoy had lengthy discussions with Parnell at Bologne in early
March and again in Dublin (with Davitt also present) on 6 April
and 1 June 1879. Devoy was endeavouring to extract concessions
from Parnell (those spelled out in the new departure telegram)
in return for fenian support, but he could neither deliver official
I.R.B. support to the parliamentarian nor deny him I.R.B. rank-
and-file support. Parnell did not need to concede anything, but
the goodwill of the Clan na Gael leader was worth having:
fenian support would obviously come much more resoundingly
with his approval; and then there was American money to consider. So, Devoy was treated to nods and winks and apparently
meaningful silences, and he returned to America in July 1879
beaten hands down at the political game but with his dignity
intact.[18] While Devoy was eager to have the land question agitated as part of a new open campaign with essentially separatist
final ends, Davitt came during 1879 to value the agrarian issue as
worthy of being agitated in its own right. So, T.W. Moody sees
the new departure of October 1878 being 'overshadowed' during
1879 by another new departure spearheaded by Davitt.[19]
    The agricultural recession of the late 1870s[20] led to a break-
down in the conventions of landlord-tenant relations in the first
instance in Mayo, in the spring and summer of 1879. It was a
county in which a high proportion of land-holders had little to
lose – and could hope to gain something – from such a breakdown. With this thought in mind (and without any great concern for separatist republicanism) thousands of them had joined
the I.R.B. Since the late 1860s the county had produced a very
effective élite of lay political leaders, almost all of them fenians

(one notable exception being James Daly of Castlebar, proprietor of the *Connaught Telegraph*), whose principal achievement had been the election of John O'Connor Power to parliament in 1874. These people scarcely needed any 'new departure' headlines from America. When Davitt visited the county for a second time in February 1879, he discovered that Daly and some of the leading fenians of Mayo were making plans for a mass-meeting at Irishtown to exert pressure for reduction of rents. Davitt intruded himself into the preparations (perhaps on invitation). He did so with the purpose of capturing the incipient Mayo movement for the planned 'new departure' and to this end he consulted intensively with Devoy and with two prominent Dublin-based fenians, Patrick Egan and Thomas Brennan (formerly clerk in the Castlebar office of Egan's milling company).[21] While most of the preparatory organising was done locally, Davitt and his friends concentrated on achieving platform arrangements that would conform with their larger plans. They vetted the list of speakers and dictated for adoption at the meeting two resolutions which have been summarised as a 'rather circuitous claim to self government . . . followed by a resounding challenge to the landlord system'.[22] The approved speakers included Matt Harris, Thomas Brennan and O'Connor Power, M.P. The latter was the most obvious choice of all, and but for Davitt's intervention he would almost certainly have become the figurehead of the emerging movement in the west. There is no evidence at this stage of any personal animosity against O'Connor Power on Davitt's part, but Devoy had detested him for years. By keeping O'Connor Power off the pedestal they reserved it for Parnell.

Davitt himself did not attend the Irishtown meeting, which took place on 20 April 1879, but he obviously made sure to be informed of what transpired there. His figure for the attendance was 7,000,[23] not an enormous number by the standards of the age. However, it was gratifying for the chairman, James Daly, who had been endeavouring for years to persuade the Mayo tenantry to combine in this way. They were doing so now because severe economic hardship (with the threat of worse to come) had been added to other predisposing conditions. The third resolution adopted by the meeting – one drawn up locally – called for the only short-term relief that was practicable: a reduction in rents.[24] In the speeches there was talk of resisting evictions and of the infamy of those who took the farms of the evicted. Even if the Irishtown meeting was originally directed against high rents and evictions on one particular estate, the effect attributed to it was more widespread, as many landlords granted rent reductions in subsequent weeks.[25] A similar meeting at Westport on 8 June was a matter of repeating a successful formula, and it initiated a spate of similar events in Mayo and Galway, at all of which Davitt himself spoke.

The meetings received extensive popular support primarily because they offered the prospect of short-term relief, namely, rent reductions and the warding off of evictions. Even though the need for such relief was more pressing in the west, it was also being felt elsewhere throughout the country and was producing appeals to, and bargaining with, landlords. By contrast the campaign in Mayo and Galway was an endeavour to obtain concessions through intimidation. Platform attacks on the legitimacy of landlordism raised prospects of a redistribution of property which could be entertained with equanimity only by those with little or nothing to lose, and which was probably the only remaining hope for many of the demonstrators who could no longer afford to pay rents, however reduced, or expect to eke a living from their impoverished holdings. This rejection of the fundamental basis of landlordism was the kind of land agitation that Devoy had declared for in his new departure telegram and subsequently, but its beginnings were owing to local factors, including local fenianism, and had nothing to do with the new departure. In the spring and early summer of 1879 Davitt and Devoy seized this incipient movement and nurtured it in the hope that Parnell would provide a wider political dimension. Insofar as they looked beyond that, they probably believed their own rhetoric and had some vague notions about a great national movement culminating in withdrawal from Westminster and popular armed struggle. To glorify this muddle with the description of 'strategy' is simply to create an illusion. In the event Davitt fell in love with the agrarian agitation and began to cultivate it for its own sake, Parnell subordinated it to a political movement of his own liking, and Devoy was left high and dry.

The agrarian movement in the west was given institutional form on 16 August 1879 when the National Land League of Mayo was formed at a meeting in Castlebar, with Davitt providing the impetus. Self-government did not feature in its published list of objectives, which included references to avoiding a clash with the constitution and to operating 'within the law'.[26] But the league stood for the repudiation of the existing basis of landownership. Its sloganising about 'the land for the people' encapsulated notions about land ownership that had for long been deeply held among 'tillers of the soil' throughout much of Europe[27] and much of Ireland. They had been given political formulation by John Mitchel and James Fintan Lalor in 1848 but without serious effect, largely because of their implications for the property of tenants of middle and higher rank. In 1879 such notions were being promulgated as practical politics (and with some success) in the west. But could their implications be swallowed by the more privileged tenant farmers and by the shopkeepers and merchants? In fact such people were in the movement from the very start. James Daly and his associates (with Davitt) were able to launch a campaign in Mayo because of the numercial weight there of desperate smallholders, but these latter never had the ranks to themselves: there were many hundreds on horseback at the Irishtown meeting. Larger farmers and townsmen, left to themselves, might not have produced such a movement, but once an antilandlord campaign started they were going to be part of it.[28] The Mayo priests were antagonists not only because of the implications of an assault on the conventions of property but because of their well-established resentment against (and fear of) the county's 'alternative' lay leadership. Sam Clark has provided some examples of priests in the west at this time guiding their parishioners in conventional efforts to secure reductions or abatements of rent — essentially respectful petitions and appeals to landlords.[29] As early as July 1879, however, priests were beginning to overcome their distaste for the confrontational approach and to make their way onto land meeting platforms.

By summer 1879 Davitt was focussing single-mindedly on the evils of landlordism in which he now discerned the source of all Ireland's national and social ills. This conviction changed the agrarian movement in his eyes from a mere tactical weapon into a crusade. This resolved his need for a meaningful role in life and provided him with an outlet (one far more realistic than preparations for a rather dubious war of national liberation) for what proved to be amazing reserves of energy. Parnell's calculations were obviously much colder, although like the other actors he was for the most part merely putting one foot in front of the other. The agrarian campaign was a vehicle which could carry him to triumph against the moderate home rulers at the next election. His attendance at the Westport meeting of 8 June 1879 was evidence of keen interest. But before committing himself he had to be as certain as possible that the movement would actually be a success. Davitt's efforts to secure his definite commitment bore fruit with the launching of the Irish National Land League on 21 October 1879 with Parnell as president. There were some important intimations of moderation. The league dedicated itself to owner occupiership, but while the logic of Davitt's views was that the landlords should be left with little more than the clothes they stood up in, the new league's policy advocated the buying out of the landlords. The 54-strong committee of the league included 14 priests.

Soon the league absorbed the Central Tenants' Defence Association — the central body of the moderate tenant-right associations of the 1870s — with an understanding that if peasant proprietorship proved unattainable the three Fs would not be scorned.[30] A fund-raising visit by Parnell to America in early 1880, organised by Clan na Gael, was a reminder of the wilder elements among his following at home and abroad, but, in the event, playing up to Clan na Gael was matched by careful gestures of distancing.[31]

The general election of 1880 was an important stage in the history of Parnell's rise to influence on the strength of the land question, but it was not by any means a plebiscite either on that question or on the leadership. Isaac Butt had for long identified himself very successfully with the interests of tenant farmers, but after his death in May 1879 the obstructionist wing of the home rule party had a virtual monopoly of this role. The moderate (anti-obstructionist) wing, and especially the new leader, William Shaw, were characterised by distaste for the Land League and by a basic, if unspoken, preparedness to support the Liberals in parliament. Gladstone might very well have chosen in 1880 to seek a secure Irish flank, as in 1868, by offering the version of 'home rule' that he then approved of, namely, local government reform and some limited administrative devolution.[32] However, Disraeli made an alarmist feint about the home rule threat to United Kingdom unity, thereby rendering the subject too hot for Gladstone to handle, even if he wished to do so.[33] In the event the only Irish reference in the Liberal leader's election address was a riposte to Disraeli to the effect that it was the behaviour of past Conservative administrators that had put the union at risk.[34] The moderate home rulers, then, entered the election without any rallying point. Only half-a-dozen of them were actually challenged at the polls by adherents of Parnell but many others anticipated and headed off potential difficulty by gesturing towards 'forward' policies. (This was, indeed, the last Irish election to be marked by that old haphazard style of selection of popular candidates which permitted them, when returned, to enjoy considerable freedom of movement as far as policies and parties were concerned.) The new candidates on the home rule side were predominantly unequivocal admirers of Parnell's line: nineteen of the twenty-one new home rule M.P.s were Parnellites.[35]

Trends in Ulster at the 1880 election parallel in an instructive way what happened within the home rule camp. Powered by the tenant-farmer interest, the Liberals held their 1874 gains in Londonderry county and took two seats in Donegal, two in Monaghan, and one each in Counties Armagh and

Tyrone. The other M.P. for Tyrone was an independent Conservative standing on a tenant-right platform. The Liberals lost
their 1874 gain in Down, but by a mere twenty votes, and in
Antrim they were, as in 1874, less than two hundred votes
short of a seat. The new Liberal standard-bearers came mainly
from the professions and business and did not include that ad-
mixture from lower social strata that had entered the home rule
ranks in 1874 and was increased in 1880.[36] Nevertheless, even
the Ulster comparison would suggest that within the home rule
camp a strong swing against the landlord interest was certain in
1880, even if Parnell had never 'taken off his coat'. Parnell's
success was that he had placed himself in a position to draw
maximum benefit from the trend. Single Conservative seats
held on the basis of deference in predominantly catholic counties
disappeared in Wicklow and Sligo, as did two of them in Carlow,
though it is worth noting that the home rule assault on the
Carlow constituency was headed by a well-known protagonist
of tenant demands who had shown considerable reluctance
about endorsing the Land League, namely, Edmund Dwyer
Gray, who had succeeded his father, Sir John, as proprietor of
the *Freeman's Journal*. In all sixty-three seats were won by
home rulers of one kind or another. Of these no more than 24
could be definitely claimed for Parnell, but their occupants
constituted an inspired, purposeful group as against an in-
coherent and confused majority. On 17 May 1880 Parnell was
chosen to replace Shaw as chairman of the party by 23 votes
to 18.

Meanwhile the land agitation was entering a new phase. It
was from early summer 1880 that the Land League began to ex-
pand significantly in Leinster and Munster. This involved the
shift in favour of the interests of more prosperous farmers that
Paul Bew has so rightly highlighted.[37] Their fears of a redistribution and of inroads by the small holders and the landless
were still real, but did not constitute a reason for inaction:
once a large-scale movement got under way they could best protect their interests by joining it. There were some less abstract
considerations. With the hope of a good harvest those numerous
landlords who were owed rent from previous years were preparing to recover the balance in the Autumn of 1880. Typically,
landlords and tenants — like most people at most times — had
been living at, or beyond, the edge of their means in the good
years.[38] Caught up in the throes of retrenchment, disappointed
expectations, and mounting arrears of debt, large numbers of
both categories were in dire straits. To many tenants the Land
League offered the prospect of financial relief (deferment and/or
reduction of rents) and of security against the ultimate sanction

for financial failure — eviction. By distinguishing ideologically between agricultural rents and all other forms of debt the Land League reassured both tenants, who were themselves rural capitalists, and also their creditors — the banks, shopkeepers and merchants — that there was no general assault on property. This also reassured the priests. The occasional visionary or opportunist who suggested extending the attack to urban rack-rents or to debts owed to banks, moneylenders, or shopkeepers was quickly put back in line.[39] Thus apparently secure from attack from below, one class of Irish capitalists waged economic war against another class of Irish capitalists.

The greater part of the Land League's income (of nearly one quarter million pounds) was donated for avowedly 'political' ends and was spent on organisation and on the provision of financial aid for resistance to the landlords at local level, especially the indemnification of tenants incurring loss in pursuit of particular local campaigns.[40] Up and down the country the land war was fuelled by outside money, not least importantly in the form of expenses for peripatetic agitators. The greater portion of this money (perhaps over ninety percent) came from the U.S.A.,[41] and if it was used to cause trouble in Ireland rather than to ease difficulties, the donors' only cause for complaint was that in the final analysis it did not create as much trouble as they would have wished. During the twelve months of greatest distress (ended by the abundant potato harvest of 1880) the Land League had received from America, in addition, considerable sums for relief. These probably amounted to less than ten percent of all the relief money raised at the time: the easing of hardship and distress was preponderantly the work of other bodies, groups, and individuals.[42] Its own relief funds gave the league a foothold in a number of places, but the 'political' money from America was what really mattered: without it there would have been no sustained land war.

The accession to office of an administration headed by Gladstone as a result of the election of March-April 1880 provided an ideal political environment for the agrarian agitation in Ireland. Disraeli's government had shown more than a little awareness of the need for Irish relief measures, but there was no question of the Conservatives legislating for major change in the land law. By contrast, Gladstone was the living symbol of Irish concession, and, as surely as he had legislated for landlord-tenant relations in Ireland before, he could do so again. The belief that the new government would not put up much fight against 'Irish ideas' was confirmed by the announcement in the queen's speech of 20 May that long-standing Irish coercion measures due to lapse on 1 June 1880 would not be

H.M.S. *Valorous*, under the command of the Duke of Edinburgh distributing relief stores on the Connemara coast, April 1880. (*Illustrated London News*, 24 April 1880)

renewed.[43] In England the 1870s had witnessed a strong wave of political opinion hostile to the status of landed property: later in 1880 Disraeli was to declare that one of the prime political issues of the day was that of 'the principles on which the landed property of this country should continue to be established'.[44] Irish hopes for anti-landowner legislation did not have to depend, or so it seemed, solely on the strength of Irish demand. On 18 June the government introduced the Compensation for Disturbance (Ireland) Bill which held out the promise of a stay on evictions for non-payment of rent. Because it was introduced to replace a similar bill of O'Connor Power's, this measure carried no weight even with Liberal peers and it was rejected by the house of lords on 3 August 1880, leaving the government in the position of having acknowledged a grievance and having failed to provide a remedy. Gladstone would be under moral pressure to try again. The setting up of a commission to enquire into the working of the 1870 land act could be taken as another indication that the land agitators had already won half the battle (even if the composition of the commission under the earl of Bessborough, was deemed by them to be unsatisfactory). The indecisiveness and conciliation of the Liberal government in 1880 is likely to have done at least as much to promote the fortunes of the Land League as did the coercion to which the same government switched in February 1881.

Behind the impressive united front presented by the Land League, division was rife. The agricultural labourers had to be fobbed off with promises and gestures on a number of occasions when they threatened to push their own claims too strongly.[45] The tensions between the interests of larger and smaller farmers were never wholly suppressed, being especially evident in the west. This was one factor in the fragmentation of the Mayo Land League that had taken place by 1881.[46] Maura Murphy has shown how the Cork trades in due course turned against the Land League, notwithstanding their colourful participation in the impressive demonstration that welcomed Parnell to the city on 5 October 1880. He came again in October 1881, but when the league set about arranging another triumphal visit to the city for Parnell in late 1882 the plan had to be dropped because the trades refused to participate. They had learned that the Land League was not necessarily good for everyone who might feel attracted by its rallying flag. In 1882 the league had enforced a ban on foxhunting over much of County Cork. The gentry were no doubt annoyed, but they were also saved much expenditure on unnecessary consumption which most of them could ill afford. The certain losers were the farriers, shoemakers, tailors and other traders deprived of 'their usual seasonal employment in providing the gentry with the requirements of the hunting season'.[47] (A complete balance sheet of the effects of the land war would have to include now irrecoverable estimates of the additional economic hardship that it caused in town and country at a time of already severe loss.)

There is yet another respect in which the apparent unity of the Land League was deceptive. An indeterminable amount of its support at local level was achieved by means of fear and coercion.[48] And there is no telling how many of the local campaigns (by boycott, supporting opposition to evictions, and so on) against 'the stooges of landlordism' were really the continuation by means newly-to-hand of pre-existing vendettas. Davitt admitted — by publicly denouncing it at league committee meetings — the fact that the coercive activities of the league were being utilised in furtherance of old private feuds.[49] An incisive study of the Land League in County Kildare has illustrated how the campaign could mean different things to different people: for not-so-badly-off tenants, the pleasant surprise of an excuse for holding on to the rent; for the Athy town commissioners, the opportunity of getting their own man into parliament; for shopkeepers somewhere else the possibility of diverting business from competitors.[50] Even the most thorough local studies cannot uncover the full complications of the period thanks to (among other things) the impenetrable reticence that can suddenly envelop rural matters. Thus, in the case of one of the most celebrated of all the land war happenings, there appears to be no way of determining against whom exactly the Irishtown meeting of April 1879 was directed.[51] There may be something to be learned by exploring the psychology of the land movement. Looking at the enthusiastic league activity of some individual strong farmers and shopkeeper-farmers it is difficult not to be reminded of *conversos* making demonstrations of zeal at an *auto-da-fe*. How many of those who joined most vehemently in the attack on land grabbers were themselves in possession of land that had been scooped up in comparatively recent times?

The Land League had from the start proclaimed owner occupiership as the objective of its agitation, rent reductions being presented merely as an interim expedient. As a voluntary business transaction between individual landowners and farmers, owner-occupiership ('peasant proprietorship') had no revolutionary implications (being from the legal point of view part of a continuum with territorial landlordism), and had been encouraged by the 1870 land act. The universal compulsory owner-occupiership demanded by the league was a very different matter. Platform orators sometimes gave audiences the impression that it would mean fee simple land for next to nothing, though this was never official league policy. The majority of tenants seem to have been quite unenthusiastic about obtaining fee simple, accepting they would have to pay for it. An immediate abatement or reduction of rent was the major aim of such people: for a long-term solution they favoured the three Fs. Unlike the three Fs, occupying ownership could be interpreted to imply redistribution, and so it appealed to the smallholders. When clothed in rhetoric about 'rooting the people in the soil', it implied rejection of all the works and pomps of landlordism, and so gave satisfaction to the league's American backers. And at the same time it was a good rhetorical and bargaining stance when actually seeking a more moderate end. The Land Law (Ireland) Act of 1881[52] provided just such a moderate gain. An independent commission working through sub-commissions would be available to determine equitable rents in disputed cases: tenants paying such rents would be, in practice, secure from eviction; and tenants could sell their interests in their holdings with a minimum of reference to their landlords. This practical concession of the three Fs was in effect accepted by the great majority of Irish tenants as a satisfactory solution to the land agitation — especially when it emerged that the sub-commissioners were fixing rents noticeably lower than those prevailing formerly, and after the arrears of rent accumulated by smallholders in the course of the recession had been wiped out by further act of parliament.[53] A reduction in rent and the return of better seasons brought respite to all tenants but did not resolve the fundamental predicament of those on uneconomic holdings. The marginal men among whom the land war had started were still marginal, at best. Many had been finally ruined. The outcome was a disappointment to most of those key non-agricultural personages in the Land League for whom the war on the landlords was either an end in itself or a means of triggering a struggle for separation from Britain. Parnell disarmed their opposition by throwing cold water on the land act (while at the same time putting no effective impediment in its way). Michael Davitt who was best placed to organise continued resistance ruined his chances by reinterpreting 'the land of Ireland for the people of Ireland' to mean nationalisation of land.[54] Like every other idea about land law in modern Ireland this was derived from contemporary debates in Britain and America. Davitt's willingness to take up a theoretically excellent idea that was politically unsaleable did immense credit to his intellectual integrity, and it was, by the same token, an implicit admission that the land war had been very largely a misconceived venture.

The smallholder fenians of the west and north-west appear to have entered the Land League campaign *en masse* and, in effect if not formally, to have abandoned the I.R.B. In Dublin and in the towns an indeterminable proportion of the rank and file remained loyal to the supreme council majority and joined it in an occasionally bitter feud with the Land Leaguers. At Davitt's insistence the supreme council had agreed in May 1879 that I.R.B. members might participate as individuals in the agrarian campaign, but in practice the council majority displayed no toleration towards the league. The reasons for this opposition are complicated.[55] For a start, the 'new departure' telegram of October 1878 had caused antagonism by the manner in which it seemed to belittle the supreme council. In reaction to that the rhetoric of intransigence had been invoked: a fenian had no business in any line other than preparation for armed assertion of the rights of Irish nationhood. This view was sincerely held by Kickham and O'Leary, which is not to say that they would not have seen the matter differently, given a different set of circumstances. Anybody predisposed to be critical had no difficulty finding much to dislike in the land war, including greed, anarchy, deception, violence, injustice to individuals, 'communism' and 'claptrap'. Kickham and O'Leary saw all of these things. In particular they were conscious of injustice being done to many reasonable landlords, and of the way in which the landlords were being attacked as a class in the name of 'the people of Ireland'.

Davitt's break with the I.R.B. was gradual and only partly deliberate. It parallels his transformation from being a physical-force nationalist using the land question to being an agrarian reformer who was also a nationalist, and no definite point of transition can be identified. He ceased to attend meetings of the supreme council during 1879, but well into 1880 he was still apparently implicated in the importation and distribution of guns.[56] He claimed that Kickham and O'Leary were interfering with this work; if that was so, the reason was undoubtedly that the weapons were going to Land League fenians.[57] What use, if any, he expected these guns to be put to is not certain, and he probably had no clear mind on the subject himself. The general election of March-April 1880 brought a further deterioration in relations between the I.R.B. and the 'new departure' people, as the former discountenanced support for Parnellite candidates. At a Land League conference in the Rotunda on 29 April 1880 proceedings were interrupted by fenian protestors who managed to push Davitt off the platform.[58] In the

great Parnellite demonstration at Cork on 5 October 1880 the
fenians interfered menacingly without actually interrupting the
proceedings.[59] In July 1880 an unnamed partisan of the supreme
council gave an interview to a visiting American journalist which
was clearly intended to damage the Land League at home and
in the U.S.A.[60] There is no evidence that members of the
supreme council were implicated in such activities but they displayed the same animus against the league as their subordinates
did. Davitt and Matt Harris had been dismissed from the supreme
council in May 1880.[61] Up to his death in August 1882 the
president of the supreme council, C.J. Kickham, remained
passionately opposed both to the Parnellites themselves and to
fenian dealings with them.

As with the supreme council of the I.R.B., the new departure
was presented to the executive of Clan na Gael as *fait accompli*.
Devoy and Carroll had more than enough weight to carry the
Clan with them on the project, at least for as long as it seemed
to be a success. Devoy returned to America from his transatlantic
trip of 1878-9 in time to report to a Clan na Gael convention,
but without anything very encouraging to relay about the new
departure. In his report he concentrated on the apparently more
reassuring and more basic matter of I.R.B. organisation.[62] The
gathering subsequently endorsed support for public agitation
in Ireland in a somewhat unenthusiastic fashion. The success of
Parnell's all-important American tour in January-March 1880
was based on preparatory work carried out by Clan na Gael.
Parnell's appeal transcended any individual organisation and he
avoided identification with the Clan. Before his hasty departure
he set in train the establishment of an American Land League to
collect and forward funds. This and other aspects of his tour
offended William Carroll who at this point turned against the
alliance with Parnell of which he had been one of the principal
authors.[63] When Davitt arrived in the U.S.A. two months later
to consolidate Parnell's work, he found Carroll engaged in a
campaign of criticism of the Land League, aided by John O'Leary
who had come across from Paris for that purpose.[64] However,
Devoy was still able to keep Clan na Gael securely on Davitt's
side.

In America the most outspoken opponent of the Land League
from the 'intransigent' side was O'Donovan Rossa. It is difficult
to believe that, given first-hand experience, Rossa would not
have enjoyed the mayhem produced by the league over much
of rural Ireland. In fact his attitude was determined by his feelings about Devoy and the Clan na Gael leadership, who (among
other offences), had taken possession of his skirmishing fund.
The new departure provided him with a pretext for denouncing

Devoy and his friends as deviationists. In June 1880 he founded the United Irishmen of America and renewed the call for 'skirmishing'. On 14 January 1881 followers of his set off an explosion at Salford barracks in Lancashire, killing a child and causing damage to property. Other attempts with less serious consequences followed — on the Mansion House (London), Liverpool police station, and Liverpool town hall.[65] The attacks were extremely annoying to Clan na Gael, not on grounds of principle but because the Clan was itself just then preparing for an explosives campaign in Britain and possibly in Ireland also.[66] William Mackey Lomasney came to Europe in February 1881 to reconnoitre for this campaign and possibly to place the necessary dynamite in safe storage. In Paris he was in touch with John O'Leary, who, presumably, did not know what his precise business was. However, John O'Connor, secretary of the I.R.B., cooperated so closely that he must have been fully party to what was happening. Lomasney met Parnell in Paris on 18 February and like others came away with the impression that at heart the parliamentarian was an extremist.[67] Parnell would have been glad of the opportunity to be friendly with a Clan na Gael emissary. He is not likely to have been fully briefed on Lomasney's mission but must have guessed its general purpose. A few weeks earlier Devoy had issued a widely-reported warning that, if land agitators resisting police harassment were shot, reprisals would be taken against cabinet members' lives and against English cities.[68] In December 1880 Davitt had at least given Devoy the impression that he envisaged attacks in Britain as a possible option, if the government were to take really drastic action against the Land League in the clearly signalled and anxiously expected coercion drive.[69] Lomasney, who on other occasions proved himself a most reckless desperado, was full of doubts and caution in reporting back to Devoy at this time, and he returned to America in July 1881 without having caused any explosions. The caution must have been inculcated by his close contacts such as O'Connor. Another likely explanation for Lomasney's abstention from action had to do with Rossa's campaign. Rossa having got in first, anything that Clan na Gael did would be inextricably confused in public and official preceptions with the unpredictable actions of his agents.[70] Indeed, the Clan na Gael initiative may have been partly intended in the first instance to head off a fresh flow of Irish-American support for Rossa. Internal Clan na Gael politics may also have been involved. The year 1881 saw the accession of Alexander Sullivan of Chicago to the presidency of the Clan and the beginning of a phase in the organisation's history which included a series of major bomb attacks in London (1883-85) overlapping with a similar campaign by followers of O'Donovan Rossa.[71] The comparative decline in Devoy's influence with the Clan was a predictable result of the petering out of the new departure in Ireland. His new departure gamble had produced no armed uprising, no withdrawal from Westminster, no expropriation of the landlords.

The detention of Parnell and some of his principal lieutenants in October 1881 under the terms of the coercion legislation was followed within a few days by the 'no rent manifesto' in which they called for a witholding of all agricultural rents. Next came the proclamation of the Land League on 20 October. There ensued a winter and spring of confusion and disorder over much of the countryside. Many tenants were moving towards accommodation with their landlords. But the arrears legislation had not yet come, so for many thousands of tenants there was still no improvement in sight. Deprived of central direction, the league became even more obviously than before a localised affair with many branches increasingly the play things of local faction and even individual malice. The alternative central organisation offered by the Ladies' Land League possibly served only to make matters worse. The chief secretary, W.E. Forster, committed himself to a restoration of something like universal law and order and when the effort failed he paid the political price. In May 1882 Gladstone accepted Forster's resignation after the cabinet had entered into an informal agreement with Parnell, who undertook to promote the ending of disorder and to act in a cooperative manner in return for his freedom and arrears legislation.

Parnell faced a demanding task in securing the adherence to this compromise of all those hot-headed, outspoken, individuals, inside and outside parliament, whose enthusiasm had powered his progress. Just how difficult the work might be was underlined in devastating fashion on 6 May when the new chief secretary (Lord Frederick Cavendish) and the permanent under-secretary at Dublin Castle (T.H. Burke) were assassinated in the Phoenix Park by the Irish Invincibles — a previously unheard-of group but one obviously deriving from the world of secret conspiracy and extremist organisation with which Parnell had so purposefully dabbled. The murders, and especially that of Cavendish, were a violation of near-sacred conventions. The land war had inculcated detestation of aristocracy but that in itself would scarcely explain the resort to the idea of attacking the rulers of the land in their own persons. The inspiration almost certainly came from international example. Following on Nobel's work with dynamite production, the late 1870s and the 1880s witnessed an upsurge of terrorism and the flourishing of small anarchist groups in many European countries. Russian anarchists set a headline with the assassination of Czar Alexander II on 13 March 1881. A few months later President Garfield of the U.S.A. was mortally wounded by an assassin. The Phoenix Park murders constitute part of this series, that continued into the following few years.

There is, however, no question of the Invincibles depending directly on other nationalities. They were indebted to foreigners for the headline and nothing more. Foreign example received an Irish response thanks to a number of factors, most of which were caused by the land war. The notion of retaliating against the government in the event of a crackdown on the Land League leadership had been current for at least a year before the arrest of Parnell and company in October 1881. The unreliable sources which are all we have to go on for the history of the Invincibles[72] suggest that some leading Land League supporters — including members of parliament — meeting in London shortly after the arrests gave vent to their anger with talk of retaliatory assassination of ministers or Dublin Castle officials. As early as November 1881 the Dublin police heard reports of fanatical plotters who had Gladstone himself on their list of targets.[73] One of those involved was Frank Byrne, secretary of the Land League of Great Britain; shortly after he emerges as the effective head of a closely knit, carefully structured, secret society — the Irish Invincibles. Through an agent, he recruited a four-man Dublin directory with authority to recruit in turn a maximum membership of fifty. Similar cells were to be formed elsewhere in the country, but unconnected with the Dublin group. C.J. Kickham repudiated the Phoenix Park murders and is reported to have replied, when asked if the culprits were fenians that, if so, they were 'fenians seduced by the Land League'.[74] In fact, the original Dublin directory included at least one fenian who had followed Kickham's line of disapproval of the land war — James Mullett. Recruits were available for the Invincibles not so much because the Land League had 'seduced' them as because it had demoralised the I.R.B. By 1881 the Dublin I.R.B. had deteriorated into a miscellany of purposeless gangs, some of them all too ready to use revolvers against one another and against suspected informers. The Invincible society offered to a select number in this milieu heightened levels of conspiracy, a sense of immediate and exhilarating purpose, and a plentiful supply of money.

The financial factor lends weight to the suspicion that Patrick Egan, the treasurer of the Land League (and based in Paris since February 1881), was among the originators or patrons of the society. P.J. Sheridan was almost certainly one

of the organisers of the Invincibles in Ireland: in a different context he admitted to having visited the country on Egan's behalf
in late 1881-early 1882.[75] Egan's complicity, however, has
never been proved.[76] Which or whether, there was a number of
Land League activists at the promotional level (safely insulated
from the 'working' groups). They included, in addition to Byrne
and Sheridan, John Walsh of Middlesbrough. Also implicated,
to what degree it is not easy to say, was Captain John McCafferty,
the Irish-American veteran of 1867. The most controverted
question of all about the Invincibles in subsequent years (after
five of the Dublin group had been executed and others sent to
jail for the Phoenix Park murders) was Parnell's relationship
with the society. The ordinary members do appear to have
believed that they were in the service of the parliamentary
leaders and the Dublin group was allegedly quite taken aback
by the severity with which Parnell, Davitt and the others
denounced the murders.[77] The *Times* v Parnell special commission of 1888 gave Parnell's enemies every opportunity to
link him to the Invincibles, if that could be done. They failed.[78]
In trying to establish this and other subversive links they were
endeavouring to prove in one tangible and potentially damning
instance a wider charge in the intangible realm of political
morality. In his rise to power he had consorted with fenians
and law-breakers; he had flouted the conventions of politics
and of parliament; and he had got away with it. Whether or not
anyone could 'get away with it' indefinitely remained to be seen.

When all has been said, the unity of the Land League was no
more deceptive than that of most 'popular' movements in
modern history. The divisions that it harboured within its
ranks notwithstanding, the league succeeded in harnessing the
sense of national and communal identity of Irish catholics,
and therein lies its greatest success. The conviction of dis-
possession was an essential feature of this and was felt irrespective
of the actual amount of property possessed by an individual
catholic. It had been a factor in the land question for generations. The appeal of the land war transcended the financial
problems of individuals and the economic preoccupations of
classes to meet the psychological needs of a community. So,
townsmen and rural labourers, shopkeepers, priests, and even
bishops, joined enthusiastically in a campaign which on purely
social, economic or moral terms many might have found less
than attractive. Thomas J. Croke, archbishop of Cashel from
1875, became a revered national figure because he came to
symbolise the identification of the church with the agrarian
campaign. Patrick McCabe who had succeeded Paul Cullen as
archbishop of Dublin in 1878 opposed the identification but

was powerless to prevent it. Here was the collapse of Cullen's formula for the accommodation of catholicism and political power in Ireland. Emmet Larkin has explored the way in which a new formula was arrived at over a period of a few years.[79] The widely-held assumption that this was a 'great leap forward' is a matter of opinion and emotional allegiance rather than one of reason or faith.

The Land League also brought a definite end to the Cullen era in that it rendered obsolete his hope of catholic social progress through infiltration of the landed class. In the heat of the land war the Irish catholic sense of identity was redefined to exclude landlords, even catholic landlords. The change was most memorably represented by the defeat of The O'Connor Don in Roscommon at the general election of 1880 by a Dublin-born Parnellite journalist, the I.R.B. man J.J. O'Kelly. While this anti-aristocratic posture can be lauded as marking a stage of egalitarian progress, there was also loss. In the nature of things the landlord class was equipped to perform functions in society that nobody else could fulfill. It possessed assets (not all of them material) that could not be redistributed overnight without being greatly diminished in the process. In general Irish landowners had been much remiss (by English standards) in their wider social obligations, but their forced exclusion as a class was an undoubted source of further impoverishment of an already underendowed country. The sight of Parnell, a protestant landlord, presiding over the Land League ought not to distract from analysis of what was actually happening underneath. Parnell is an example of an important phenomenon of the nineteenth century that Harold Perkin has described as the 'social crank', an individual from one class background adopting and becoming spokesman of an opposing class.[79]

The attitude of protestant farmers in the land war years is of some significance. They had never been noticeably slower than catholics to push for financial and legal gain at the expense of landlords. Throughout the 1870s predominantly presbyterian tenant-right associations had been strong in Ulster. There as over most of the country farmers reacted to their financial problems at the end of the decade by seeking rent abatements. When the Land League with its more bellicose approach reached the province, its catholic-nationalist dimension provoked the orange order to immediate hostility, which took the form of counter-demonstrations against league meetings. To the great majority of Ulster protestant farmers the political content of the Land League was indeed unacceptable. But they attached so much importance to the agrarian question that they were not to be stampeded into attacking a potentially useful ally.

A small number even joined the league. For the most part they gladly tolerated this separate pressure that strengthened their own continuing conventional campaign, of which the highlight was the impressive showing of tenant-right candidates in the 1880 general election. The triumphs and near-triumphs at the polls were possible because catholic farmers in nothern counties that did not have home rule candidates were prepared to join presbyterians in voting Liberal.

The phase of co-operation based on mutual economic interest gave way in short time to the division which Land League attitudes made inevitable. A crucial test came with the publication of the 1881 land bill. This was welcomed by the Ulster tenant-righters as a very great boon, but was reviled and, apparently, even put at risk by the parliamentary representatives of the Land League. By 1882 the period of good-will was past.[80] The league, together with the National League that took its place, was successful precisely as a political movement of the Irish catholic collectivity. Davitt and other league leaders — like so many others similarly placed, before and since — were reluctant to acknowledge the essentially confessional basis of their movement's strength and made professions of non-denominational intent that were utterly genuine and utterly unrealistic. Far from building any worthwhile bridges between the confessions, the Land League and Parnell failed to forge permanent links even with presbyterian farmers who were themselves in a phase of very determined and active antagonism to the landlords.

The Land League was 'nationalist' in a number of the senses of that many-sided term. That is certainly not to say that the tenants expected no satisfaction prior to national self-government. But the rhetoric of the league did link the 'solution' of the land question to various formulations of 'freedom for Ireland'; and the league was intimately linked with politicians who had been operating under the banner of one such formulation, namely, 'home rule'. Much of the energy of the movement came from fenians, who were accustomed to rationalising their activities with reference to nationalist ideas. The political community whose support gave the Land League its mass power was one that on-and-off over at least half a century had had its ambitions defined for it in terms of Irish self-government (most notably as 'repeal of the union'). When, in October 1882, Parnell finally discarded the Land League banner and raised that of a new Irish National League devoted to home rule, his mass following scarcely considered the change worth noticing. The financing of the new league is of special significance. With the winding down of the land war, the flow of dollars that had boosted the Land League virtually dried up. But in the quiet years that followed, the National League was able to raise substantial income from home sources.[81] This was precisely the test by which all the nationalist endeavours of the previous thirty years had failed; for the first time since O'Connell's death the great majority of the priests were using their influence on behalf of a political movement, and catholics with purses were regularly loosening the strings to support a cause. A dormant power had been mobilised and Parnell had succeeded in placing himself at the head of it.

Given the wider history of the age it is safe to say that the Irish catholic community of the mid-nineteenth century was virtually certain to be mobilised for political objectives behind somebody. What was not at all inevitable was the extent (if any) to which these objectives would be 'nationalist'. The events of 1879-82 had made Irish catholic opinion not only positively anti-aristocratic but also more bitterly anti-English than before and to that extent more 'nationalist'. The catholic body had for long identified its own perceived deprivations as wrongs done to 'Ireland', which were blamed with more or less vehemence on 'England', and, logically or otherwise, the vehemence had been greatly increased during the land war, with the 'class enemy' being ever more closely associated with English rule. Instinctive respect for existing constitutional arrangements, simply because they existed, was shaken by Parnell's flouting of parliamentary and constitutional conventions. And yet the foundation document of the Irish National League framed the 'national demand' in terms that Isaac Butt might have used: 'the restitution to the Irish people of the right to manage their own affairs in a parliament elected by the people of Ireland'.[82]

The land war underlined the extent to which the 'farming ideal' had taken hold of society over much of the island. The model of the independent family farm was cherished not only by those who benefited from such an amenity, but also by those who had only uneconomic holdings and by landless labourers — the latter a large element in many land meetings. The dream of the ambitious labourer was not of combination for higher wages and better conditions, but of possessing a patch of land for himself. To occupy land and to own livestock were the essential criteria of dignity for the Irish rural dweller, pride in labour for its own sake being at a discount. This attitude was the product of socio-economic conditions of many years' standing, but its status was confirmed by the land war. Shopkeepers, and priests, acquiesced in the same notion of what constituted the standard of 'Irish' social, economic and moral existence. The 'family farmer' ideal owed its strength not simply to the economic and numerical weight of the farming class but to the absence of propaganda for any alternative ideal, aristocratic, entrepreneurial, statist, or proletarian. Shopkeeping and the church were alternatives for individuals, but in overall terms they were not alternatives but ancillaries.

If the support of farmers, priests, bishops and shopkeepers was the essence of the success of Parnellism, the movement owed most of its vitality to rather different people – the numerous outsiders (many, but by no means all, of them fenians) that it had enabled to 'come in from the cold'. The Land League, the National League and the parliamentary party provided numerous frustrated individuals and elites with the opportunity for significant role-playing. Up and down the country the land war called forth a string of village Davitts many of whom remained active in local or national politics for a generation. At the intermediate leadership level were the travelling organisers of the Land League, some fenian and some not, who burned up impressive quantities of previously un-utilised energy – P.J. Sheridan, Michael Boyton, John Heffernan, J.W. Walshe, P.J. Gordon, Jeremiah Jordan and others. The neo-fenian elite of the late 1860s turned up in force in the national leadership of the leagues and (in 1880 or afterwards) in the parliamentary ranks at Westminster – Davitt himself, O'Connor Power, J.J. O'Kelly, James O'Connor, J.F.X. O'Brien, not to mention the already-established O'Connor Power and F.H. O'Donnell. They were joined by others of the same general background and vintage such as T.P. O'Connor, Thomas Sexton, Tim Healy and William O'Brien (all four of them journalists). There, too, were the self-made businessmen-fenians of the 1870s – Joseph Biggar, Patrick Egan, Thomas Brennan, John Barry and John Ferguson.

These formed the backbone of the new catholic political establishment. Scarcely any of them belonged to the farming class that in a very real sense was the dominant social group over much of the island. But their position was conditional on their upholding of the interests and values of that group, which was unable or unwilling to provide its own political leadership. (Proprietors of successful family farms are notoriously disinclined towards regular active participation in public affairs: their lives are already too full.) If there is continuity between the fenianism of the nineteenth century and the upheavals of the 1916-21 period it rests on this structural basis. A new set of outsider elites ousted the post-1882 political establishment, with the aid of the catalyst that had eluded the fenians – a great European war involving Britain. Like O'Connor Power and Biggar and Parnell and Davitt and the others, they were permitted to scorn or abuse constitutional conventions as they wished; but it was *sine qua non* that they should accept and uphold the catholic, rural-oriented, and property-conscious values of the dominant social ideal.

The survival of the I.R.B. influenced the forms used by the later generation; writings by, and songs and stories about, 'bold fenian men' contributed richly to the rhetoric. But continuity of names and forms means little and these things were not of the essence. It is true of Irish history as of every other country's history that people interact with contemporary circumstances, even when they believe themselves to be taking cues from the past. Certainly the fenians of the mid-nineteenth century were not answering the call of any inexorable national spirit, but rather were they, by-and-large, trying to find, through the invocation of nationalism, a more significant place for themselves in the world.

NOTES TO THE TEXT

Chapter One

1. See, for example, M. Bergman, 'The potato blight in the Netherlands' in *International Review of Social History*, xii (1967), pp 390-431; J. Mokyr, 'Industrialisation and poverty in Ireland and the Netherlands' in *Jn. of Interdisciplinary Hist.*, x (1980), pp 429-58.

2. B.M. Walker, *Parliamentary election results in Ireland, 1801-1922* (Dublin, 1978): Dr Walker's invaluable work of reference has provided essential material for every chapter of this book; for an authoritative account of the background to the 1847 elections, see K.B. Nowlan, *The politics of repeal* (London, 1965).

3. Jacqueline R. Hill, 'Artisans, sectarianism and politics in Dublin, 1829-48' in *Saothar*, vii (1981), p. 22; Maura Murphy, 'Fenianism, Parnellism and the Cork trades, 1860-1900', ibid., v (1979), p. 29.

4. *11 Vict.*, c. 12.

5. *11 & 12 Vict.*, c.35; see C.G. Duffy, *Four years of Irish history* (London, 1883) pp 641 and ff.

6. This entire episode is the subject of numerous reports among the Out-

rage papers, 1848, Co. Tipperary (S.P.O., Police and crime records).

7. J.S. Donnelly Jr, *The land and people of nineteenth-century Cork* (London, 1975), p. 90.

8. Constabulary report, Kilkenny, 10 June 1850 (S.P.O., Outrage papers, 1850, Co. Kilkenny).

9. T.P. O'Neill, 'Fintan Lalor and the '49 movement', in *An Cosantóir*, x (Apr. 1950), pp 173-9; Marcus Bourke, *John O'Leary: a study in separatism* (Tralee, 1967), pp 20-29.

10. *11 Vict.*, c. 2.

11. *19 & 20 Vict.*, c. 36.

12. Tom Garvin, 'Defenders, ribbonmen and others: underground political networks in pre-famine Ireland' in *Past & Present*, no. 96, pp 133-55; Michael Beames, 'The ribbon societies: lower-class nationalism in prefamine Ireland', ibid., no. 97, pp 128-43; the evidence for later periods is considered in W.C. Vaughan, *Sin, sheep and Scotsmen* (Belfast, 1983), pp 31-33.

13. *13 Vict.*, c. 2.

14. T.P. O'Neill, *Fiontán Ó Leathlobhair* (Dublin, 1962).

15. J.H. Whyte, *The independent Irish party, 1850-9* (Oxford, 1958), p. 6.

16. *11 & 12 Vict.*, c. 48; *12 & 13*

Vict., c. 77.

17. *13 & 14 Vict.*, c. 60.

18. See *Freeman's Journal* and *Nation*, Sept.—Oct. 1850.

19. Whyte, *Indep. Ir. party*, pp 14-6.

20. Ibid., p. 32.

21. The Co. Down election is examined in Stephen Stewart, 'Presbyterian radicalism, landlord influence and electoral politics in C. Down in the mid-nineteenth century' (M.A. thesis, Maynooth, 1981); see also, Liam McNiffe, 'The politicisation of Leitrim, Sligo and Mayo in the general election of 1852' (M.A. thesis, Maynooth, 1979); Co. Clare is dealt with by M.P. O'Connor in an undergraduate project (Maynooth, 1979).

22. See Whyte, *Indep Ir. party*, pp 86-92.

23. For example, see: *Irishman*, 17 July 1858 on murder of Ellis; *Nation*, 10 May 1862 on murder of Maguire and 30 May 1863 on murder of Grierson.

24. See Bew and Wright in Clark and Donnelly, *Irish peasants*, p. 194.

25. Clark and Donnelly, *Irish peasants*, p. 273.

26. *Kilkenny Journal*, 17 Oct. 1849.

27. J.H. Whyte, 'Political problems, 1850-60' in P.J. Corish (ed.), *A History of Irish Catholicism* (Dublin, 1967), pp 26-33.

28. *Nation*, 18 Aug. 1855.

29. In this area I am indebted to undergraduate work by James H. Murphy (Maynooth, 1980).

30. Whyte, 'Political problems', pp 1-10.

31. D'Arcy, *Fenian movement*, pp 5-8.

32. Mitchel, *Jail journal* (Dublin, 1918), appendix, pp 377-9.

33. Joseph Denieffe, *Personal recollections of the Irish Revolutionary Brotherhood* ... (New York, 1906).

34. MS 331; John Lalor to J.L. O'Ferrall, 11 Nov. 1861 (Cullen papers, Dublin Diocesan Archives).

35. See Jacqueline R. Hill, 'The intelligentsia and Irish nationalism in the 1840s' in *Studia Hibernica*, no. 20 (1980), pp 73-110.

36. T.D. Sullivan, *Recollections*, p. 12.

37. Ryan, *Fenian chief*, pp. 1-10.

38. B. Ó Cathaoir, 'John O'Mahony, 1815-77' in *Capuchin Annual 1977*, pp 180-93; James Maher (ed.), *Chief of the Comeraghs* (Mullinahone, 1957).

39. John Savage, *Fenian heroes and martyrs* (New York, 1868), p. 307; this is a compilation of rushed pieces written for the Irish-American press in 1865-6.

40. Quoted in Ryan, *Fenian chief*, p. 62.

41. MS 331.

42. *Weekly Freeman*, 6 Oct. 1883 and ff.

43. F. Davys to Lord Naas, 26 Jan. 1859 (Mayo papers, N.L.I., MS 11187).

44. *Weekly Freeman*, 6 Oct. 1883 and ff.

45. Blanche Tuohill, *William Smith O'Brien and his Irish revolutionary companions in exile* (Columbia and London, 1981), p. xii.

46. Seán Ó Luing, *Ó Donnabháin Rosa I* (Dublin, 1969), pp. 66-7.

47. *Irishman*, 7 Sept. 1867.

48. Ó Luing, *Ó Donnabháin Rosa I*, pp 16-33.

49. Ibid., pp 64-5.

Chapter Two

1. Peter Singer, *Marx* (London, 1978), p. 7.

2. P.M. Kennedy, *The rise and fall of British naval mastery* (London, 1976), pp 172-3.

3. See R.V. Comerford, 'Anglo-French tension and the origins of fenianism' in *Varieties of tension*, pp 152-3.

4. See, for instance, a spate of letters to William Smith O'Brien at this time (MS 447).

5. *Nation*, 27 Mar.-29 May 1958.

6. P.J. Smyth to John Martin, 3 Feb. 1859 (N.L.I., Hickey collection, MS 3226).

7. Denis Gwynn, *Cardinal Wiseman* (London, 1929), pp 265-7.

8. Ibid.; see also *The sermons, lectures and speeches delivered by his eminence Cardinal Wiseman ... during his tour of Ireland ...* (Dublin, 1859).
9. Quoted in *Irishman*, 8 Jan. 1859.
10. MS 331: Joseph Denieffe, *A personal narrative of the Irish Revolutionary Brotherhood . . .* (New York, 1906), p. 17.
11. Ryan, *Fenian chief*, pp 61-2.
12. Denieffe, *Personal narrative*, p. 87.
13. Ibid., pp 159-40.
14. Ibid., p. 12.
15. Original in Stephens collection among the Davitt papers in T.C.D. Library.
16. MS 331; Denieffe, *Personal narrative*, p. 125.
17. J.H. Lepper, *Famous secret societies* (London, 1932), p. 175.
18. MS 331.
19. Lord Tenterden, 'The fenian brotherhood: an account of the Irish American revolutionary societies in the United States from 1848 to 1870' (Printed Foreign Office memorandum, Feb. 1871).
20. *Irishman*, 23 Oct. 1858.
21. Denieffe, pp 25-6.
22. MS 331.
23. Seán Ó Luing, *Ó Donnabháin Rosa I*, pp 84-8.
24. Constabulary reports: Kenmare, 3 and 7 Nov. 1858; Skibbereen, 27 Dec. 1858; undated statement of Robert Cusack (S.P.O., Police reports on secret societies, 1857-9).
25. The episode is covered by numerous items in the S.P.O. collection 'Police reports, on secret societies, 1857-9', and among the Mayo papers (N.L.I., especially MSS 11187 and 11188).
26. Ó Luing, *Ó Donnabháin Rosa 1*, p. 103.
27. See Co. Kilkenny file in 'Police reports on secret societies, 1857-9' (S.P.O.).
28. MS 331.
29. Ibid.
30. Ryan, *Fenian chief*, pp 128-40; D'Arcy, *Fenian movement*, p. 12.
31. Document in hand of Stephens and Meagher (T.C.D., Davitt add.).
32. Document of 9 Dec. 1858 (T.C.D., Davitt add.).
33. Meagher to Stephens, 26 Jan. 1859 (T.C.D. Davitt add.).
34. MS 331.
35. *Irishman*, 16 Aug. 1862.
36. Document commissioning Stephens, New York, 9 Dec. 1858 (Davitt add., T.C.D.); letters of Stephens, January and April 1859 quoted in D'Arcy, *Fenian movement*, pp 12-13.
37. See *Irishman*, 12 Feb. 1959.
38. MS 331; D'Arcy, *Fenian movement*; Kevin Quigley, 'American financing of fenianism in Ireland 1858-67' (M.A. thesis, Maynooth, 1983), pp 11-12.
39. MS 331.
40. Ryan, *Fenian chief*, p. 156.
41. Diary of James Stephens, 1859 (Public Record Office of Northern Ireland: photostat in N.L.I., MS 4148).
42. William Dillon, *Life of John Mitchel* (2 vols, London, 1888), ii, 132-8, 142 and ff; Ministry of the Interior to Ministry of Foreign Affairs, 3 Sept. 1859 (Archives Ministère des Affaires Etrangeres, Affaires diverses politiques, Angleterre).
43. MS 331.
44. Ibid; Denieffe, *Personal narrative*, pp 46-8.
45. *Nation*, 19 Apr. 1862, supplement.
46. Ibid; Sullivan to W.S. O'Brien, 25 Oct. 1858 (N.L.I., W.S. O'Brien papers, MS 446).
47. Ibid; A.M. Sullivan, *New Ireland* (popular edition), pp 201-2.
48. *Nation*, 30 Oct. 1858.
49. *Irishman*, 9 Oct. 1858; *Nation*, 19 Apr. 1862.
50. MS 331.
51. John Vincent (ed.), *Disraeli, Derby and the conservative party: journals and memoirs of Edward Henry, Lord Stanley, 1849-69* (Hassocks, 1978), p. 40; Whyte, *Indep. Ir. party*, p. 56.
52. Ibid., pp 33-4.
53. *21 & 22 Vict.*, c. 103.
54. *Nation*, 3 July 1858.
55. Ibid., 26 June 1858.

56. Whyte, *Indep. Ir. party*, p. 153.

57. *Nation*, 7 and 14 May 1859.

58. *Irishman*, 17 Dec. 1859.

59. For a thorough exposition see K.T. Hoppen, 'Tories, catholics and the general election of 1859' in *Hist. Jn.*, xii, no 1 (1970), pp 48-67.

60. See *Nation*, 6 June 1857 and 16 Jan. 1858.

61. *Irishman*, 21 Aug. 1858; *Evening News* (Dublin), 20 Jan. 1859.

62. *Nation*, 19 Feb. 1859; *Tipperary Examiner*, 5 Mar. 1859.

63. See, for example, *Nation*, 16 Jan. 1858 and 22 Jan. 1859.

64. *Dundalk Democrat* cited in *Nation*, 9 Mar. 1861.

65. Sir Bernard Burke, *Genealogical and heraldic history of the landed gentry of Ireland* (4th ed., London, 1958), pp 533-4; T.D. Sullivan, *Recollections of troubled times in Irish politics* (Dublin, 1905), p. 148.

66. See R.V. Comerford, 'Anglo French tension and the origins of fenianism' in *Varieties of tension*, p. 163.

67. *Irishman*, 3 Sept. 1859.

68. *Nation*, 15 Sept. 1860.

69. Ibid., 8 Oct., 17 Dec. 1859; *Irishman*, 19 Nov., 10 Dec., 1859.

70. *Irishman*, 3 Mar. 1860; Archbishop Cullen to Fr. Kirby, 28 July 1860 ('Irish College, Rome: Kirby papers; guide to material of public and political interest, 1836-61' ed. by P.J. Corish in *Archivium Hibernicum*, xxxi (1973), p. 79).

71. G.F.H. Berkeley, *The Irish battalion in the papal army of 1860* (Dublin and Cork, 1929), p. 6.

72. E.R. Norman, *The catholic church and Ireland in the age of rebellion, 1859-73* (London, 1965), pp. 49-50.

73. Quoted in Christopher O'Dwyer 'Archbishop Leahy of Cashel, 1806-75' (M.A. thesis, Maynooth, 1971).

74. Cullen to Kirby, 10 Apr., 5 June 1860 (Kirby papers, *Arch. Hib.*, xxxi, pp 76, 77).

75. Cullen to Kirby, 18 May, 1 June 1860 (Kirby papers, *Arch. Hib.*, xxxi, p. 77).

76. Berkeley, *Irish battalion*, pp 22 and ff.

77. Ibid., 107-215.

78. *Times*, 25 Sept. 1860; *Nation*, 22, 29 Sept. 1860.

79. Cullen to Kirby, 5 Oct. 1860 (Kirby papers, *Arch. Hib.*, xxxi, p. 79).

80. 29 Sept. 1860.

81. *Irishman*, 10 Nov. 1860.

82. Cullen to Kirby, 6 Nov., 7, 27 Dec. 1860 (Kirby papers, *Arch. Hib.*, xxxi, pp 80-81).

83. Norman, *Catholic Church and Ireland*, p. 63.

84. *Irishman, Nation*, 17 Dec. 1859.

85. 17 Dec. 1859.

86. Cullen to Kirby, 7 Dec. 1860 (Kirby papers, *Arch. Hib.*, xxxi, p. 80).

87. Norman, p. 37.

88. Cullen to Kirby, 3 Feb. and 16 Mar. 1860 (Kirby papers, *Arch. Hib.*, xxxi, pp 94-5).

89. 19 May, 30 June 1860.

90. *Nation*, 1 Sept. 1860.

91. Ibid., 7 July 1860; *Irishman*, 30 June, 7 July 1860.

92. Journal of W.J. O'Neill Daunt (N.L.I., MS 3041).

93. *Irishman*, 8 Dec. 1860.

94. *Nation*, 26 Jan. 1861.

95. *Irishman*, 12 Jan. 1861.

96. Ibid., 2 Mar. 1861.

97. Ibid., 11 May 1861.

98. *Nation*, 5 June 1861.

99. *Census of Ireland 1861*, part V, pp xiv, xvii, xxvii and 464.

100. *Irishman*, 13 July 1858; *Nation* 21 Aug. 1858.

101. *Irishman*, 31 Nov. 1858.

102. John Devoy's recollections in *Irish Freedom*, Mar. 1913.

103. *Nation*, 20 Mar. 1858, 1 Sept. 1860.

104. Ibid., 20 Mar., 3 Apr. 1858.

105. Ibid., 1 Sept. 1860; *Irishman*, 18 Dec. 1858 and 19 Jan. 1861.

106. *Irishman*, 18 Dec. 1858.

107. Ibid., 1 June 1861.

108. Ibid., 2 Jan. 1864.

Chapter Three

1. T.C. Luby to John O'Mahony, 25 Aug. 1860 (New York Public Library, O'Donovan Rossa papers; on microfilm in N.L.I.).
2. MS 331.
3. MS 331; Denieffe, *Personal narrative*, p. 60.
4. Stephens to Anon., 16 June 1850 (Davitt addenda, T.C.D., MS 9695d); Geoffrey Best, *War and Society in Revolutionary Europe, 1770-1870* (London, 1982), p. 271.
5. MS 331; Devoy, *Recollections of an Irish rebel* (New York, 1929), p. 26.
6. Ibid.
7. MS 331.
8. J.E. Pigot to W.S. O'Brien, 21 Dec. 1858 (N.L.I., W.S. O'Brien papers, MS 446); J.E. Pigot to W.S. O'Brien, 4 Sept. 1860 (N.L.I., W.S. O'Brien papers, MS 447).
9. Copy of G.H. Moore to W.J. O'Neill Daunt, 10 Feb. 1863 (N.L.I., O'Neill Daunt journal, appendix, MS 3042).
10. E.g., *Nation*, 17 Aug. 1861.
11. *Celt*, Mar., May 1858.
12. See ch. 2 above; see Sullivan, *New Ireland* (popular edition), p. 248 for reference to their close association at this time.
13. *Nation*, 9 Mar. 1861.
14. Underwood to W.S. O'Brien, 21 Dec. 1857 (N.L.I., W.S. O'Brien papers, MS 446); *Nation*, 5, 12 Dec. 1857.
15. *Irishman*, 21 May 1859.
16. Ibid., 8 Dec. 1860.
17. Ibid., 26 Jan. 1861.
18. Ibid., 2 Mar. 1861.
19. Ibid., 9 Mar. 1861.
20. J.C. Waters to W.S. O'Brien, 22 Mar. 1861 (N.L.I., W.S. O'Brien papers, MS 447).
21. *Nation*, 19 Mar. 1859.
22. *Irishman*, 26 Jan., 23 Mar. 1861.
23. Ibid., 23 Mar. 1861.
24. *Irishman*, 9 Mar. 1861.
25. J.C. Waters to W.S. O'Brien, 22 Mar. 1861 (N.L.I., W.S. O'Brien papers, MS 447).
26. *Irishman*, 23 Mar. 1861.
27. Ibid.
28. *Nation*, 23 Mar. 1861.
29. *Irishman*, 23 Mar. 1861.
30. Ibid., 23, 30 Mar. 1861.
31. Ibid., 13 Apr. 1861, 15 and 22 Feb. 1862.
32. Ibid., 25 May 1861.
33. Ibid., 22 Oct. 1859; police report, 11 Nov. 1861 (S.P.O., Chief secretary's office, Registered papers, 1877/3591); J.F. Maguire, M.P., to W.S. O'Brien, 28 June 1858 (N.L.I., W.S. O'Brien papers, MS 446).
34. P.J. Smyth to W.S. O'Brien, 1, 10 and 14 Oct. 1859 (N.L.I., W.S. O'Brien papers, MS 446).
35. *Irishman*, 22 Oct. 1859; 15 Aug. 1859 was the ninetieth anniversary of the birth of Napoleon I.
36. Ibid., *Nation*, 17 Sept. 1859.
37. *Irishman*, 26 Nov. 1859.
38. *Irishman, Nation*, 14 Apr. 1860.
39. T.G. McAllister, *Terence Bellew MacManus. 1811(?)-1861: a short biography* (Maynooth, 1972), p. 41
40. *Irishman*, 23 Feb. and 2 Mar. 1861; *Nation*, 23 Feb. 1861.
41. *Irishman, Nation*, 25 May 1861.
42. D'Arcy, *Fenian movement in U.S.*, p. 19; *Irishman*, 25 May 1861.
43. *Irishman*, 31 Aug. 1861.
44. L.R. Bisceglia, 'The funeral of Terence Bellew MacManus' in *Eire-Ireland*.
45. MS 331.
46. *Irishman, Nation*, 25 May 1861.
47. *Nation*, 1 June, 8 June 1861; *Irishman*, 8 June 1861.
48. MS 331; *Irishman*, 20 July, 3 Aug. and 7 Sept. 1861.
49. MS 331.
50. *Irishman*, 20 July, 3 Aug. 1861.
51. Ibid., 28 Sept., 12, 19 Oct. 1861.
52. *Nation*, 5 Oct. 1861.
53. *Irishman*, 21 Aug. 1869.
54. See, e.g., letter in *Irishman*, 1 June 1861.
55. E.J. Ryan to Archbishop Cullen, Oct. 1861 (D.D.A., Cullen papers, Incoming correspondence, 1861); MacManus funeral committee to Cullen, 19 Oct. 1861 (D.D.A.,

Cullen papers, Incoming correspondence, 1861).
56. *Irishman*, 2 Nov. 1861.
57. *Nation*, 26 Oct., 9 Nov. 1861.
58. MS 331; Seamus Pender, 'Luby, Kenyon and the MacManus funeral' in *Cork Hist. and Arch. Soc. Jn.*, lvi, no. 183 (June 1951), pp 52-65.
59. *Irishman*, *Nation*, 16 Nov. 1861.
60. Police reports, 6, 8 and 9 Nov. 1861 (S.P.O., Chief secretary's office, Registered papers, 1877/3591).
61. *Irishman*, 9 Nov. 1861.
62. T.N. Underwood to W.S. O'Brien, 1 Jan. 1862 (N.L.I., W.S. O'Brien papers, MS 447).
63. *Irishman*, 16 Nov. 1861.
64. Denieffe, *Personal narrative*, p. 70; Police report, 11 Nov. 1851 (S.P.O., Chief secretary's office, Registered papers, 1877/3591).
65. Police report, 11 Nov. 1861 (S.P.O., Chief secretary's office, Registered papers, 1877/3591).
66. Ibid.
67. *Freeman's Journal*, 23, 24 Aug. 1861.
68. Ibid.
69. Police report, 20 July 1862 (S.P.O., Chief secretary's office, Registered papers, 1877/3591).
70. *Nation*, *Irishman*, 12, 19, 26 July 1862.
71. Norman, *Catholic church and Ireland*, pp 94-5.
72. *Irishman*, 22 Feb. 1862.
73. Ibid., 30 Mar. 1861, 22 Feb. 1862.
74. *Nation*, 22 Mar. 1862; *Irishman*, 29 Mar. 1862.
75. MS 331; *Irishman*, 5 Apr. 1862.
76. T.N. Underwood to W.S. O'Brien, 1 Jan. 1862 (N.L.I., W.S. O'Brien papers, MS 447); The O'Donoghue to W.S. O'Brien, not dated, but clearly 1862 (N.L.I., W.S. O'Brien papers, MS 447); *Irishman*, 5 Apr. 1862.
77. T.N. Underwood to W.S. O'Brien, 1 Jan. 1862 (N.L.I., W.S. O'Brien papers, MS 447); see above, ch. 1.
78. *Nation*, 28 Aug. 1858.
79. *Irishman*, 22 Mar. 1862, 21 Mar. 1863, 19 Mar. 1864.
80. Denieffe, p. 56; Devoy, *Recollections*, p. 35.
81. *Nation*, 6 Apr. 1861.
82. Ibid., 25 May 1861.
83. Ibid., 13 July 1861.
84. Ibid., 13 July 1861.
85. *Nation*, 17 Aug. 1861.
86. John Mitchel to John O'Mahony, 8 May 1861, quoted in Denieffe, *Personal narrative*, pp 164-5.
87. Ibid.
88. *Irishman*, 8 Dec. 1860.
89. Ibid., 15 Dec. 1860.
90. *Nation*, 9 Feb. 1861.
91. *Irishman*, 15 Dec. 1860, 13 Apr. 1861.
92. J. Mitchel to J. O'Mahony, 8 May 1861, quoted in *Denieffe*, pp 164-5.
93. Ibid.
94. American paper quoted in *Irishman*, 12 Oct. 1861.
95. *Nation*, 16 Nov. 1861.
96. T.N. Underwood to W.S. O'Brien, 1 Jan. 1862 (N.L.I., W.S. O'Brien papers, MS 447).
97. *Nation*, 30 Nov., 14 Dec. 1861.
98. Ibid; MS 331.
99. *Irishman*, 7 Dec. 1861; J. Stephens to John O'Mahony, 25 Feb. 1862 quoted in Denieffe, pp 167-79; MS 331.
100. *Irishman*, 7 Dec. 1861; MS 331; Denieffe, pp 167-79.
101. *Irishman*, 28 Dec. 1861, 16 Feb., 12 Apr. 1862.
102. *Irishman*, 19 Apr. 1862; *Nation*, 17 May 1862.
103. *Irishman*, 31 May 1862.
104. Ibid., 3 May 1862.
105. *Nation*, 17 May 1862.
106. E.G., *Nation*, 12 July 1862, 24 Jan., 28 Mar. 1863; *Irishman*, 31 May 1862, 9 May, 22 Aug. 1863.
107. *Fenian chief*, pp 57-105; MS 331.
108. 21, 28 May, 4, 25 June, 19 Nov., etc.
109. *Nation*, 6 Sept. 1862.
110. Ibid., 2 Apr. 1864.
111. Smith O'Brien to secretary, Cork National Reading Room, 20 Oct. 1860 (N.L.I., W.S. O'Brien

papers, MS 447).
112. Dillon to Smith O'Brien, 23 July 1864 (N.L.I., MS 8657).
113. E.g., *Irishman*, 4 Jan. 1862.
114. Ibid.
115. Cato (i.e. P.J. Smyth) in *Irishman*, 14 Jan. 1865.
116. MS 331.
117. Sullivan, *New Ireland*, p. 248.
118. MS 331.
119. *Irishman*, 22 Sept. 1866.
120. *Nation*, 26 July 1862.
121. Ibid.
122. *Nation*, 27 Sept. 1862; *Irishman*, 18 Oct. 1862.
123. *Irishman*, 18 Oct. 1862.
124. Ibid., 8, 29 Nov. 1862.
125. Mullen to J.P. McDonnell, 31 July 1863 (S.P.O., Fenian briefs).
126. *Nation*, 7 Jan. 1865.
127. *Irishman*, 25 May 1861.
128. Ibid., 16 Aug. 1862.
129. *Irishman*, 12 May 1860; *Nation*, 19 May 1860.
130. *Irishman*, 22 Dec. 1860; *Nation*, 29 Dec. 1860.
131. *Irishman*, 22 June, 3 Aug. 1861, 28 Mar. 1863.
132. Ibid., 26 Apr. 1862.
133. *Nation*, 21 June 1862; *Irishman*, 28 June 1862.
134. *Irishman*, 4, 18 Apr. 1863.
135. C.J. Kickham to E.J. Ryan, 14 Dec. 1861 (S.P.O., Fenian briefs).
136. Printed address of central association of National Brotherhood of St. Patrick, 1 Apr. 1863 (S.P.O., Fenian briefs).
137. J. Warren [i.e. J. Stephens] to T.C. Luby on 14 Aug. 1863 (S.P.O., Fenian briefs).
138. MS 331.
139. J. Warren [i.e. J. Stephens] to T.C. Luby, undated (S.P.O., Fenian briefs).
140. MS 331.
141. *Tipperary Advocate*, 8 Aug. 1863.
142. *Nation*, 8, 15 and 22 Aug. and 3 Oct. 1863.
143. M. Bourke, *John O'Leary: a study in Irish separatism* (Tralee, 1967).
144. J.S. Donnelly, Jr., 'The Irish agricultural depression of 1859-64', in *Ir. Econ. and Soc. Hist.* iii (1976), pp 33-54.

Chapter Four

1. *Irishman*, 30 May, 20, 27 June, 11 July, 1 Aug. 1863.
2. Martin to Smith O'Brien, 4 July 1863 (N.L.I., W.S. O'Brien papers, MS 447).
3. *Irishman*, 26 Sept., 17 Oct., 12, 19 Dec. 1863; *Nation*, 24 Oct. 1863.
4. Police report, January 1864 (N.L.I., Larcom papers, MS 7725).
5. *Nation*, 27 Feb. 1864.
6. Ibid., 23 Jan. 6 Feb. 1864; *Irishman*, 30 Jan. 1864.
7. Journal of W.J. O'Neill Daunt, 3 Jan. 1865 (N.L.I., MS 3041).
8. *Irishman*, 18 Jan. 1868.
9. *Irishman*, *Nation*, 27 Feb. 1864; MS 331.
10. MS 331.
11. *Nation*, 7 May 1864.
12. Ibid., 28 Jan., 4 Feb. 1865.
13. Ibid., 25 Feb. 1865.
14. Police report, August 1865 (C.S.O., R.P. 1864/18377 on 1877/3591).
15. Brendan Mac Giolla Choille, 'Dublin trades in procession, 1864' in *Saothar*, i, no. 1, pp 18-30.
16. *Irishman*, 6 Aug. 1864.
17. Dorrian to Kirby, 10 Aug. 1864 (Kirby papers: *Arch. Hib.*, xxx, p. 43).
18. *Freeman's Journal*, 9 Aug. 1864.
19. *Nation*, *Irishman*, 14 May 1864.
20. Norman, *Catholic church and Ireland*, pp 177-180; P.J. Corish, 'Political problems, 1860-78' in *A History of Irish Catholicism*, v, fasc. 2, p. 30.
21. Christopher O'Dwyer, 'Archbishop Leahy of Cashel, 1806-75' (M.A. thesis, Maynooth, 1971), pp 286-7.
22. Norman, *Catholic church and Ireland*, p. 137.

23. Ibid., pp 142-3.
24. Ibid., p. 150.
25. Ibid., pp 152-62.
26. Ibid., p. 150.
27. Ibid., p. 141.
28. *Nation*, 29 July 1865.
29. Norman, *Catholic church and Ireland*, p. 140.
30. Ibid., p. 136.
31. Ibid., pp 185-6.
32. O'Dwyer, 'Leahy', pp 284-5.
33. J. Warren [i.e. James Stephens] to T.C. Luby, 7 Sept. 1863 (S.P.O., Fenian briefs); MS 331.
34. MS 331.
35. *New Ireland*, p. 249.
36. MSS 331, 333.
37. *Nation*, 24 Oct. 1863.
38. *Nation*, 24 Oct. 1863.
39. 19 Mar. 1864, 14 Jan., 9 Sept. 1865.
39. See R.V. Comerford 'Patriotism as pastime: the appeal of fenianism in the mid-1860s' in *I.H.S.*, xxii, no. 87 (Mar. 1981), pp 239-50.
40. See Maurice Agulhon,*Penitents et francs-macons de l'ancienne Provence* (Paris, 1968).
41. O'Dwyer, *Leahy of Cashel*, pp 440-42.
42. R.V. Comerford, *Charles J. Kickham (1829-82): a study in Irish nationalism and literature* (Dublin, 1979), pp 69-76.
43. Corish, Political problems 1860-78', pp 6 and ff.
44. W.E. Vaughan and André Fitzpatrick (ed.), *Irish historical statistics: population 1821-1971* (Dublin, 1978), p. 161.
45. See *Irish People*, 23 Jan., 6 Feb., 5 Mar. 1864; J.M. Hernon, *Celts Catholics and copperheads: Ireland views the American Civil War* (Ohio, 1968), pp 26, 28, 34.
46. D'Arcy, *Fenian movement*, p. 59.
47. 25 Feb. 1865.
48. *Nation*, 5 June 1858.
49. 'An address to the members of the National Brotherhood in Ireland and in exile . . .', 24 Sept. 1863 (S.P.O., Police and crime records, Fenian briefs).
50. Draft address of P.S. Banaghan, 11 April 1864 (S.P.O., Police and crime records, Fenian briefs).
51. Marjolein 't Hart, '"Heading for Paddy's green shamrock shore": the returned emigrants in nine-teenth-century Ireland' in *Ir. Econ. and Soc. Hist.*, x (1983), pp 96-7. (Thesis abstract).
52. Doheny to W.S. O'Brien, 20 Aug. 1858 (N.L.I., W.S. O'Brien papers, MS 446).
53. Here I am drawing on the work of Brian Griffin for his M.A. thesis 'The I.R.B. in Connacht and Leinster 1858-78' (Maynooth, 1983).
54. MS 331; See Seán Ó Luing, 'A contribution to a study of fenianism in Breifne' in *Breifne*, iii, no 10 (1967), pp 155-74, especially the excerpt quoted from *Irish Republic* (Chicago), 22 Feb. 1868 on pp 160-62.
55. See Brendán MacGiolla Choille, 'Fenians, Rice and ribbonmen in Co. Monaghan, 1864-67' in *Clogher Record*, vi, no 2 (1967), pp 221-52.
56. See map page 208.
57. *Irishman*, 12 Apr. 1862, 18 Apr. 1863; Police report, 5 Sept. 1864 (S.P.O. Police and crime records, Fenian police reports, 1864-65); D'Arcy,*Fenian movement*, pp 63-4.
58. J.M. Hernon, *Celts, catholics and copperheads*, p. 11.
59. D'Arcy, *Fenian movement*, pp 36-8.
60. Kevin Quigley, 'American financing of fenianism in Ireland, 1858-67' (M.A. thesis, Maynooth, 1983), pp 46-50.
61. D'Arcy, *Fenian movement*, pp 40-43.
62. See Brian Jenkins, *Fenians and Anglo-American relations during reconstruction* (Ithaca, 1969).
63. British consular report, New York, 5 May 1865 (S.P.O. fenian police reports, 1864-5).
64. D'Arcy, *Fenian movement*, pp 98, 174-5.
65. John Vincent (ed.), *Disraeli, Derby and the conservative party: journals and memoirs of Edward Henry, Lord Stanley, 1849-69* (Hassocks, 1978).
66. See, for example, Constabulary crime records, Fenian briefs).

reports, 29 May, 29 August, 21 Sept., 25 Oct. 1865 (S.P.O., Fenian police reports, 1864-5).

67. MS 5964.

68. D'Arcy, *Fenian movement*, pp 44-50.

69. Ibid., pp 59-60: MS 5964.

70. MS 5964; MS 331.

71. *Contemporary Review*, lxxxi, pp 680-93.

72. D'Arcy, *Fenian movement*, pp 44-51.

73. Constabulary report, Carrick on-Suir, 23 Feb. 1865 (S.P.O.. Fenian police reports, 1864-5).

74. MS 5964.

75. A.J. Semple, 'The fenian infiltration of the British army in Ireland, 1864-7' (M. Litt. thesis, T.C.D., 1971), pp 47-52.

76. John Devoy, *Recollections of an Irish rebel*, pp 128 and ff.

77. Semple, 'Fenian infiltration', p. 170.

78. Ibid., p. 31.

79. MS 333.

80. MS 5964.

81. D'Arcy, p. 70.

82. Stephens to the Clonmel 'Bs', 8 Sept. 1865 (S.P.O., Police and crime records, Fenian briefs).

83. D'Arcy, pp 76-7.

84. MS 5964.

85. Denieffe, *Personal narrative*, pp 126-7; Devoy, *Recollections*, pp 88-97.

86. Ryan, *Fenian chief*, pp 228-42.

Chapter Five

1. William D'Arcy, *The fenian movement in the United States, 1858-86* (Washington, 1947), pp 79-81.

2. Ibid., p. 84.

3. Ibid., p. 107.

4. Ibid., pp 169-79.

5. Ibid., p. 214.

6. *29 Vict.*, c. 4.

7. *Irish Republic* (Chicago), 22 February 1868 quoted in Ó Luing, 'Fenianism in Breifne', pp 160-62; Anonymous [Duffy] to Stephens, 1 and 14 Aug. 1866 (T.C.D., Davitt add.).

8. Leon Ó Broin, *Fenian fever: an Anglo-American dilemma* (London, 1971), pp 96-7.

9. Government memo, June 1867 (N.L.I., Larcom papers, MS 7697).

10. Ryan, *Fenian chief*, pp 243-54.

11. 'Summary of the progress of fenianism up to 1868' (N.L.I., Larcom papers, MS 7517).

12. Ó Broin, *Fenian fever*, pp 129-32.

13. 'Summary of the progress of fenianism' (N.L.I. MS 7517); 'Memoir' of dates of Col. Octave Fariola, Adj. General, F.B. and I.R. (T.C.D., Davitt add.); D'Arcy, *Fenian movement*, pp 251 and ff.

14. *Irishman*, 9 Mar. 1867.

15. 'Summary of the progress of fenianism' (MS 7517).

16. Geoffrey Best, *War and society in revolutionary Europe, 1770-1870* (London, 1982), pp 298-9.

17. Ó Broin, *Fenian fever*, p. 137 and ff.

18. Ibid., pp 143-55.

19. Ibid., pp 157-73.

20. *Nation*, 14 Oct., 16 Dec. 1865.

21. *Freeman's Journal*, 8 June 1865.

22. See chapter two, above.

23. *Freeman's Journal*, 19 Apr. 1866.

24. *Nation*, 5 May 1866.

25. Ibid., 9 June 1866.

26. Norman, *Catholic church and Ireland*, pp 205, 294.

27. John Vincent, *The formation of the British Liberal party* (London, 1966), pp 192-4, 227-32.

28. *Nation, Irishman*, 3 Nov. 1866; *Freeman's Journal*, 31 Oct. 1866.

29. *Nation, Irishman*, 3, 10 Nov. 1866.

30. Lord Strathnairn to Duke of Cambridge, 16 Mar. 1867 (quoted in Ó Broin, *Fenian fever*, p. 164).

31. Ó Broin, *Fenian fever*, p. 179.

32. *Nation*, 24 Aug. 1867; the subsequent history of *Speeches from the dock* is a bibliographical study in itself.

33. *Hansard 3*, clxxxvi, coll 1929-33.

34. *Hansard 3*, clxxxvi, coll 1945-87.

35. *Report of the commissioners on the treatment of the treason felony convicts in the English convict prisons* [3880], H.C. 1867, xxxv, 673-98.

36. *Irishman*, 20 July 1867.

37. *Irishman*, 31 Mar. 1866.

38. *Freeman's Journal*, 16 Sept. 1867; *Irishman*, 21 Sept. 1867.

39. Ó Broin, *Fenian fever*, p. 156.

40. *Irishman*, 12 Oct. 1867.

41. Quinlivan and Rose, pp 37-73; J. Vincent (ed.), *Journals of Lord Stanley*.

42. Journal of O'Neill Daunt (N.L.I., MS 3041).

43. *Irishman*, *Nation*, 30 Nov. 1867.

44. *Freeman's Journal*, 7 Dec. 1867.

45. Ibid., 9 Dec. 1867.

46. Ó Broin, *Fenian fever*, pp 206-7.

47. See *Irishman*, 21 Dec. 1867.

48. *Freeman's Journal*, 9 Dec. 1867.

49. J.L. Hammond, *Gladstone and the Irish nation*, pp 80-81.

50. Norman, *Catholic church and Ireland*, p. 242.

51. Ibid., pp 272-3.

52. *Hansard 3*, cxc, coll 1764 (16 Mar. 1868).

53. Norman, *Catholic church and Ireland*, p. 273.

54. Quoted in *Dublin Review* (new series), x (Apr. 1868), p. 488.

55. *Hansard 3*, cxcvi (31 May 1869). An exchange of letters on the subject with Lord Grey in April 1869 which has recently come to light exhibits the same lack of clarity: see *The Gladstone diaries*, viii (Oxford, 1982), pp 60-61.

56. J.R. Vincent, 'Gladstone and Ireland' in *Proceedings of the British Academy, London* lxiii (1977) pp 401 and ff.

57. Ó Broin, *Fenian fever*, p. 225, 234.

58. *Freeman's Journal*, 17 Apr. 1868.

59. Ó Broin, *Fenian fever*, pp 234-5.

60. *Irishman*, 14 Mar. 1863.

61. Ibid., 18, 25 Apr. 1868.

62. Ó Broin, *Fenian fever*, p. 192.

63. J.L. Porter, *Life and times of Henry Cooke* (London, 1871), p 488 cited in Norman, *Catholic church and Ireland*, p. 304.

64. *Irishman*, 31 Aug. 1867, 29 Aug. 1868.

65. Ibid., 31 Aug. 1867.

66. Ibid., 29 Aug. 1868; (Robert Anderson), 'Fenianism, a narrative by one who knows' in *Contemporary Review*, xix (1872), pp 638-9.

67. *Irishman*, 31 Aug., 29 Aug. 1868; 'Summaries of the history of fenianism down to 1868' (N.L.I., MS 7517); Devoy, *Recollections*, pp 238-9.

68. *Irishman*, 8 Aug. 1868; [Anderson] 'Fenianism: a narrative by one who knows', pp 639-41.

69. Memo to Irish government, 18 Feb. 1868 (N.L.I., Mayo papers, MS 11188); Message from I.R.B. supreme council to the Irish people, 24 Apr. 1868 (S.P.O., F papers, 2906 R); Police report, 7 Mar. 1868 (N.L.I., Mayo papers, MS 11188); Constabulary Reports 28.6.1868 (S.P.O., F papers, 2919 R, 2922 R, 2924 R, 2944 R, 2900 R).

70. Ó Broin, *Fenian fever*, pp 217 ff.

71. Denieffe, *Personal narrative*, pp 44-5.

72. Ó Broin, *Fenian fever*, pp 222-3.

Chapter Six

1. Representation of the People (Ireland) Act (*31 & 32 Vict.*, c.49); Brian Walker, 'The Irish electorate, 1868-1915' in *I.H.S.*, xviii, no. 71 (Mar. 1973), pp 372-3.

2. *32 & 33 Vict.*, c. 42.

3. Quoted in Norman, *Catholic church and Ireland*, p. 382.

4. Ibid., p. 383.

5. Ibid., p. 382.

6. *Irishman*, 7 Nov. 1868.

7. David Thornley, *Isaac Butt and home rule* (London, 1964), pp 53-5.

8. Maurice Johnson, 'The fenian amnesty movement, 1868-79' (M.A. thesis, Maynooth, 1980, pp 94-9).

9. Ibid., p. 118.

10. Constitution of the I.R.B. supreme council, 18 Aug. 1869

(S.P.O., F papers, 6001 R).
11. Address of the I.R.B. supreme council to the people of Ireland, Jan. 1870 (S.P.O., F papers, 6450 R); notwithstanding the dating of this document, the meeting it refers to almost certainly took place on 27 Dec. 1869: police report, 30 Dec. 1869 (S.P.O., F papers, 5388 R).
12. [Robert Anderson] 'Fenianism: a narrative by one who knows' in Contemporary Review, xix (1872), p. 640; Irishman, 8 Aug. 1868.
13. Irishman, 4, 14, 19, 26 June 1869; Kickham to John O'Mahony, 28 Sept. 1869 (Catholic University of America, Washington, Fenian papers).
14. Irishman, 24 Oct. 1868.
15. Constitution of the I.R.B. supreme council, 18 Aug. 1869 (S.P.O., F papers, 6001 R).
16. Police reports, 1870 (S.P.O., F papers, 5599 R and 6935 R); return of arms surreptitiously brought into Ireland for fenian purposes, 1871 (S.P.O., F papers, 6890 R); T.W. Moody, Davitt and Irish revolution, 1847-82 (Oxford, 1981), pp 53-77.
17. Johnson, 'Amnesty movement', pp 125-47.
18. Ibid., pp 154-6.
19. Irishman, 22, 29 May, 5, 12 June 1969.
20. Report of the commissioners appointed to inquire into the treatment of treason-felony convicts in English prisons, together with appendix and minutes of evidence, Vol I [C-319], H.C. 1871, xxxii, pp 14-16, 30-32.
21. Ibid., pp 10-12.
22. Ibid., p. 12.
23. See The O'Donoghue to Gladstone, 9 Aug. and J.F. Maguire to Gladstone, 17 Sept. (British Library, Gladstone papers, Add MSS 44421 and 44422).
24. Johnson, 'Amnesty movement', p. 212.
25. See note 8 above.
26. Irishman, 23 Oct. 1869.
27. Johnson, 'Amnesty movement', pp 252-3.

28. E.D. Steele, Irish land and British politics: tenant-right and nationality 1865-70 (London, 1974), p. 63.
29. Homer Socolofsky, Landlord William Scully (Lawrence (Kansas), 1979), pp 52-4.
30. Hansard 3, cxcv, col 2010 (30 Apr. 1869).
31. Butt, The Irish people and the Irish land: a letter to Lord Lifford.
32. See Nation, 17 July, 20 Aug., 4 Sept., 2 Oct. 1969.
33. Johnson, 'Amnesty movement', p. 261.
34. Isaac Butt, Ireland's appeal for amnesty (Dublin, 1870).
35. Irishman, 6 Nov. 1869; Irish Freedom, Oct. 1912.
36. Irishman, 13 Nov. 1869.
37. Nation, 18 Dec. 1869.
38. Thornley, Butt, p. 72.
39. For more details see R.V. Comerford, Charles J. Kickham, (Dublin, 1979), pp 105-16.
40. Thornley, Butt, pp 72-3.
41. Steele, Land and politics, pp 271-4 analyses a wide range of reactions.
42. Hansard 3, cxcix, coll 122-52 (10 Feb. 1870).
43. Nation, 5 Feb. 1970; Steele, Land and politics, p. 295.
44. Thornley, Butt, pp 75-7.
45. Nation, 2 Apr. 1870.
46. 33 & 34 Vict. c. 46.
47. See W.E. Vaughan, Sin, sheep and Scotsmen: John George Adair and the Derryveagh evictions, 1861 (Belfast, 1983).
48. Ó Broin, Fenian fever, p. 248.
49. See P.J. Corish, 'Political problems, 1860-78' in A history of Irish catholicism, v, fasc. 3 (Dublin, 1967), pp 41-3; E. R. Norman, Catholic church and Ireland, pp 129-33.
50. Corish, 'Political problems', pp 46-7.
51. See Report from the select committee on Westmeath . . . , p. 9, H.C. 1871 (147), xiii, p. 565; constabulary report, Co. Armagh, 6 Oct. 1869 (S.P.O., F papers 4690 R); police report, 18 Sept. 1869 (S.P.O., F papers 4593 R); Brendan

Mac Giolla Choille, 'Fenians, Rice and ribbonmen in Co. Monaghan, 1864-7' in *Clogher Record*, vi, no 2 (1967), pp 226-7.

52. John O'Leary, *Recollections of fenians and fenianism* (2 vols, London, 1896), i, III and ii, 27.

53. *33 Vict.*, c. 9.

54. *34 & 35 Vict.*, c. 25.

55. Sean Daly, *Cork 1870-72*.

56. *Freeman's Journal*, 20 July 1870.

57. Máire Corkery, 'Ireland and the Franco-Prussian war' in *Etudes Irlandaises*, vii (1982), pp 127-44.

58. *Irishman*, 1 Oct. 1870.

59. Johnson, 'Amnesty campaign', pp. 390-99.

60. *Report of the commissioners appointed to enquire into the treatment of treason-felony convicts in English prisons, together with appendix and minutes of evidence* [c 319] and [c 391-1], H.C. 1871, xxxii.

61. Cormac Ó Grada, 'Fenianism and socialism: the career of Joseph Patrick McDonnell', in *Saothar*, i, no i (May 1975), pp 31-41.

62. William O'Brien and Desmond Ryan (ed.), *Devoy's Post Bag* (2 vols, Dublin, 1948, 1953), i, 42.

63. *Irishman*, 5 Nov. 1870.

64. Ryan, *Fenian chief*, p. 236.

65. T.F. MacCarthie's *People of Ireland*, Sept.-Dec. 1869.

66. Police report, 22 Sept. 1870 (S.P.O., F papers, 6852 R).

67. Police reports, 19 Oct., 8 Nov., 7 Dec. 1870 (S.P.O., F papers, 6903 R, 6956 R, 7019 R); draft letters of Stephens to unnamed correspondents in Ireland, 14 Feb., 22 Feb., 19 Apr. 1871 (T.C.D. Davitt add.).

68. See various items among papers of J.P. McDonnell 1863-4 (S.P.O., Fenian briefs).

69. Summaries of police reports, 1867-71 (S.P.O., fenianism: index of names, 1866-71); Police report, 21 May 1870 (S.P.O., F papers, 6450 R); letter of J.J. O'Kelly, 30 Nov. 1872 (*Devoy's post bag*, i, 60-61).

70. Thornley, *Butt*, p. 97; McCaffrey, 'Irish federalism in the 1870s' in *Transactions of the American Philosophical Society*, (1962), pp 1-58.

71. Constabulary report, Apr. or May 1870 (S.P.O., F papers 6344 R); see Comerford, *C.J. Kickham*, pp 122-3.

72. Thornley, *Butt*, p. 90.

73. Mark Ryan, *Fenian memories* (Dublin, 1945), p. 41.

74. Address of the I.R.B. supreme council, 20 Jan. 1870 (S.P.O., F papers, 6450 R).

75. Comerford, *C.J. Kickham*, pp 112-4.

76. Thornley, *Butt*, pp 105-6.

77. Ibid., pp 113-6.

78. Ibid., pp 117-8.

79. Mark Ryan, *Fenian memories*.

80. Quoted in *Annual Register*, 1872, p. 12.

81. See ibid., pp 79-85.

82. *Hansard 3*, ccxii col. 1763 (26 July 1872).

Chapter Seven

1. Norman, *The catholic church and Ireland in the age of rebellion, 1859-73* (London, 1965), pp 431-6.

2. P.J. Corish, 'Political problems, 1860-78' in *A history of Irish catholicism*, v, fasc. 3 (Dublin, 1967), p. 56.

3. Ibid.; Thornley, *Butt*, p. 153.

4. Thornley, *Butt*, p. 159.

5. Ibid., p. 179.

6. For a discussion of the topic see Michael Hurst, 'Ireland and the Ballot Act of 1872' in *Hist. Jn.*, viii, no. 3 (1965), pp 326-53.

7. Thornley, *Butt*, p. 192.

8. See Brian M. Walker, 'The land question and elections in Ulster, 1868-86' in Clark and Donnelly, *Irish peasants*.

9. Thornley, *Butt*, p. 207.

10. Moody, *Davitt*, pp 131-2.

11. Mark Ryan, *Fenian memories*.

12. Ibid.

13. Thornley, *Butt*, p. 213.

14. Ibid., pp 212-26.

15. Ibid., pp 227-8.
16. Ibid., pp 230-34.
17. Ibid., pp 279-84.
18. *41 & 42 Vict.*, c. 66; *42 & 43 Vict.*, c. 65. See T.J. Morrissey, *Towards a national university: William Delany S.J. (1835-1924) and an era of initiative in Irish education* (Dublin, 1983), pp 33-60.
19. Address of the I.R.B. supreme council to the officers and men of the I.R.A., [17 March 1873] in T.W. Moody and Leon Ó Broin (ed.), 'The I.R.B. supreme council, 1868-78' in *I.H.S.*, xix, no. 75 (Mar. 1975), pp 310, 13 (from Doran papers).
20. Amended constitution of the I.R.B. and of the supreme council, 17 March 1873 (Ibid., pp 313-7).
21. Thornley, *Butt*, pp 160-62.
22. Ibid., pp 164-5.
23. Ibid., pp 165-8.
24. Comerford, *C.J. Kickham*, pp 121-3.
25. MS among Doran papers reproduced in Moody and Ó Broin, 'I.R.B. supreme council', p. 294; for further detail on the episode see Comerford, *C.J. Kickham*, pp 131-2.
26. *Devoy's Post Bag*, i, 5, 26.
27. Ibid., i, 58-9, 114.
28. See *Irishman*, Feb. and Mar. 1876.
29. Comerford, *C.J. Kickham*, p. 131.
30. Kickham to Devoy, 6 July 1876 (*Devoy's Post Bag*, i, 191-3).
31. Sean Ó Luing, *Ó Donnabháin Rosa II* (Dublin, 1979), pp 61-8.
32. *Devoy's Post Bag*, i, 284-337.
33. Moody, *Davitt*, pp 156-8.
34. Johnson, 'Amnesty movement', pp 457-8.
35. Johnson, 'Amnesty campaign', pp 457-8.
36. Ibid., pp 455-6, 459-70.
37. Ibid., pp 481-5.
38. Address of the I.R.B. supreme council to the people of Ireland, Jan. 1870 in Moody and Ó Broin, 'The I.R.B. supreme council', p. 310.
39. Report of Mr Stritch, R.M., 25 Mar. 1870 (S.P.O., F papers, 6438 R).
40. Address of the I.R.B. supreme council to the officers and men of the I.R.A., [17 Mar. 1873] in Moody and Ó Broin, 'The I.R.B. supreme council', pp 310-11.
41. Address of the I.R.B. supreme council to the people of Ireland, January 1870 (Ibid. p. 310).
42. Devoy report 20 July 1879 (N.L.I., Devoy papers, MS 18039); in these pages I am considerably indebted to the work of Brian Griffin (M.A., Maynooth, 1983).
43. Report of Mr Stritch, R.M., 28 Feb. 1870 (S.P.O., F papers, 5773 R).
44. Irish Office memo., 23 Apr. 1878 (S.P.O., A files, A 574-6); resident magistrate's report, Tuam, 15 Apr. 1878 (C.S.O., R.P., 1878/7308).
45. Moody, *Davitt*, p. 191.
46. Thornley, *Butt*, pp 229-230.
47. *Annual Register, 1875*, pp 8-11.
48. Thornley, *Butt*, pp 265-8.
49. Ibid., p. 241.
50. D.A. Thornley, 'The Irish home rule party and parliamentary obstruction, 1875-87' in *I.H.S.*, xii, no. 45 (Mar. 1980).
51. *Freeman's Journal*, 15, 16 Jan. 1878.
52. John Vincent, 'Gladstone and Ireland' in *Proceedings of British Academy* lxiii (1977), p. 205.
53. Ibid., pp 205-9.
54. Thornley, *Butt*, p. 279.
55. Ibid., pp 310-15.
56. Ibid., pp 360-63; *Nation*, 10 Aug. 1878.
57. *Devoy's Post Bag*, i, 209-12.
58. Ibid., 293-4.
59. Resident magistrate's report, 15 Apr. 1878 (S.P.O., C.S.O., R.P. 1878/7308).
60. Ibid.
61. Ryan, *Fenian chief*, pp 273-81.
62. *Devoy's Post Bag*, i, 284-5. I have drawn on undergraduate research by F. Burns (Maynooth, 1979).

Chapter Eight

1. W.E. Vaughan, 'An assessment of the economic performance of Irish landlords, 1851-81' in *Varieties of tension*, p. 181.
2. David Thornley, *Isaac Butt and home rule* (London, 1964), p. 207.
3. See W.L. Feingold, 'The tenants' movement to capture the Irish poor law boards, 1877-86' in *Albion*, 7, no. 3 (1975).
4. Moody, *Davitt*, pp 186-220.
5. Ibid., p. 204.
6. J.J. O'Kelly to John Devoy, 5 Aug. and 21 Aug. 1877 (*D.P.B.*, i, 266-70).
7. Carroll to Devoy, 30 Mar. 1878 (*D.P.B.*, 323-5); Moody, *Davitt*, pp 205-6.
8. See chapter 7 above.
9. Moody, *Davitt*, pp 221-327.
10. Ibid., p. 225.
11. Ibid., pp 230-63.
12. Copy of Devoy's telegram provided to Dublin Castle by postmaster-general, 15 Nov. 1878 (S.P.O., Police and Crime Records, A. files, no. 550).
13. Moody, *Davitt*, p. 267.
14. Ibid., p. 256.
15. See ibid., p. 252.
16. See R.V. Comerford, *C.J. Kickham (1828-82): a study in Irish nationalism and literature* (Dublin, 1979), pp 141-2.
17. Moody, *Davitt*, pp 278-81.
18. Ibid., pp 280-300.
19. Ibid., p. 325.
20. For a survey see J.S. Donnelly, Jr., *The land and people of nineteenth-century Cork: the rural economy and the land question* (London and Boston, 1975) pp 251-5.
21. Moody, *Davitt*, p. 284.
22. Ibid., p. 291.
23. Michael Davitt, *The fall of feudalism in Ireland* (London and New York, 1904), pp 146-7.
24. *Connaught Telegraph*, 26 Apr. 1879.
25. See Moody, *Davitt*, p. 296.
26. Moody, *Davitt*, pp 317-8.
27. William Doyle, *The old European order*, p. 103.
28. See Sam Clark, *Social origins of the Irish land war* (Princeton, 1979), pp 259-60.
29. Ibid., p. 287.
30. *Freeman's Journal*, 17 Dec. 1879.
31. Moody, *Davitt*, p. 358.
32. John Vincent, 'Gladstone and Ireland' in *Proceedings of the British Academy, London*, lxiii (1977), p. 209.
33. See Moody, *Davitt*, p. 370.
34. John Vincent, 'Gladstone and Ireland', p. 210.
35. C.C. O'Brien, *Parnell and his party* (Oxford, 1974 edition), pp 26, 40-41.
36. Ibid., pp 18, 13; B.M. Walker, 'The land question and elections in Ulster, 1868-86' in Clark and Donnelly, *Irish peasants*, pp 244-6.
37. Paul Bew, *Land and the national question in Ireland, 1858-82* (Dublin, 1978), especially chs. 6, 7 and 8.
38. See L.P. Curtis, Jr., 'Incumbered wealth: landed indebtedness in post-famine Ireland' in *American Historical Review*, lxxxv, no. 2 (Apr. 1980), pp 332-67; and Moody, *Davitt*, pp 329-30.
39. See, for example, *Freeman's Journal*, 20 Oct. 8 and 15 Dec. 1880.
40. Moody, *Davitt*, p. 545.
41. C.C. O'Brien, *Parnell and his party*, pp 134-5.
42. Foster, *Randolph Churchill*, p. 50.
43. *Hansard 3*, cclii, col 67 (20 May 1880).
44. Harold Perkin, *The origins of modern English society, 1780-1880*, p. 452; Perkin points out that 'the land reform movement bulked much larger in contemporary politics and public opinion than it does in the histories of Victorian Britain' (p. 451, note 3).
45. Bew, *Land and the national question*, pp 142-3, 174-5.
46. Ibid., pp 133-4.
47. Maura Murphy, 'Fenianism, Parnellism and the Cork trades, 1860-1900' in *Saothar*, v, (1979), pp 30-31.
48. For a sample catalogue see

Donnelly, *Land and people of nineteenth century Cork*, pp 282-6.

49. *Freeman's Journal*, 15 Dec. 1880.

50. Undergraduate research work by T. Nelson, Maynooth, 1979.

51. Moody, *Davitt*, pp 292-5.

52. *44 & 45 Vict.*, c. 49.

53. *45 & 46 Vict.*, c. 47.

54. Moody, *Davitt*, pp 519-21.

55. I have endeavoured to tease them out in the case of C.J. Kickham, president of the supreme council, in *C.J. Kickham (1828-82)*, pp 142-55.

56. Moody, *Davitt*, pp 379-80.

57. Davitt to John Devoy, 6 Feb. 1880 (*D.P.B.* i, 482-4).

58. *Freeman's Journal*, 30 Apr. 1880.

59. Maura Murphy, 'Fenianism, Parnellism and the Cork trades, 1860-1900' in *Saothar*, v, (1979), p. 29.

60. Moody, *Davitt*, pp 402-3; see *Freeman's Journal*, 23 Aug. 1880.

61. Ibid., pp 381-412.

62. *Special commission act, 1888: reprint of the shorthand notes of the speeches, proceedings and evidence* . . . (12 vols, London, 1890), iv, 505-11.

63. Carroll to John Devoy, 12 Mar. 1880 (*D.P.B.*, i, 499-500).

64. John Devoy to James Reynolds, 21 June 1880 (*D.P.B.*, i, 533-4); Marcus Bourke, *John O'Leary: a study in Irish separatism* (Tralee, 1967), pp 163-4.

65. K.R.M. Short, *The dynamite war: Irish American bombers in Victorian Britain* (Dublin, 1979), ch. 2.

66. Ibid., pp 48 ff.

67. Lomasney to Devoy, 18 Feb. 1881 (*D.P.B.*, ii, 39-40).

68. Quoted in F.S.L. Lyons, *Charles Stewart Parnell* (London, 1977), p. 154.

69. Davitt to Devoy, 16 Dec. 1880 (*D.P.B.*, ii, 21-5).

70. Lomasney to Devoy, 31 Mar. 1881 (*D.P.B.*, ii, 56-9); Short, *Dynamite war*, p. 59; Henri Le Caron, *Twenty years in the secret service; the recollections of a spy* (Reprinted, Wakefield, 1974), p. 156.

71. Short, *Dynamite war*, chs. 4-8.

72. Tom Corfe, *The Phoenix Park murders: conflict, compromise and tragedy in Ireland 1879-82* (London, 1968), p. 135, sets out the problem.

73. Report of Detective-Inspector John Mallon (S.P.O., Fenian papers, B files, no. 267).

74. R.B. O'Brien, *The life of Charles Stewart Parnell* (London, 1898), p. 355.

75. *Irish World*, 24 Mar. 1883, cited in Bew, *Land and the national question*, p. 201.

76. Corfe, *The Phoenix Park murders*, p. 214.

77. Ibid., p. 230.

78. Lyons, *Parnell*, pp 390-432.

79. Perkin, *The origins of modern English society 1780-1880*, p. 220.

80. R.W. Kirkpatrick, 'Origins and development of the land war in mid-Ulster, 1879-85' in *Varieties of tension*, pp 201-35; Paul Bew and Frank Wright, 'The agrarian opposition in Ulster politics, 1848-87' in Clark and Donnelly, *Irish peasants*, pp 192-227; B.M. Walker, 'The land question and elections in Ulster, 1868-86', ibid., pp 230-68; for a reference to protestant farmers in Cork see Donnelly, *Land and people of nineteenth-century Cork*, p. 278.

81. C.C. O'Brien, *Parnell and his party*, pp 134-5.

82. Lyons, *Parnell*, p. 236.

BIBLIOGRAPHY

Primary Sources: I Manuscripts

PUBLIC RECORD OFFICE OF NORTHERN IRELAND, BELFAST: Diary of James Stephens, 1859. DUBLIN DIOCESAN ARCHIVES: Cullen papers (for selected periods). NATIONAL LIBRARY OF IRELAND: Thomas Clarke Luby's recollections. William Smith O'Brien papers and correspondence. Report by the inspector-general of constabulary, 1863. Journals of William Joseph O'Neill Daunt. Charles Gavan Duffy letters. William Hickey papers. John O'Mahony correspondence. Samuel Lee Anderson papers. Sir Thomas Larcom papers. Isaac Butt papers. Alexander Martin Sullivan letters. J.P. Leonard correspondence. J.F.X. O'Brien papers. Earl of Mayo papers. John Devoy papers. Land League papers. STATE PAPER OFFICE, DUBLIN CASTLE: Chief Secretary's office: registered papers. Police and crime records, fenian papers, including: Reports on secret societies, 1858-9; Fenianism: index of names, 1864-5; Fenianism: index of names, 1866-80; Habeas corpus suspension act, index, abstracts of cases, 1866-8; Fenian crown briefs; 'F' papers 1866-79; 'A' files, 1877-82. Police and crime records: Irish National Land League and Irish National League papers. TRINITY COLLEGE LIBRARY, DUBLIN: Dillon papers. Davitt deposit (James Stephens papers). IN PRIVATE POSSESSION: Charles Guilfoyle Doran papers (property of Mr. John C. Elliott). PUBLIC RECORD OFFICE, LONDON: Home Office papers: Prison registers, 1866-71. Colonial Office records: Dublin Castle papers. BRITISH LIBRARY: Gladstone papers. QUALITY HOUSE (NATIONAL REGISTER OF ARCHIVES): Palmerston papers (courtesy of the Broadlands Trust). NEW YORK PUBLIC LIBRARY: Margaret McKim Maloney collection: O'Donovan Rossa papers. (On microfilm in National Library of Ireland) PUBLIC ARCHIVES OF CANADA, OTTAWA: Correspondence between Timothy Daniel Sullivan and Thomas Darcy McGee, 1862. (On microfilm in National Library of Ireland). MINISTÈRE DES RELATIONS EXTERIEURES, PARIS: Mémoires et documents: Angleterre, 1863-79. Affaires diverses politiques: Angleterre 1851-59. CATHOLIC UNIVERSITY OF AMERICA, WASHINGTON: Fenian papers (otherwise O'Mahony papers). (On microfilm in National Library of Ireland).

Primary Sources: II Published Letters and Papers

P.J. Corish (ed.), 'Irish College, Rome: Kirby papers; guide to material of public and political interest, 1862-83' in *Archivium Hibernicum*, xxx (1972), pp 29-115; '... 1836-61' in *Archivium Hibernicum*, xxxi (1973), pp 1-94.

P. MacSuibhne (ed.), *Paul Cullen and his contemporaries, with their letters from 1820 to 1902* (5 vols, Naas, 1961-77).

Karl Marx and Friedrich Engels, *Ireland and the Irish question* (Moscow, 1971).

H.C.G. Matthew (ed.), *The Gladstone diaries*, vols VII and VIII (Oxford, 1982).

T.W. Moody and Leon Ó Broin (ed.), 'The I.R.B. supreme council, 1868-78' in *Irish Historical Studies* xix, No. 75 (Mar. 1975), pp 286-332.

P.F. Moran (ed.), *The pastoral letters and other writings of Cardinal Cullen* (3 vols, Dublin, 1882).

William O'Brien and Desmond Ryan (ed.), *Devoy's post bag* (2 vols, Dublin, 1948 and 1953).

Agatha Ramm (ed.), *The political correspondence of Mr Gladstone and Lord Granville, 1876-86* (2 vols, Oxford, 1962).

J.R. Vincent (ed.), *Disraeli, Derby and the conservative party: The political journals of Lord Stanley, 1849-69* (Hassocks, 1977).

Primary Sources: III Contemporary Newspapers and Periodicals

Catholic Telegraph (Dublin). *Celt* (Kilkenny). *Connaught Patriot* (Tuam). *Connaught Telegraph* (Castlebar). *Cork Examiner. Dublin Review* (London). *Evening News* (Dublin). *Freeman's Journal* (Dublin). *Galway American* (Galway). *Irish-American* (New York). *Irishman* (Belfast, later Dublin). *Irish People* (Dublin). *Irish People* (New York). *Irish Times* (Dublin). *Kilkenny Journal. Nation* (Dublin). *Tablet* (Dublin and London). *Times* (London). *Tribune* (Dublin). *United Irishman and Galway American* (Dublin). *Weekly Freeman* (Dublin).

Primary Sources: IV Published Works of Contemporaries

Robert Anderson, 'Fenianism: a narrative by one who knows' in *Contemporary Review*, xix (1872), pp 301-16, 624-46.

F.M. Bussy, *Irish conspiracies: recollections of John Mallon (the great Irish detective) and other reminiscences* (London, 1910).

Isaac Butt, *Land tenure in Ireland: a plea for the celtic race* (London, 1866); *The Irish people and the Irish land: a letter to Lord Lifford* (Dublin, 1867); *Irish federalism: its meaning, its object and its hopes* (Dublin and London, 1870); *Ireland's appeal for amnesty* (London, 1870).

John Daly, Recollections in *Irish Freedom*, Feb. 1912—May 1913.

W.J. O'Neill Daunt, *Eighty-five years of Irish history, 1880-85* (2 vols, London, 1886).

Michael Davitt, *The fall of feudalism in Ireland* (London and New York, 1904).

Joseph Denieffe, *A personal narrative of the Irish revolutionary brotherhood giving a faithful report of the principal events from 1855 to 1867, written at the request of friends* (New York, 1906).

John Devoy, *Recollections of an Irish rebel* (New York, 1929); Reminiscences in *Irish Freedom*, Mar. 1913–Dec. 1914.

Michael Doheny, *The felon's track* (New York, 1849).

Charles Gavan Duffy, *Four years of Irish history, 1845-49* (London, 1883); *The league of north and south: an episode in Irish history, 1850-54* (London, 1886).

Charles J. Kickham, *Knocknagow, or the homes of Tipperary* (first edition, Dublin, 1873).

Henri Le Caron, *Twenty five years in the secret service* (London, 1892).

John Mitchel, *Jail Journal* (Dublin, 1910).

John Martin and W.S. O'Brien, *Correspondence between John Martin and Smith O'Brien relative to a French invasion* (Dublin, 1861).

William O'Brien, 'Was fenianism ever formidable?' in *Contemporary Review*, lxxi (1897), pp 680-93.

Frank Hugh O'Donnell, *A history of the Irish parliamentary party* (2 vols, London, 1910).

Jeremiah O'Donovan Rossa, *Rossa's recollections, 1838 to 1898* (New York, 1898).

John O'Leary, *Recollections of fenians and fenianism* (2 vols, London, 1896).

Richard Pigott, *Personal recollections of an Irish national journalist* (2nd ed., Dublin and London, 1883).

Frank Roney, *Frank Roney, Irish rebel and California labour leader*, ed. Ira B. Cross (Berkeley, 1931).

John Rutherford, *The secret history of the fenian conspiracy, its origins, objects and ramifications* (2 vols, London, 1877).

Mark Ryan, *Fenian memories* (Dublin, 1945).

John Savage, *Fenian heroes and martyrs* (Boston, 1868).

A silent politician [J.E. Pigot] , *On the future of Ireland and on its capacity to exist as an independent state* (Dublin, 1862).

James Stephens, Reminiscences in *Weekly Freeman*, 6 Oct. 1883 and foll.

A.M. Sullivan, *New Ireland* (London, 1877).

T.D. Sullivan, *Recollections of troubled times in Irish politics* (Dublin, 1905); *A.M. Sullivan: a memoir* (Dublin, 1885).

Lord Tenterden, 'The fenian brotherhood: an account of the Irish-American revolutionary societies in the United States from 1848 to 1870' (Printed Foreign Office memo, Feb. 1871).

P.J.P. Tynan, *The history of the Irish National Invincibles and their times* (London, 1894).

Nicholas Wiseman, *The sermons, lectures and speeches delivered by Cardinal Wiseman during his tour in Ireland* . . . . (Dublin, 1859).

Primary Sources: V Official Publications

The census of Ireland for the year 1851 (. . . . 1861, 1871, 1881).

Hansard's parliamentary debates, third series.

Report of the proceedings at the first sitting of the special commission for the county of the city of Dublin, held at Green Street, Dublin, for the trial of Thomas Clarke Luby and others . . . . (Dublin, 1866).

Report of the commissioners appointed by the Home Department to inquire into the treatment of certain treason-felony convicts in the English convict prisons, H.C. 1867, (3880), xxxv.

Report of the commissioners appointed to inquire into the treatment of treason-felony convicts in English prisons, together with appendix and minutes of evidence [C 319] H.C. 1871, xxxii.

Report from the select committee on Westmeath . . . . together with proceedings of the committee, minutes of evidence and appendix, H.C. 1871 (147), xiii.
Special Commission Act, 1888: reprint of the shorthand notes of the speeches, proceedings and evidence taken before the commissioners (12 vols., London, 1890).

Primary Sources: VI Works of Reference

Annual Register 1848 etc (London, 1859 etc).
Henry Boylan, *A dictionary of Irish biography* (Dublin, 1978).
Sir Bernard Burke, *Genealogical and heraldic history of the landed gentry of Ireland* (4th ed., London, 1958).
Dictionary of national biography (22 vols., London, 1908-9).
Public general acts and measures (London, annual).
Thom's Irish Almanac and Official Directory, 1848 etc (Dublin, 1848 etc).
W.E. Vaughan and A.J. Fitzpatrick, *Irish historical statistics: population, 1821-1971* (Dublin, 1978).
B.M. Walker, *Parliamentary election results in Ireland, 1801-1922* (Dublin, 1978).

Secondary Sources

(This list gives a selection of standard works together with various items not in the notes to the text, where most of my secondary sources are indicated.)

J.C. Beckett, *The making of modern Ireland 1603-1923* (London, 1966).
G. Best, *Mid-Victorian Britain* (London, 1971).
P. Bew, *Land and the national question in Ireland, 1858-82* (Dublin, 1978).
M. Bourke, *John O'Leary: a study in Irish separatism* (Tralee, 1967).
D.G. Boyce, *Nationalism in Ireland* (London, 1982).
A. Briggs (ed.), *Chartist studies* (London, 1959).
S. Clark, *Social origins of the Irish land war* (Princeton, 1979).
R.V. Comerford, 'Irish nationalist politics, 1858-70' (Ph.D. thesis, Trinity College, Dublin, 1977); *Charles J. Kickham (1828-82): a study in Irish nationalism and literature* (Dublin, 1979).
P.J. Corish (ed.), *A history of Irish catholicism* (Portions of six vols in fasciculi , Dublin, 1967-71).
L.M. Cullen, *An economic history of Ireland since 1660* (London, 1972).
H. Cunningham, *The volunteers* (London, 1965).
W. Dillon, *Life of John Mitchel* (2 vols., London, 1888).
F. D'Arcy, 'Charles Bradlaugh and the Irish question' in A. Cosgrove and D. McCartney, *Studies in Irish history presented to R.D. Edwards* (Dublin, 1979), pp 228-56.
W. D'Arcy, *The fenian movement in the United States, 1858-86* (Washington, 1947).
J.S. Donnelly, *The land and the people of nineteenth century Cork: the rural economy and the land question* (London, 1975).
O.D. Edwards, 'Ireland' in O.D. Edwards (ed.), *Celtic nationalism* (London, 1968).
R.F. Foster, *Charles Stewart Parnell: the man and his family* (London, 1976).

D. Gahan, 'The estates of Co. Wexford in the nineteenth century: an analysis of their changing financial situation in the decades prior to the land war' (M.A. thesis, Loyola University of Chicago, 1979).

T. Garvin, *The evolution of Irish nationalist politics* (Dublin, 1981).

M. Harmon (ed.), *Fenians and fenianism: centenary essays* (Dublin, 1968).

J.L. Hammond, *Gladstone and the Irish nation* (London, 1938).

E.J. Hobsbawm, *The age of capital, 1848-75* (London, 1975).

K.T. Hoppen, 'National politics and local realities in mid-nineteenth century Ireland' in A. Cosgrove and D. McCartney (ed.) *Studies in Irish history presented to R. Dudley Edwards* (Dublin, 1979).

D. Jordan, Land and politics in the west of Ireland: County Mayo, 1846-82 in *Irish Economic and Social History*, x (1983), pp 94-5. (Thesis abstract).

R. Kee, *The green flag: a history of Irish nationalism* (London, 1972).

E. Larkin, *The Roman Catholic church and the creation of the modern Irish state, 1878-86* (Philadelphia, 1975).

J.J. Lee, *The modernisation of Irish society* (Dublin, 1973).

M. Leo, 'The influence of the fenians and their press on public opinion in Ireland, 1863-70' (M. Litt. thesis, Trinity College, Dublin, 1976).

D. Leonard, 'John Mitchel, Charles Gavan Duffy and the legacy of Young Ireland' (Ph.D. thesis, University of Sheffield, 1975).

F.S.L. Lyons, *Charles Stewart Parnell* (London, 1977).

D. McCartney, 'The church and fenianism' in *University Review*, iv (Winter 1967).

W. McGrath, 'The fenian rising in Cork' in *Irish Sword*, viii, no. 33 (1968), pp 322-35.

T.F. Martin, 'A.M. Sullivan, 1829-84' (M.A. thesis, University College, Cork, 1981).

J. Moloney, 'The National Brotherhood of St Patrick and the rise of Dublin fenianism' (M.A. thesis, University College, Galway, 1976).

T.W. Moody, (ed.) *The fenian movement* (Cork, 1968); *Davitt and Irish revolution, 1846-82* (Oxford, 1981).

G.P. Moran, 'The land question in Mayo, 1869-90' (M.A. thesis, University College, Galway, 1981).

J.A. Murphy, 'The influence of America on Irish nationalism' in D.N. Doyle and O.D. Edwards (ed.), *America and Ireland, 1776-1976* (New York, 1980).

J. Newsinger, 'Old chartists, fenians and new socialists' in *Éire-Ireland*, xvii, no. 2 (Summer 1982) pp 19-46.

C.C, O'Brien, *Parnell and his party* (Oxford, 1974 edition).

L. Ó Broin, *Fenian fever: an Anglo-American dilemma* (London, 1971); *Revolutionary underground: the story of the Irish Republican Brotherhood 1858-1924* (Dublin, 1976).

S. O Lúing, *Ó Donnabháin Rosa* (2 vols., Dublin, 1969 and 1979).

T.P. O'Neill, *Fionntán Ó Leathlobhair* (Dublin, 1962).

J. O'Shea, *Priest, politics and society in post famine Ireland: a study of County Tipperary, 1850-91* (Dublin, 1983).

P. Ó Snodaigh, 'Eireannaigh sa chogadh chathartha 'sna Stait Aontaithe' in *Studia Hibernica* x (1970), pp 95-107.

G. Ó Tuathaigh, 'Nineteenth-century Irish politics: the case for normalcy' in *Anglo-Irish Studies*, i (1975) pp 71-81.

H. Perkin, *The origins of modern English society, 1780-1880* (London, 1969).

D. Ryan, *The fenian chief: a biography of James Stephens* (Dublin, 1967); *The phoenix flame: a study of fenianism and John Devoy* (London, 1937).

B.L. Solow, *The land question in the Irish economy, 1870-1903* (Cambridge, Mass., 1971).

E.D. Steele, *Irish land and British politics: tenant-right and nationality, 1865-70* (London, 1974).

E. Strauss, *Irish nationalism and British democracy* (London, 1951).

D. Thornley, *Isaac Butt and home rule* (London, 1964).

H.H. van der Wusten, *Iers verzet tegen de staatkundige eenheid der Britse eilanden, 1800-1921* (Amsterdam, 1977).

W.E. Vaughan, *Sin, sheep and Scotsmen: John George Adair and the Derryveagh evictions, 1861* (Belfast, 1983).

J.R. Vincent, 'Gladstone and Ireland' in *Proceedings of the British Academy*, lxiii (1977), pp 193-238.

J.H. Whyte, *The independent Irish party, 1850-59* (Oxford, 1958); 'Landlord influence at elections in Ireland, 1760-1885' in *English Historical Review*, lxx (1965), pp 740-60.

T.D. Williams (ed.), *Secret societies in Ireland* (Dublin, 1973).

INDEX